Pointers & Setters

Pointers & Setters

Derry Argue

SWAN·HILL
PRESS

To Hedy

Copyright © 1993 by Derry Argue

First published in the UK in 1993
by Swan Hill Press
an imprint of Airlife Publishing Ltd

British Library Cataloguing in Publication Data
   A catalogue record for this book
   is available from the British Library.

The author has asserted his moral rights to be
identified as the author of the work.

ISBN 1 85310 239 3

Printed by Livesey Ltd, Shrewsbury.

Swan Hill Press
an imprint of Airlife Publishing Ltd
101 Longden Road, Shrewsbury SY3 9EB

Contents

Introduction

Nearly thirty years ago I attended my first field trial. I can vividly recall the sight of a black-and-white pointer dog running so fast it seemed incredible that it could scent a bird, let alone point one. As I thought to myself that the dog must run into game at any moment, it slammed on the brakes and spun round in an abrupt and skidding halt. The pointer hesitated a moment, then stalked forward three or four paces with increasing intensity and came to a final, rigid point. Head up and tail out-stretched, every muscle of the dog's back and thighs taut and quivering, there was no doubt at all that the dog was saying, 'Here they are and I'll bet my life on it'.

That was my first introduction to the traditional British pointing dogs. These include the pointer, sometimes called the 'English pointer', and the Gordon, Irish, and English setters. These are the specialists. Fast, stylish, game-finding dogs with a unique history and evolution for the single purpose of finding game birds. These, as I will explain, were bred to find game with such efficiency that no other breed can compete on equal terms. They were bred to perform this function with such perfection as to bring dog-work to as near an art as any field sport can get. And in saying this I do not denigrate the pointer-retrievers, or HPR breeds, just emphasize that the aims are different. To suggest that the fiddle player is different to the concert violinist is not to claim that one gives any less pleasure than the other to his or her listeners. The traditional British bird dogs are the supreme stylists created by generations for which style was everything.

That dog positively shook with the excitement of the close proximity of game; and that elation conveyed itself to the on looking crowd so there seemed to be some common emotional involvement. For the first time I found myself experiencing the thrill of seeing a top class bird-dog in action. It was the start of a love affair that was to change the course of my life.

As ordered by the judges, the handler came up beside the dog, spoke a few soft words to it and told it to go forward. The pointer ran forward in a series of exciting dashes, halting after each advance of a few yards to wait for its handler. From its action, the dog seemed almost to want to catch the grouse but at the same time seemed fearful of flushing them. It was wonderful to me, a complete novice, to see such excitement and power in a dog yet to see it working in such obvious sympathy with its handler.

So absorbed was I in the spectacle of the dog working that I forgot completely about the birds. When they rose in unison it took me utterly by surprise. At the same instant the dog hit the ground as if shot and the Official Gun, appointed for the occasion to act out the role of the hunter, fired into the air. The whole sequence was neat and snappy and very exciting and I was rather relieved that it was just a field trial and I had not been expected to shoot the grouse. They might have looked easy to the casual observer, but so exhilarating had the sequence been that the grouse presented very testing targets. The whole performance had knocked the breath out of me and I knew that, one day, I was going to own a dog like that.

The late Donald McLean, as famous for his Migdale spaniels as for his pointers and setters. (Derry Argue)

Some years later, discussing the thrills of this sport, the late Donald McLean, then gamekeeper on Benmore and Assynt Estates in Sutherland, Northern Scotland, summed it up by saying, 'If only some of these big landowners could see these dogs in action on their grouse moors, they would all be at it!' What more can I say? Fortunately, it is not necessary to be a big landowner, or even to own your own grouse moor, to experience the thrill of running a top class pointer or setter. The myth that these dogs can only be used for the few weeks during the short grouse season was exploded long ago.

This book is about the traditional British working pointers and setters as they are used for shooting under British and Irish conditions. That might seem to limit the book's appeal to a very small minority of privileged people but pointing dogs are once again becoming popular and the trend is likely to continue as land is taken out of agriculture and the heather moorlands are managed to produce the single most profitable enterprise – grouse shooting. The principles involved in using one of the traditional breeds of working pointers or setters for red grouse shooting on a first class dogging moor in Britain are not so different from those involved in using a pointing dog for more mundane work on any acreage that will hold a bird or two. I hope that the book will be of interest to any owner of a working gundog for my research into breeding and training pointers and setters has led me on to study a wide range of subjects from animal psychology to pedigree breeding. Over the years I have had the privilege of corresponding with many breeders and trainers in other lands, not just about pointing dogs, or even gundogs, but of many other breeds of working dogs, of hawks and falcons, even horses, and, just once, of training bumble bees to amuse a classroom of school children!

But it is not enough to begin to understand the way a dog's mind works. You also have to study the human element because man-and-dog is a partnership so firmly cemented over the millennia that our affinity to communicate with dogs almost passes unnoticed. How easy it is to fall into the trap of assuming that dogs are 'almost human'. Fortunately for our canine friends, that is a gross libel!

Pavlov called the dog 'the small man'; an understanding of your canine companion will certainly lead to a better understanding of the human psyche. But this does not claim to be a scientific book and I can produce no elaborate proof as to why some training techniques work and why others, commonly accepted and generally advocated, are less successful. All I can say is that they work for me and I can only guess at the reasons why they do work. It is the journalists' maxim to 'tell it like it happened' and that is all I can do. I have mostly omitted the usual discussions of modern kennels and bird-dog characters and, except in passing, I have left out any reference to dog shows or dogs bred for the show bench as this is a subject of which I know little. The modern gundog scene, except for general comment, I have left strictly alone; I have no wish to be dragged through the defamation courts!

This book is written primarily to benefit the breeds of dogs that have given me so much fun and if it helps owners to breed, train, and handle better dogs, it will inevitably succeed in that aim. In my opinion, the real thoroughbred bird-dogs are getting scarcer by the minute and are being replaced by less talented dogs because they are less easily spoilt by bad or ignorant trainers and more easily produced to compete in the five minute heat at a field trial.

Chapter 1
The Pursuit of Style

There are now only three recognised British breeds of setters – the Irish, Gordon, and English; and one pointer, sometimes called 'the English pointer'. Over the centuries, these dogs have been exported from Britain to sportsmen all over the world and they still hold their own against increasing competition from more modern breeds. Just what makes the traditional pointing dogs so special?

These are the dogs bred to find and point game; but that is all too simple a definition. The pointing instinct is not unique to pointers and setters. There are also a large number of general purpose pointing dogs, officially designated by The Kennel Club in London as those which 'hunt-point-and-retrieve' (colloquially known as 'pointer-retrievers' or 'HPRs'), that have been imported to Britain in recent years, all seeming to rival our native pointing dogs.

And why should we need pointing dogs at all? As a falconer wanting to fly my peregrines at grouse, I needed a dog which would find and point game birds but I needed a lot more besides. I needed a dog which would search wide areas of open country where game was scarce, leaving no birds behind. Just to do that, the dog needed a superb physique and the courage and stamina to run for long periods. I needed a dog which would readily respond to my commands and work *with me*; a dog with the sensitivity and intelligence to respond not just to signals but also to the slightest body language or gesture because most of my attention had to be focussed on the falcon. The ideal dog would respond to the falcon and me without the need for harsh restraint or control. I would not have time to control a wilful dog. It had not only to point but point unerringly, without mistake, and to hold that point until I approached or the falcon was in position for a successful flight. The dog needed the inborn instinct to hunt for game in a methodical manner, searching the air for scent, and to have the sagacity to outwit the wildest of game birds, the Scottish red grouse. Not least, the dog had to have that almost indefinable quality, style, because it was to be part of a team intended to participate in a sport which is a spectacle in itself. There are a lot more requirements in a bird dog that I had not even come to realize at that time.

This element 'style' is an intangible quality that is difficult to define. It is what field sports should be all about and what the casual observer so often fails to understand. The quality of the sport is seldom proportional to the size of the bag so where birds are scarce it is even more important that the dog should make a fair contribution to what we call style. As some sportsman whose identity was forgotten long ago remarked, 'It is not the frequency of the occurrence but the quality of the performance'.

To some, there is no doubt about the quality of the dog which does its task superbly well, so it can truly lay claim to the title of a stylish performer. To others, the fussy, showy work of a moderate dog will be claimed stylish. If beauty is in the eye of the beholder, then style must be something each values for himself. But there can be no doubt about the first-class experienced game shot who crumples those high, curling cock pheasants at the driven shoot. No doubt at all about the peregrine falcon which mounts almost to the clouds and plummets in a vertical stoop when the grouse are flushed. But does the game shot need to kill every bird or the falcon unerringly strike down its chosen victim every time? If it was as easy as that there would surely be no sport at all.

The culmination of the hunt is the kill but the final achievement of that goal is a comparatively minor part of the whole in terms of sport. Killing more does not increase the sport whatever some might think. If it did, the salmon fisher would use a net instead of a fly rod, the deer stalker a machine gun. The bird dog field trialer concentrates his attention on everything *but* the kill. Although field trials are purported to be conducted 'as an ordinary shooting day', at most trials for pointers and setters in Britain the final shot is fired into the air and the bird escapes with scarcely a feather out of place! Yet there is no doubting the enormous pleasure enthusiasts of this sport experience when working their dogs. Some participants never become involved in shooting at all and their dogs never see a bird killed to their points. On the other hand, killing birds over a dog, especially a setter, undoubtedly *makes* the dog and we should never lose sight of the *raison d'etre* of the pointer or setter which is to put birds into the game bag. When we lose sight of that objective, the dogs it has taken centuries to create are half way lost.

Advie Annan points a grouse amongst the rushes. (Derry Argue)

Style has a great deal to do with how those intentions are pursued, if not achieved. North American sportsmen would call it class. Style is a quality they attribute to the stance and demeanour of the dog on point. Style, to us in Britain, applies to the action, poise, the whole concept of dog work. Bill Brown, late editor of *The American*

Field, writing in 1977, defined class in a bird dog as 'the ability to do, at great speed and with unusual accuracy, what the average can only do slowly and under particularly favourable circumstances'.

Many a casual observer will recognize style, and class, in a gundog the moment he sees it; others will be in the sport all their lives (yes, and judge trials!) and fail ever to recognize the difference between the common shooting dog and a dog with real style.

All these pointing and bird finding functions can be performed by many breeds of pointing dogs. Pointing alone is no particular talent. Arkwright, in his famous book *The Pointer and His Predecessors* mentions the New Forest pig that was taught to find and point partridges within a fortnight and also his own fox terrier which he trained to stand (i.e. point) partridge. I have owned collies and lurchers that I trained in odd moments to point quite acceptably. So you can see there is nothing special in a dog pointing. Omit style and bird finding and shooting over a pointing dog degenerates into mere pot-hunting and the dog becomes no more than an instrument with the sole function of setting up the next shot. At that point, to my mind, sport ceases to exist and at this stage of my career I would require a substantial fee to induce me to go shooting *without* a dog, not just any dog either.

Not so long ago I was admiring a very nice looking English setter at a field trial. It was certainly a very smart dog and although I was taken with its looks and work there was obviously something not quite right. My companion remarked what a wonderfully stylish animal the setter was and I agreed . . . with the proviso that it was certainly a wonderful dog *if* the point it had now come to produced grouse. As it happened, there were no grouse there and everyone had had their expectations raised only to be disappointed with the anti-climax. It would have been easy to have said 'bad luck' but these were August grouse and there was no reason why the dog should have been congratulated for doing what could only be described as a bad job.

Later the same dog did it again, hesitating in a stylish way with its tail outstretched and flag extended in 'true setter glory', it was almost impossible for any onlooker with the hint of sportsmanship in his blood not to catch his breath. But at the same moment, his brace mate, one of those rough-and-ready, work-hardened, no-nonsense pointers from Ireland galloped past him and declared by his every demeanour and with no hint of hesitation, 'nothing there'. Of course, the pointer was promptly put out of the stake for not backing but for all his lack of manners he had shown up the English setter for a liar and a fool, a poseur that did not know its job. I should perhaps add that the fault was probably caused by bad training but that did not alter the situation. At no stretch of the imagination, in my opinion, could that dog be said to have had style, pretty though he might have appeared to the unenlightened. And unenlightened people exist for that dog went on to become a field trial champion and a famous stud.

A full realization of just how unacceptable the behaviour of such a dog is, despite his good looks, would be brought home to the reader more forcibly if he had had to walk to such an 'unproductive point' half way up a Perthshire hillside for the umpteenth time during the same day's shooting! Such deficiencies are far from obvious at an English field trial because the dog has only to walk upwind, continuing to pose for the admiring onlookers, for another twenty or thirty yards to be sure of chancing on another covey, so thick are the birds on the ground at such meetings. Nearly every field trial currently run in Britain for pointers and setters is held on what can only be classed as a good driving moor. The moor in question yielded a bird per acre.

Advie Dick, lemon-and-white Llewellin dog, and Advie Annan share a point on grouse.
(Derry Argue)

Above all else, a pointer's or a setter's point should be definite and true. If he points, there should be birds, though it is no fault to the dog if, through some delay in the Guns getting up, the game has moved. The object of the exercise is to 'present the game to the Gun'. If the birds move, the dog may re-locate. It is even possible to have a moving point, though it may seem a contradiction in terms. What the dog must not do is to disturb the game so much that it moves off altogether, by flying or running, so the Guns are denied the chance of a shot. That requirement, for a definite point, is even more exacting in the sport of falconry and I would go so far as to say that a flush is infinitely preferable to the falconer than a false point which would have the effect of disappointing the falcon.

It is open to debate whether the rough-and-ready pointer mentioned above could ever be called stylish. As it really was an ugly brute my own opinion is that it had no style no matter how well it did its work. There is something of a tradition in British field trials that it is the work that matters and 'never mind the looks'. I cannot agree and I have taken some care in choosing pictures for this book which illustrate what is possible if looks are given due consideration. Nor do I believe the ideal can be described in words or that all dogs in a certain breed should adhere to some committee's idea of what constitutes a 'standard' for the breed. I have never understood that. Do such people go home from their committee meetings to be greeted by 'standard' spouses, a row of children each conforming to 'the standard', with 'standardized' cats and dogs asleep on the hearth rug? The libraries are full of law books which will testify to the difficulties of interpreting the written word and history is all against there being any single 'ideal' for a pointer or a setter.

In nature, pointing is the pause between a predator locating its prey and the final rush or attack. Man has extended this pause in pointing dogs through selective breeding and training. But there is more to it than that. A dog is essentially a pack animal. Wild dogs have perfected a method of hunting in a group or pack. Group hunting is more efficient than hunting alone because each member of the pack can perfect a different role in the proceedings so the whole working together create a unified force able to tackle larger and more difficult prey. Some dogs select the victim, others take priority in cutting it out from the herd, yet others pursue, wear down and tire the selected target. But it may be only a few individuals in the pack which take that dangerous first bite to disable and bring down the quarry so the rest can kill it and break it up. Then, the pack will start to feed from the carcass in strict order according to the social hierarchy. Nature is seldom haphazard.

This pack relationship is quite complex and we will be coming back to it later but it is a fact that most dogs prefer to hunt in company, hence the increased dangers of allowing two or more dogs to stray in sheep country. Dogs quickly revert to nature and that quiet, domesticated pet can rapidly become an accomplished killer. The terrier, or terrier-cross, partnership with another dog of collie ancestry is particularly lethal; the one rounding up and cornering the sheep, the other specializing in killing.

Pointing dogs are no less pack animals but they prefer, through selective breeding for that propensity, to share their hunting with a single partner. The true bird dog lacks the killer instinct. It is not uncommon for a pointer to be trained to work with a coursing dog; the pointer finding and pointing the hares and the greyhound coursing and killing. It is a peculiar characteristic of some bird dogs that they are almost completely indifferent to game once it has been killed. It is a characteristic which can be exasperating in the extreme when you *know* birds are down, your spaniel has been left at home, but your bird dog flatly refuses to have anything to do with finding them! Fortunately, a little forethought and training can prevent the problem but that is another matter.

The pointing dog has a peculiarly generous nature in that it hunts *for* its human handler, delegating almost completely the act of killing. Hunting alone, a pointing dog is not an efficient killer of mature game birds. But combine its hunting skills with those of the human hunter and the result can be murderous in the extreme . . . and I choose my words carefully. This partnership between man and pointing dog is vital if the sport is to succeed. The dog is not a machine. That is why adding a pointer or a setter to a line of walking Guns is doomed to failure. The dog starts to work well enough but when it tries to relate to its handler, looking back for directions or reassurances all it sees is a sea of wax-proofed jacketed figures, all similar, from which it is virtually impossible for anyone to distinguish the handler, let alone for the dog to do so. From there, matters deteriorate. I remember one sporting agent who purchased two pointers from Lord Rank's kennel (at that time probably the top kennel in the country) and used them in front of a line of walking Guns. By the end of the season the dogs were completely ruined and could not be given away.

The partnership between handler and dog is no more apparent than when walking in to a point. The dog has found and pointed the birds, the handler now approaches, checks to see that the Guns are in position, then walks forward in unison with the dog to put the birds up. In the USA, the dog is trained to stand while the handler goes forward to flush the birds. The different styles are due to variations in the behaviour of game in the two countries and to tradition. But on the British scene, the dog hands responsibility to the handler and both then proceed to put up the birds together but with the handler dictating the pace.

I well remember some overseas clients I had out with me one day when this characteristic was demonstrated in rather an amusing way. At every point, the Guns raced forward, ran ahead of the dog and fired wildly as the birds rose. I remonstrated with them to go slowly as there was no need to run. The birds were lying well and there was no danger of the dog, an old experienced pointer, flushing the birds prematurely. But it was no good. So I bided my time and in due course my chance came.

By the dog's demeanour I knew she was pointing a big covey of grouse a long way off and I knew she would not move until I told her to no matter what anyone else might say or do. So I sat down on a rock and watched the fun. As usual, my clients ran up to the dog, ran ahead of her and charged around in the heather trying to find the grouse. I just sat there with a broad grin on my face indicating, every time they glanced in my direction, that if they wanted to do it their way perhaps they ought to put a bit more energy into their scampering about. It was a hilarious situation and it took all of twenty minutes to convince them that I might actually know best when, to their credit, they shared in the joke.

After that I had no more trouble. I believe we walked forward fifty yards from where the dog had pointed, way ahead of where they had assumed the birds to be, before a very good covey rose in front. Later that day we got a similar point on the very top of a hill where the heather was short. I walked in beside the dog for all of two hundred yards before a large covey that had been running ahead of us decided to take to their wings. By that time, my clients had decided that both my dog and I were telling lies and they had lost interest to the extent that they missed with four shots! Under such conditions it is clearly nonsensical to think of the Gun raising the birds independently of the dog. This, of course, indicates that the true bird dog character is almost devoid of killer instinct and subjects itself completely to the control of the handler. Time and time again I have brought my dogs to within inches of birds which have lain tightly for some reason or other. And when the dog has flatly refused to move forward any further, I have generally found the bird inches from its nose, sometimes buried deep in the heather. On one such occasion, I easily caught a full grown red grouse which lay motionless directly under my dog's nose. When released the bird flew off as strongly as any I have seen. I can only conclude that it had never before seen dog or man and had assumed we were as harmless as the black-faced sheep it was so used to seeing on the mountain.

This generosity of spirit is the hallmark of a pure-bred bird dog. The dog hunts for and to its handler and it is not unusual to see a look of ill-concealed horror on the face of a young pure-bred pointer or setter which has accidentally flushed birds. Sandy (portrayed on the cover of this book), a young pointer in my kennel as I write, is a case in point. A very sensitive dog which was sold and roughly handled by an ignorant trainer, Sandy had learnt to hunt but was not steady when I purchased him back. As soon as Sandy realized what was required he became a very sure and careful bird finder. In fact, my training had to be geared to reduce his seriousness.

Working him on a neighbouring moor one day he ran over a small rise and out of sight. A few moments later, a single grouse flew from roughly his direction and I knew that Sandy had either run into birds or had otherwise flushed one accidentally. Sandy had grown out of the stage when he deliberately ran up his birds and he was very serious in his work with only an occasional lapse as might be forgiven any young dog.

I ran to where I judged Sandy to be and found him with his head buried in the heather. The expression on his face was as eloquent as if he had spoken the words, 'Oh my god, what have I done! I have flushed a bird'. So mortified was he that I had to spend a few moments consoling him. Later that day, I allowed a young setter to run in on one of Sandy's points (for reasons too elaborate to tell here) and again I saw that look of horror as the pointer realized what the setter was about to do. Dogs which take bird finding so seriously are worth their weight in gold as, with experience and careful handling, they can only improve. With ignorant handling, they are very rapidly destroyed in mind and spirit.

As anyone who has ever worked a dog on game will readily testify, bird work is seldom as simple as it sometimes appears. An experienced dog worked on grouse early in the season can make things look extraordinarily easy. And so they often are. A covey of grouse in August is very innocent. The scent emanating from a strong covey of, say, fifteen birds on a good day must positively stink to any reasonable dog and be almost impossible to miss in a favourable wind. I have seen dogs scent such coveys at ranges in excess of one hundred and fifty yards and once paced out a point from the find to where the *pair* of birds rose at over eighty yards. I do not believe these birds had run in front of the dog at all as the heather was deep and these distances fairly represented the length of the dog's nose.

But it is a different thing when scenting conditions are bad, when old birds run, perhaps downwind to confound the dogs, when everything is against the dog coming to a decisive point. It is these conditions which extract that last hint of instinct and inbred genius from our pointers and setters. It is the extremes of endurance, the extremes of scent, the scarcity and the wildness of the birds, and the harshness of the conditions which separate our native breeds of pointers and setters from those recent hunter-retriever imports. I refer here, of course, to the best of both breeds. One the supreme specialist, the other the all-rounder. Surely, there can be no comparison? Perhaps in the future it will be possible to test the two types together in the same trial. Now that would be a test worth seeing and dispel a lot of arguments.

Complete obedience in a pointer or a setter is required at a field trial though things have progressed, or deteriorated (depending on your point of view), since the late George Abbott judged trials. George was trainer and handler to the late Mrs Florence Nagle of Sulhampstead d'Or Irish Setter fame and he is reputed to have been a stern judge and worthy opponent. 'Drop your dog', he would tell a competitor, and if the dog did not drop instantly on command out it would go for being 'out of control'. How many dogs would be put out of a trial these days if that test were strictly applied? It ought to be possible to drop a trained pointer or setter at one hundred yards at least. Yet it is quite possible to successfully shoot over a bird dog that has received no formal training whatsoever. Many come to hunt and point naturally, needing only the opportunity to work. In the days when nearly all shooting in Britain was over pointers and setters, bird dogs were considered to be the easiest of all gundogs to train. Now the opposite is the case. What has gone wrong?

In the old days in Britain, pointers and setters were trained to drop flat in response to the sound of the shot or to the sight of a bird flying off and that tradition continues in this country to this day. In the past, dropping to wing was required by netsmen who would, at the moment the birds tried to fly, drop their nets over both the dog and the bird. Then, later, when shooting became more popular the sportsman needed time to reload his muzzle-loading shotgun in preparation for the next shot. In fact, it still makes sense to train these dogs to drop to wing and shot because the common game birds hunted in Britain tend to be found in coveys and do not necessarily all fly off together when one or two are disturbed. A dog which will drop the instant a bird flies up gives the Gun a chance to re-load and compose himself if there are more left. Training the dog to drop to shot covers the eventuality where birds flush unseen by the dog though it ought to be said that it is bad practice to shoot at any birds except those which rise to the point.

Personally, I like to see a dog trained in this way and there is no doubt that it looks very snappy. There are also sound psychological reasons for directing the dog's natural instincts to 'do something' when game is disturbed rather than have him stand there apparently taking no further part in the proceedings. But where the game hunted is not found in coveys (snipe, woodcock, etc.) it really makes little difference in practical terms whether the dog drops, stands, or runs in to shot. Even if a dog runs in to shot, little harm is done and it is said that allowing dogs to do this makes them keener and they often retrieve naturally as they feel it is *their* bird. Personally, I would suspect such explanations as excuses for the lazy trainer. There is also the possibility that such dogs will not take training. But the choice is a personal one. Of course, running in to shot is quite a different thing to chasing and there are those who would argue that allowing a dog to run in to shot is just one step away from the more serious crime.

If dogs are to be trained to drop to wing and shot it certainly helps to have dogs which are naturally inclined to drop. This is an anathema to North American hunters who do not, generally, like a dog to go down at all. In the USA bird dogs are generally trained to 'Whoa!', or stop in the upright standing position. The only reason I can think for this divergence is that the type of cover often hunted in the States is tall and if a dog were trained to drop it might become lost to sight. We do not generally have that problem in Britain. Also, I suspect that the difference is traditional. All bird dogs in the States are trained by what I would consider to be setter training methods whereas in Britain we expect (quite wrongly in my opinion) all pointers and setters to be trained like pointers. The two types are as different as chalk and cheese which I hope will become clearer as we proceed. Is it possible for a whole nation to get it wrong?

In my experience, the best type of dog to give a snappy performance, dropping quickly to shot or wing, is a dog which is slightly jumpy, or what some would call a nervous animal. I discussed this with the famous hackney breeder and trainer, the late 'Cluny' Crichton, and he considered this 'highly strung' temperament essential in a top bred driving horse. He preferred an animal which many would have thought nervous. Since then I have questioned many top dog trainers and the best trainers also prefer this sort of dog for reasons that will soon become apparent. Arkwright clearly agreed. In reality, such an animal, be it horse or dog, becomes confident when it is doing what it is trained to do and responds far quicker and more easily to its handler's slightest signal than the more phlegmatic animal. I would go so far as to state that I find it difficult to relate to a dog which is slow to respond and I find the training of such dogs usually proceeds with a struggle. Sensitive dogs can learn very quickly indeed, but these days they are unpopular because they are quite as quickly ruined.

Consider the temperament of the English Thoroughbred race horse compared with, say, a Highland garron. The first (although there are exceptions) is all nerves, jumping and ready for flight at every strange sound or sight. The Highlander, really a small draught horse bred for nothing more than heavy work on the Highland croft, is as phlegmatic and imperturbable as it is possible for an equine to be; steadily getting down to his work without a hint of temperament or excitability and often taking to work after only a few hours breaking. Yet which would you enter for The Grand National or choose to ride to hounds?

Sensitivity of nose is absolutely vital in a bird dog. And I use the Americanism of 'bird dog' for good reason. Pure-bred pointers and setters are bred to hunt birds, not ground 'game' such as hares and rabbits. There is a very good reason for that. On certain Scottish hillsides hares (White Hares, Blue Hares, Mountain Hares, whatever you like to call them—all *Lepus timidus* to the naturalist and all a nuisance to the dog trainer) occur in great numbers. Also, the Brown Hare (*Lepus europaeus*), which is something like the American Jack Rabbit, is fairly common on the low ground and on rough upland grazing. It used not to be unusual for organised shoots of thirty or forty Guns during the winter on some Scottish grouse moors to kill upwards of a thousand of these mountain hares in a day. Such slaughter is possible because the animals, which occur in great numbers and are a serious pest, prefer to run up hill when disturbed. Walking Guns drive the hares from their forms on the lower slopes to concealed Guns along the tops and hundreds are slaughtered. So to own a dog which points hares is no great virtue. Rather the reverse. Almost as great a pest are the hill sheep on many moors. They have earned the name 'Highland maggots' from dogmen because of their undulating, rhythmic gallop through the heather . . . similar to the blow-fly maggot in appearance! Some dogs seem to love to hasten them on their way, especially when birds are scarce and a bit of excitement seems called for!

To illustrate the issue, put yourself in the position of some paying Gun asked to walk half way up a mountainside to your dog's point and then think of your reaction when a hare jumps up in front of the dog! Never mind the client, think of your own boot leather spent, as the dog handler, in such unproductive exercise! It is an excellent tradition in Britain that he who shoots a hare, carries it home!

So a superlative nose in a bird dog is no great asset in itself, it must also be a *discriminating* nose. I was once sent an Irish setter to train that was as keen to point a sheep as it was to point a bird. I don't think there is much reason to elaborate on that story . . . . The scene was the Scottish Highlands where sheep outnumber people by probably a hundred to one. These powers of scent discrimination have been developed to the ultimate degree in tracking breeds like the Bloodhound which will follow its quarry with resolute single-mindedness through every diversion. It is quite possible to train a highly-bred pointer or setter to ignore hares completely; and as equally impossible to train such a dog that cannot discriminate between the different types of scent. Usually, dogs know from experience what they are pointing and, with practice, it is fairly easy to decide from the dog's demeanour what game he has found.

Nose alone will not find birds. The dog must have the brain and instinct to use it. He must *want* to find birds. Again, the Americanism 'desire' hits the target dead centre. But the dog which homes in solely on the scent of birds will almost certainly waste time on ground scent. For our purposes, ground scent is that retained by the soil and vegetation in which the birds have been in contact; perhaps they ran that way, stayed to feed, or even dozed a while in the afternoon sunshine.

Ground scent does not depend for its existence on the birds being there NOW. Ground scent is the easiest found. It is this scent which is generally hunted by the flushing breeds (and pointer-retrievers). All these dogs, such as the spaniels which roust out game for the sportsman within shotgun range, need to know is the *proximity* of game. Once alerted, the flushing breeds rush around until they disturb the game without any preliminary such as pointing. This is permissible because flushing dogs are trained to work within a specified distance of the handler, say fifteen yards, and the range of a shotgun is roughly double that. It doesn't matter when the birds are raised, the sportsman has plenty of time to shoot knowing from the actions of the dog that game is near.

A lot of time would be wasted if a pointer or a setter stopped on point every time it came across ground scent because the birds could have moved or flown off. Having said that, it is perfectly permissible for a bird dog to *hesitate* or briefly point ground scent until ordered on. (My own dogs regularly look back to me for reassurance when they touch on fresh ground scent. They need no such confirmation when they find air scent.) Just how confusing ground scent can be is easily understood by looking for the marks of grouse in the snow. They run here and there covering the ground with their footprints . . . and their scent. A pointing dog has to respond to the *body scent* of the game it is hunting because that is the only real indication of where the game is NOW.

Body scent disperses from all living animals very much as smoke disperses from a bonfire. The smoke is 'immediate'. Extinguish the fire and the flow of smoke ceases. The smoke already in the air continues to be carried up until it too finally disperses. But scent is not smoke and although the example explains roughly how scent behaves, in reality a complete understanding of the phenomenon and how it is detected by animals is a science in itself. We do know that scent is comprised of very small volatile particles which can be carried in the air and which gradually disperse. For our purposes, the comparison with smoke is probably enough. The important thing to realize is that body scent is immediate; it indicates the probable location of the source (bird or animal) now. Ground scent may or may not indicate the presence of game. The birds may have run or flown off moments before. As an indication of the locality of the source (i.e. the birds), ground scent is unreliable.

Because body scent is carried in the air, it is stating the obvious that bird dogs must search the air to find this type of scent. To do this, they usually carry their heads high while flushing dogs, hounds, and others bred to hunt ground scent usually carry their heads low. I say 'usually' because there are no hard and fast rules. Hence the comparison in humans said to have their noses in the air; it is a slightly derogatory explanation of high breeding. On a good day, foxhounds will race across country quite obviously following the air scent of the fox they are hunting. And even the best pointer or setter will occasionally drop its head to check ground scent. This last is no fault though it is usually wrong for a bird dog to point foot scent alone for long. But as a dog is said to be able to detect scent in concentrations from one thousandth to one millionth of that detected by man it might be rather rash to state that a dog is pointing ground scent rather than body scent carried on an air current at ground level at any particular time . . . . Though many better qualified than the author claim to be able to make such fine judgments.

To make best use of its scenting powers a bird dog must search the moving air currents for these particles of air scent. Because air scent is generally rising in the air, the higher a dog carries its head the better chance it generally has of finding this elusive form of scent. It is not unusual to see a good dog actually stand on its hind legs to check for the faintest whiff of scent carried on the breeze. Of course, to search as large an area as possible, the dog must travel at right angles to the air flow. The more efficient the dog's nose, the less likely it is to miss scent and the faster it can perform the search. The most efficient manner in which to search a given area is for the dog to hunt to-and-fro in a more or less zig-zag pattern moving forward as each parallel is covered. This pattern is easier to show in a diagram than to explain in words. (See Figure 1, page 106).

This *quartering*, as it is called, is absolutely fundamental to a pointer's or a setter's work. The dog ought to work with a degree of mathematical precision, running across in front of the handler at right angles to the wind, then turning at the extremity of its *cast*, into the wind, turning again to take in the next cast parallel to the first, and so on, the sum of this pattern being the dog's *beat*. This is especially true for British conditions. Grouse and partridges, particularly, are able to conceal themselves and lie to a dog's point even on bare ground and a stubble field or heather moorland is relatively featureless. Where game tends to be found in particular isolated areas, it follows that a dog ought to use its brain to concentrate its search on such preferred areas. In America, where conditions are different, these dogs are trained to search objectives, particular areas frequented by game, and dogs are expected to apply much more initiative than in Britain. There is much we British could learn from this approach.

The better the dog's olfactory powers the more ground it can search between parallels and the wider it can go. So the fastest dog with the best nose will search more ground in a given time than a slow dog with a poor nose. The more ground a dog covers in a given time the less walking the Guns will have to do. So, the less able the Guns are to walk, the faster and wider ranging the dogs ought to be, and not the opposite as many may suppose. The Guns actually have to walk further behind a dog that ranges close and/or slowly. When a fast dog ranges wide, the Guns may even have to stop occasionally to allow the dog time to cover the ground. Very few dogs go too wide though I have to mention that there are exceptions. I have seen dogs range across a front nearly half a mile wide in Caithness. That could mean an eight hundred yard hike to a point at the extremity of the beat. In my opinion that is too far, especially if the birds are not lying too well. Better still to have an intelligent dog that will work wide or close according to the conditions. On flat moors, such as are found in Caithness in the far North of Scotland, a dog ought to go wide. But the same dog ought to have the sense to work close when, for example, working scrub for woodcock later in the season, or for snipe in some boggy corner of rushes. As they say, it all depends.

An intelligent dog will quickly learn that crossing the wind in this regular way is the most efficient method for finding birds. All these dogs need is the opportunity to learn and they will teach themselves. A stupid dog will never learn. But it is generally assumed by British trainers that pointers and setters must be trained to quarter correctly for field trials and I shall say no more on the subject until we get to the chapter on training. An intelligent dog soon learns to handle the wind, and it has to do this if it is going to work downwind as there is no way a handler can train or help his dog in that situation.

And so the picture of the traditional British bird dog begins to emerge. Apart from differences in character and style, pointers and setters do the same job in much the same way. Here we have a dog which has a great passion for bird finding that is only eclipsed by its love for its handler. A dog which has the courage to hunt long and hard for birds under the most demanding of conditions and when it has found them, to remain staunchly on point for long as is needed to allow its handler to get to it. Only then will it hand over responsibility to its handler, moving in with him to flush on command. The dog must not only have tremendous olfactory powers but the ability to discriminate between different scents and search with a preference for air scent. Natural quartering with a high head is wanted. I would add to this a natural sagacity to interpret the escape behaviour of wild game. But not least, good looks and stylish performance to inspire the Guns to walk and watch the dog work even though game may be scarce and the ground hard going.

There is, of course, much more. In Britain, our bird dogs are not generally trained to retrieve. But they often do so naturally and would do so regularly if only we trainers would take the trouble to teach them. Before the last world war, British breeds were trained for Continental field trials in which the dogs had to retrieve a live brailed duck from water, retrieve a dead fox or cat over a distance of one thousand metres, retrieve a dead hare, follow the blood spore of boar or roe, and much more. These were the ancestors of the dogs we own today, so please do not tell me it cannot be done. Pointers from my kennel exported to the Continent have successfully competed in such trials. My own Irish setters often retrieved better than the specialist breeds. We British are probably unique in *not* training our pointers and setters to retrieve. It is tradition only and has nothing to do with ability. Most pointers and setters are natural retrievers but they are prevented from doing the job by owners who do not believe it can be done or that it will cause unsteadiness.

My Irish setters beat the retrieving specialists on more than one occasion. One day, a partridge was shot which fell into a gorse bush. My setter had been ordered on the lead because she was 'too wild'. In fact, she was merely working as a bird dog should and it was the shoot organizer who did not understand the work of a setter. In this case about a dozen labradors and spaniels failed to pick the partridge and I felt justified in timidly enquiring whether I might try my dog. 'You can't do much harm now,' said my host with great magnanimity, whereupon the setter was released. She went straight to the bush, picked the partridge immediately, and brought it right back to hand. No great feat really, as all the retriever breeds had been searching for ground scent and my dog had naturally sought for and found the partridge by air scent. There were many similar exploits, the late Captain Parlour relating how one of his setters pointed another bird while in the act of retrieving one that had been shot. Again, the softer, more controllable dog is best or the retrieving bird dog quickly becomes one that runs in to shot.

The pointers and setters are the specialists, required to find game birds in open country where the birds are considered too scarce for driving or walking up and this can only be a thumbnail sketch of how much they can or will do if properly trained. Before we go any further, it will certainly be valuable to know how and why these dogs came to be bred to do this exacting type of work on one of the world's wildest and most demanding of game birds, the red grouse.

Chapter 2
Origins of the Bird Dogs

I remember very little of the history I was taught in school. Mostly it seemed to comprise long lists of kings and dates which meant very little to me except tedious hours of detention when the attempts to engrave this comparatively useless information into my memory proved futile. Now I wish I had paid more attention. In spite of what they tried to teach me thirty-odd years ago I have since discovered that some of those long dead kings were very interesting characters indeed. Many shared my own passions for dogs, hawks, and hunting!

Few sportsmen in the past had the time or inclination to write about dogs and getting at the facts is a matter of splicing together what few details and snippets of information do exist in the light of what makes sense from one's own experience. This sort of speculation is often worthwhile because a knowledge of the past can help to solve today's problems. Knowing how a breed of dog evolved and what it was used for makes it easier to train one today. Knowing what characteristics were valued centuries ago and what has been introduced since to 'improve' a breed for shows or trials can guide our assessment of strains extant today. Approach the training of all strains of pointers and setters in the same way and you are soon find yourself in difficulties.

In the real world, it may take decades, even centuries for new ideas to become generally accepted and for things to change. That was certainly true of the rural society of medieval England. The changes that have taken place in just my own lifetime are truly incredible; radio and television, space research, and so on. In comparison, improvements in something simple like the wagon wheel changed little from Roman times right up to recent date with the introduction of roller bearings, metal spokes, pneumatic tyres, and so on. In the past any new idea, unless endorsed by some higher authority, was regarded with suspicion. For guidance, one looked to the past, to the classics and the Bible. To have publicly claimed, in those days, what we all now know to be true would have had violent and terminal consequences!

So just getting sportsmen to accept the idea that a pointing dog might be of some use to them would have taken some doing five hundred years ago. There were other factors to inhibit the spread of new ideas. The total population of Britain in 1500 was about two million. Of these, perhaps fifty were peers, mostly militia, and another one hundred thousand gentlemen landowners, many of whom were illiterate. The rest were probably too busy worrying where the next meal was coming from to indulge in original thought.

At that early date, various types of dogs were used for driving game into nets, retrieving game shot with the bow, or for flushing game for hawks. There is evidence that there were pointing dogs from the earliest time, but probably used for locating large game animals in cover as an aid to traditional hunting with hounds rather than hunting birds. These were the brachs, a type of pointing dog bred as an off-shoot from the hounds and the progenitors of such breeds as the German Shorthaired Pointer. Modern stag hunts use 'tufters', old experienced hounds, to locate and single out huntable stags in a vaguely similar manner. I would suggest that the use of such dogs was quite different to the use of modern pointing dogs and that is why they evolved separately. A professional roe stalker of my acquaintance used various breeds of dogs, including lurchers and collies, to assist in deer stalking in woodland. The dogs were either held on a lead or trained to stay close and the stalker was alerted to the presence of deer up wind by the actions of the dogs. Probably the brachs were used in a similar way: a primitive but reasonably effective method of hunting. The old-time hunters would have wanted to drive game into open country where it could be coursed, hardly the role of a pure-bred pointing dog. Some of the modern pointer-retriever breeds were bred up from these brachs with judicious introductions of English bird dog, bloodhound, and other breeds. Such dogs were always considered the general purpose dogs of the gamekeeping classes, as well able to follow the spore of a wounded roe or boar as to point a bird, retrieve a hare, or kill a marauding cat or fox. By British standards, such dogs were bred to be as tough as old boots, in general constitution and in temperament, and the method of training adjusted accordingly. My Continental friends expect to use force training methods on such dogs; indeed, they tell me the dogs are bred to accept such training methods. In Britain, the same breeds have been bred to accept softer methods of training. I mention this because some people occasionally obtain books on training these dogs and then apply these same methods to the education of British bird dogs with predictably disastrous results. The soft natured pointers and setters are quickly ruined; the hard-headed versions survive. But to whose benefit?

The English seem to have had pointing dogs for hunting birds from before 1500 but these were probably spaniels trained to point without any great refinement. Some spaniels today will point, especially if encouraged to do so; and there are of course specialist pointing spaniels like the Brittany. There was really no need for a fast, wide ranging specialist bird finding dog at this stage of our history. Guns were far too heavy and inefficient to be in general use and far too cumbersome to be practical hunting weapons for those who owned them. Most game was shot with the longbow or crossbow as it sat on the ground, arrows and bolts being a lot easier to procure than powder and shot. Richer harvests could be got by using nets or traps in a variety of ways. Dogs might have been useful in driving out cover, the birds being caught in flight nets set where they were expected to fly, but their use was limited to specialist applications as this cannot generally be expected to produce a rich harvest. Concentrations of birds on migration might be caught in large numbers, perhaps woodcock found in concentrations before land drainage destroyed habitat, so the cocker or springer spaniel got its name from hunting or springing these birds for the netsmen. Other game birds increased as agriculture improved, no doubt widening the possibilities for the use of such dogs.

If netting game was a reasonably efficient way of killing birds, catching game with hawks was more fun. Hawking with a goshawk or a sparrowhawk is more effective with a small type of flushing spaniel and although a dog trained to point might have been an interesting refinement it is not much more. Pure falconry, with the long winged hawks, was a sport for the aristocracy and it was popular amongst the upper classes while land remained relatively open and unfenced. Britain, of course, was changing; the traditional oak and pine woods either being felled for ship building, charcoal, or to rid the countryside of wolves, both two and four-legged versions. They had no need of pointing dogs (or so they thought!) because they had only to get enough people together to flush game for their falcons to get a flight. That's assuming they wanted to fly at grouse or partridges or similar birds. Game is usually well aware when hawks and falcons are about and prefers to stay hidden safely in cover. Dogs that can roust birds out of such cover can be really useful but this is not the role of the highly bred pointing dog. But let's start from the beginning and take a closer look at falconry and hawking.

Strictly speaking, falconry is the sport of flying the long winged hawks, such as the peregrine falcon, at quarry. Hawking is the use of the short winged hawks, such as the sparrowhawk and goshawk, though it is also a term used in the more general context of sport with trained diurnal birds of prey.

There are today two main branches of falconry with the true falcons. These are 'out of the hood flights' and 'game hawking' with falcons. Flights 'out of the hood' are true aerial coursing matches with the quarry identified by the falconer before the falcon's hood is removed. Dogs are seldom used in this sport though coursing dogs might be trained to work with the falcon as salukis are used by the Arabs when flying their falcons at houbara (a type of desert bustard) or at desert hares and gazelle. When the quarry is sighted the falcon is unhooded and released like a greyhound slipped on a hare. The hood, incidentally, covers the falcon's eyes keeping it from seeing the quarry before it is ready to fly. Many falconry terms survive today, for instance, in this context, 'what the eye does not see, the heart does not grieve after'.

Modern game hawking is a much more sophisticated sport altogether which I shall explain in detail in a later chapter.

Hawking, with hawks like the goshawk or sparrowhawk, is a more down-to-earth affair. The hawk is flown in straight pursuit over a relatively short distance. The hawk can be compared with the shotgun; effective within a short range. If the quarry is missed it is either driven into cover or escapes. Here a keen spaniel can be useful and game flushed repeatedly for the hawk to fly becomes increasingly demoralised making it easier for a kill. Long flights are unusual so the birds can be flown in relatively enclosed country. This is a real yeoman's sport with the end product of a pheasant, partridge, rabbit, or quail, perhaps several of each, for the pot. A friend phoned only yesterday to say he had just caught four rabbits in under an hour with his male goshawk. He might have done even better with the bigger and stronger female goshawk, a dozen or so rabbits in a similar time being nothing unusual.

I heard an interesting account of partridge and quail hawking with goshawks over pointers in pre-partition India from Mr Anoop Bedi, a post graduate student at Edinburgh University, which might indicate how early British hawking was done. These dogs were (and apparently still are for I have recently exported a pointer puppy for that very purpose) trained to hunt for and briefly point migratory quail for hawking. The brief pause before going in to flush is apparently all that is needed to alert the falconer. Spaniels can be quite easily trained to do the same job as the dogs are required to range close. Pointers, of course, would stand the heat of India better. There is no reason to believe that this sport has changed much over the centuries and events might have been similarly managed in medieval Britain when migratory quail were quite common.

A spaniel is so useful when hawking pheasants and rabbits with a goshawk that an Irish friend used to have trouble keeping up with his dog/hawk team! Both participants seemed to realize that the human element was really unnecessary! But, again, there was no pointing by the dog involved, it just flushed game from cover after it had been driven in by the hawk. But dogs do get very clever and some learn to wait until the hawk is correctly placed before rushing in to flush out the game.

Falconry is more ethereal. Flights with peregrine falcons after the kite or heron (illegal in modern times) were magnificent; true three dimensional coursing in the sky which required madcap gallops by the field if they were to witness the hunt over many miles of open country. The pursued, a relatively slow flying bird, had the ability to rise quickly in rising air currents and perform tight turns. The faster falcon can only follow by flying in wide circles. It is all to do with aspect ratios and stalling speeds which (thank goodness!) are beyond the scope of this book. I'd equate the match as something like trying to run over a rabbit in an open field with a motorcycle. The bike may be faster but the rabbit can make tighter and quicker turns and is never caught. The kite or heron, or in modern times the rook, will attempt to beat the falcon in the air; the falcon attempting to gain the advantage of height so that it can drive down and strike its intended victim with a smashing stoop. The quarry frustrates the issue by side-stepping, so to speak, and attempts to rise even higher by flying in tight circles. The full excitement of the chase is only experienced at first hand; the two birds go up and up with the occasional stoop by the falcon and side-slip by the quarry, just as the greyhound and hare alternately strike and dodge, each matching the other turn for turn, twist for twist, with the pursued more often as not escaping unscathed as the birds are blown downwind in the slightest breeze.

But have you ever tried eating kite or heron pie? An old ex-African game warden, the late Major Eustace Poles, assured me that kites delight in feeding from the latrines and open cess pits of human sewage though he admitted that carrion would suffice if these delicacies are unobtainable! Herons are only slightly more fastidious! Kite or heron hawking was unlikely to have much appeal to the common man for obvious reasons. The scrawny, fetid tasting prize, in culinary terms, scarcely merited the effort involved.

'Waiting-on' flights in the Middle Ages were to be had with peregrines trained to fly high above a hawking party and to follow the crowd of mounted sportsmen as they galloped across a rural countryside unfenced and unimproved by modern agricultural. There is the initial stoop as a half dozen mallard spring from some small lochan, then the aerial battle for supremacy if the first strike is missed. After a flight lasting perhaps twenty minutes up and down the valley, the duck puts in to some other small splash, the mounted followers galloping up to flush it out again; dogs barking, men shouting, and horses neighing. All confusion and excitement. Half the rural population of the district rushing about and getting under each other's feet. All wonderful chaotic fun no doubt, but hardly very rewarding in terms of meat for the table. But a few horsehair nooses amongst some spoilt corn in a quiet corner of the marsh would have caught more mallard in a night than the falconers could ever hope to have done in a month of

Sundays. But as a training ground for war for the aristocracy, such mad gallops across country in the name of hunting had few equals.

Or it could have been a flight at a partridge, or a covey of grouse, that the falcons followed as they flew high above the mounted hawking party. Whatever got up was fair game. The followers might enjoy themselves and have a good day, but this brand of falconry has never been a numbers game. It is too uncertain, too haphazard. So, pointing dogs were certainly not essential in early British falconry except perhaps to join the general mêlée to roust out game that had taken cover at ground level. But all this was to change with the introduction of a purpose-bred and trained, fast, long-legged, pointing dog from Europe. I cannot prove this speculation for recorded facts and dates are rare, but from the little information available it seems a likely explanation.

The Setter

The first account of pointing dogs in England is by Dr Johannes Caius, writing in *De Canibus Brittanicus*, in 1576 . Dr Caius mentions both spaniels and the closely related setters which were reported to find quail and partridges, then lie on the ground and creep forward until near them. The hunter then prepared his net (presumably setting it up, or suspending it, between two rods upwind of the birds) and the dog, on command, rose up and frightened the birds into it. This is but a slight improvement on the use of a spaniel to beat out cover in the hope of frightening game into nets prepared in advance. But what is more interesting is that Dr Caius goes on to say, under the heading of dogs that 'serve for fowling' that 'there is also at this date among us a new kind of dogge brought out of Fraunce, and they bee speckled all over with white and black, which mingled colours incline to a marble blewe'. 'To serve', in falconry parlance, is to flush. But could there be a more accurate description of the blue belton colour found in today's English setters? And why bother to import pointing spaniels if they were so similar to those already here? Clearly, these were something new and exciting.

As Arkwright concludes, setters may have originated in Spain, but they obviously came to Britain via France. There is some speculation that the English name 'spaniel' may have been derived from the word *espagniol*, literally 'Spanish', or perhaps from the French *épanier*, meaning 'to flatten', i.e. to drop down for use with the net. I prefer the first explanation.

The earliest Continental reference to a pointing dog is from a Frenchman, Gaston de Foix, Vicomte de Bearn (1331-1391). In his *Livre de Chasse*, Gaston, popularly known as 'Gaston Phebus' because of his love of hunting, wrote, 'Another kind of dog there is that is called falcon-dog (more correctly translated, 'hawk or falcon-dog') or spaniel (written *espagniol* in the original French) because it comes from Spain, notwithstanding that there are many in other countries . . .'. Gaston goes on to describe what is clearly a flushing spaniel for use with goshawk or sparrowhawk adding, almost as an afterthought, that they are good for taking partridges and quail with the net when they are taught to be couchers (i.e. droppers). This seems to confirm the earlier theory that spaniels were trained to point, not as the specialist bird-finding setters, but merely as an adjunct to hawking proper. Gaston kept between 1,500 and 1,600 dogs gathered

Billy Hossick with some of his Irish setters. (Derry Argue)

together from all over Europe, more as a student of hunting on the grand scale than as a mere collector.

It is not only possible to catch game birds using a net and a pointing dog but a very deadly method of taking game. I owned an Irish setter which took to the job like a duck to water. She would range and point in the usual manner but then wait for me and a companion to draw the net over her, and onto the covey, from behind. She would not move until she felt the touch of the net on her rump when she would walk forward at a gentle pace right up to the birds without the need for any word of command. When the first bird rose she would drop like a stone and if we were quick with the net the whole covey would be taken. This dog actually became rather sticky (something unheard of in an Irish setter) because she always seemed to expect to feel the net on her back before she was ready to move forward! (It is an interesting fact that many Irish setters, and English pointers in that country, have a rather low set tail and quite often lie down on point, both characteristics advantageous to netting. It is also interesting to speculate that the Irish setter's 'insufficiency of point' may be because they were originally bred for netting and not for gunning.) I had better add that such methods are illegal in Britain and we were doing this under licence to catch grouse for a research project! I understand that modern poachers have adapted the method using two Land-Rovers to drag a very large net between them over the stubbles of estates in the South of England. A similar method of taking grouse, without using a dog or vehicle, was told to me by crofters on Speyside when grouse were much more plentiful. On the other hand, I would think pointers generally unsuitable for this job, and few English setters would have the temperament for it. Gordon setters, which also often have the low set tail, might rather enjoy it!

The first account of a pointing dog being used in this way in England in the sixteenth century is of Sir Robert Dudley, Duke of Northumberland, though there appears to be some doubt about the exact date this took place. Mr G St G Gompertz, writing in his *The Gordon Setter; History and Character,* points out that Arkwright wrongly gives Dudley's date of birth as 1504 and he corrects this to 1574 and his death as 1649. Arkwright quotes from Hume's *History of England* that Dudley was made Duke of Northumberland by Edward VI in 1551 (twenty-three years before Mr Gompertz tells us Sir Robert was born) but this is not a history book and we do not need to be that pedantic.

The original account by Anthony à Wood states that Robert Dudley was a tall red-headed man, 'noted for riding the Great Horse, for tilting, and for his being the first of all that taught a Dog to sit in order to catch partridges . . .'. Dudley was an intelligent, well-travelled man, a surveyor and navigator, and he apparently had every opportunity to observe pointing dogs being used on the Continent which he visited regularly as an ambassador for Britain. If we assume he introduced the use of a pointing dog to Britain at the age of thirty (not a totally unreasonable assumption) that would put the first use of such a dog in Britain at around 1600 which would seem to fit quite well. This might also indicate that the pointing dogs originated somewhere in the Middle East (where concentrations of migratory birds occur) but the comment is purely speculative.

By this time, the population of Britain had increased to about four million but the country was in a pretty chaotic state and could hardly feed itself. On the other hand, it was the age of exploration and discovery. Established ideas were being questioned, tested, and very often found wanting. The Flat Earth Syndrome was beginning to shake a little. Queen Elizabeth I was on the throne and Sir Francis Drake had not only circumnavigated the world but had defeated the Spanish Armada. The country was more receptive to new ideas. But when Elizabeth died in 1603, James VI of Scotland inherited a bankrupt kingdom.

The old adage says that if you cannot make money, then you should either inherit it or marry it. Accordingly, Prince Charles, later Charles I, travelled incognito with Buckingham to Spain in 1623 in an abortive attempt to marry the Infanta and cure the cash flow crisis at home once and for all. He was even prepared to become a Catholic to make himself a more acceptable match. James was distraught and sent a court favourite, James Hay, to France to negotiate with Louis XIII for the betrothal of Charles to Louis's sister, Henrietta Maria. Hay was a good choice. An affable, charming character, Hay was also a very keen sportsman and an experienced falconer. This passion in the sport was shared by the French king whose favourite flight is said to have been the diminutive merlin after the winter lark, something that has never been emulated in modern times as it is probably the most difficult facet of falconry to succeed in. Not only are the two birds equally matched, but flights can be expected to continue over huge expanses of sky and countryside. In 1970 I was granted a licence to take two merlins for this flight but a spell in hospital nipped my ambitions in the bud. Louis is reputed to have kept hundreds of hawks so his choice was certainly not out of necessity. Louis was certainly an innovator who is said to have had little patience with his contemporaries. He is also credited with being the first man to shoot flying game.

When Louis sent Hay some falcons James intercepted them, took his pick, and sent the remainder on with a note saying what he had done mentioning that he knew Hay would not mind! Hay's motto was 'Spend and God will send' and he apparently took this literally spending his way through £400,000 during his lifetime, much of which was James I's money. No doubt James felt justified in pinching Hay's best falcons! Hay remained a bachelor all his life and died a bankrupt in 1688 (or 1666 depending on your source!). For his services in arranging Charles's marriage James made him the first Earl of Carlisle. Cumbria at that time was a famous sporting area and was later recognised for producing excellent setters as evidenced by the comments of Laverack and others of that period. But we are getting ahead of ourselves.

State papers of James I (of England) state that in 1624 'A French baron, a good falconer, has brought him (James I) sixteen casts of Hawks from the French King (Louis XIII), with horses and setting dogs; he made a splendid entry with his train by torch-light, and will stay till he has instructed some of our people in his kind of falconry, though it costs his Majesty £25 or £30 a day'. (A cast of falcons is two birds, usually trained to fly together, not necessarily of different sexes).

This is an important note. James I was no stranger to falconry and yet, although he was nearly bankrupt and in bad health, was happy to pay £25–£30 (a sizeable sum in 1624) a day to learn the French king's style of falconry. We already had setting dogs in Britain yet Louis sent over some of his own dogs with a baron to teach the English how it should be done. By March the following year, 1625, James was dead. But can there be any doubt that Louis had perfected the waiting-on flight with peregrines at game using trained setters? Is it not possible that Louis thought this sport particularly suitable for a fellow falconer who was no longer fit to follow the more usual sport of galloping across country on horseback with falcons flying randomly overhead? Quite recently I watched a trained peregrine flown at partridges over a pointer. It was possible to watch the whole flight without moving more than twenty-five yards from the car. Real wheelchair sport!

There is a painting in The Louvre entitled *Boune, Noune, and Poune – Dogs Belonging to the Pack of Louis XIV of France*, by Desportes (1666-1743). These dogs are undoubtedly setters and were probably descendants of Louis XIII's dogs. They are similar in every respect to the smaller type of field trial or Llewellin setter not uncommon today. It is difficult not to make the obvious connection between these dogs and the Llewellins which can be traced back to 1790 when the Reverend Harrison of Carlisle acquired his dogs.

But this new style of falconry needs further examination. Game hawking with pointing dogs and falcons trained to 'wait on' crystalizes the epitome of falconry; now game birds can be found, pointed, the falcon released to fly high above the point, and then, when the stage is set, the game can be sprung. The result is a total distillation of the flight, once so unpredictable, now so singularly stage-managed with that downward stoop by the falcon onto its prey taking place directly in front of the spectators! If Louis did not have this in mind as a way to entertain his sick and virtually invalid future brother-in-law then this report is the more remarkable.

Although English setters seem to have originated from French imports, no information is available on the origins of the Irish setter. Possibly it came direct from France with which Ireland had direct connections, or even from Spain. The Gordon setter, on the other hand, was merely a colour variation of the English setter as we shall learn later.

But with the royal seal of approval, so to speak, it is reasonable to assume that Louis XIII's dogs would have been distributed to favoured members of the British aristocracy to be used for falconry, hawking, or netting as the opportunity arose. I believe it is particularly relevant that the Carlisle area (and spreading right through the north of England) seems to have been a centre for the best setters. Edward Laverack mentions that his own breed which became known as The Laverack Setter was at one time known all through Cumberland, Northumberland, and the Borders. This, of course, was where James Hay came to rest. Is it too much to surmise, to hope, that Hay brought home some of Louis XIII's setters which were then distributed throughout the area? There is, of course, a gap of one hundred years, but bear in mind how slowly things changed in the country. There will be proof somewhere, but who has the time to unearth it?

It seems Charles was not the sportsman his father was and falconry appears to have taken a back seat. Seventeen years later, the Great Rebellion (or the Civil War, depending on your politics) broke out in England. Later, France was to experience a similar upheaval in the French Revolution. Oliver Cromwell, as a landowner, enjoyed hunting but he was also the man who was enough of a kill-joy to order the abolition of Christmas Day. Most of all, he condemned anything to do with royalty. The same politics were to be followed in France. Cromwell was hardly likely to have had much time for the subtler intricacies of game hawking as introduced by Louis XIII to James I using setting dogs, yet it is reasonable to believe that he might have tolerated, if not approved of, more practical ways of filling the pot by using these self-same dogs with nets. He is said to have enjoyed hawking but this was almost certain to have been pot-hunting with a goshawk. Even so, it is unlikely that he could change much in the remoter country areas and it is known that falconry continued in Scotland when it had more or less died out in England. Even though James never returned to Scotland, it is a fair guess that Scottish nobles travelled back and forth to and from the English court taking their dogs with them.

Arkwright clearly had little idea that there was a considerable difference between hawking (with goshawk or sparrowhawk) and game hawking with peregrines. He admits to translating the French for 'the bird' into 'the falcon' in English when it more

The late James Duncan, studying red grouse on Speyside. The Irish setters, bred by the author, were used to locate grouse which were then netted.
(Derry Argue)

probably meant either hawk or falcon according to the context. Yet he states that a reference to the use of pointing dogs with falcons in a book published in 1885 (*The Customes of Yorkshire*) is the first example he had found of the sport in England. He also quotes the author as saying this was hawking only as revived by Colonel Thornton, a noted sporting character of the time. If the sport had been revived, it does not need an Einstein to work out that it must have existed at an earlier date. There is no doubt that Arkwright carried out extensive research into the origins of the pointing dog and the serious student should refer to his book, *The Pointer and His Predecessors*, for more detailed information than can be included here.

To conclude, my own feeling (and it can be no more than that) is that the first importations of the long-legged specialist bird-finding setters into England took place in 1624 and that earlier references to dogs used for hawking were spaniels, not dissimilar to our modern Springers and Cockers though some undoubtedly larger and perhaps roughly similar to modern retrievers. Undoubtedly, the two types, spaniels and setters, would have been crossed from time to time giving rise to the forerunners of our modern setters.

A fast wide ranging pointing dog is almost essential for game hawking (the waiting-on flight) and it seems likely that those French blue beltons are the ancestors of some of today's top strains of English setters.

The Pointer

There is less doubt about the importation of the pointer. A long succession of wars with France and Spain had promoted improvements in firearms so that by 1700 the flintlock was not only improved to near perfection but the many ex-soldiers returning from these wars were acquainted with its use; it was at last readily available. Shooting flying had been an amusement of the eccentric aristocrat since Louis XIII who is one of the first credited with the accomplishment. By the eighteenth century the gun had been lightened and the ignition time (delay between pulling the trigger and the shot leaving the barrel) so improved that shooting flying had become not only a possibility but a reality.

There is little doubt that pointers were imported into England by these soldiers returning from war after the Peace of Utrecht around 1713. It is generally agreed that these were heavy, slow animals with excellent olfactory powers, brought into this country direct from Spain. This sounds reasonable. Setters, we will learn, can be very easy to train if you know what you are doing but they require a light touch. They generally take longer to reach their best and what they learn is not forgotten. The pointer, on the other hand, is relatively easy-going. It often points straight off on first encountering game and the mistakes the trainer makes are not so irredeemable as they might be with a setter. Although pointers need a certain amount of maintenance training, their psychology is not unlike that of a soldier drilled into his duties by repetition and kept in line by authority. The setter has far too much intellect to submit to such base treatment although he will readily participate in a fair partnership. It is easy to see which would best suit the military mind and which suited the professional fowler who, by necessity, lived in close rapport with his dog and with nature. So the pointer was taken up by the returning soldiers. They had seen them in use in Spain and had learnt how to train and work them. Interestingly, various pointer-retrievers were brought into this country by soldiers returning from the 1939-1945 war so history repeats itself.

But this slow, ponderous animal was not necessarily typical of all Spanish pointers. Arkwright quotes at length from *Arte de Ballestria y Monteria*, by Alonzo Martinez de Espinar in 1644, that describes the use of pointers to find partridges in Spain which were then shot on the ground with a crossbow. Espinar remarks of the pointer, ' . . . so good are his wind and activity that from morning to night he will not cease galloping, and there are some so swift that they seem to fly over the ground'. Fast pointers were valued by their breeders in those early times and it is only the ignorant Englishmen who wanted the slow animals because they could not manage quality. Did I say history repeats itself? A prospective purchaser called at my kennel to see some setters the other day and chose the slowest (and, I thought, the worst) because it was 'the steadiest'. Yet Arkwright reproduces the Tillemans painting of the Duke of Kingston with his liver and white pointers dated 1725. He points out that the dogs are of the type and colour of the royal pointing dogs of France and that the Duke had every opportunity of getting these dogs direct from source as he was often at the French court and kept a French mistress. The dogs in this painting would not disgrace a modern kennel and are of uniformly good type, some in the painting pointing standing, some lying, and some apparently backing. From their conformation, one can guess that they would have been quite fast enough for modern requirements.

But in Britain, as the decades slipped by, even greater things were to come. The landed aristocracy had always had its kennels of dogs and now, to quote Arkwright, 'nearly every family of position had its own breed of pointers'. From the earliest times the art of training hawks and dogs had been revered as a profession and now the estates had their families of gamekeepers who generally owned the dogs and passed them from generation to generation. Few gentlemen of standing would have stooped to train a dog or a falcon and that situation continued right up to the twentieth century. These were the professions of the specialists, artisans perhaps, but each considered as expert in his own field as the better educated doctors and lawyers. Small wonder that gamekeepers in Scotland still often enjoy a relatively privileged position in rural society as many a resident agent or shooting tenant has discovered to his cost!

But by the eighteenth century the Industrial Revolution had begun in earnest. A new rich class was being created by the industrialisation of society and fresh young markets in the colonies were opening up. Fortunes were being made every day. If the sixteenth and seventeenth centuries were the ages of discovery, this was the great age of innovation and competition. Every man who had made his fortune wished to emulate those who already had money and to ape the country squire. It was not enough to shoot flying, you had to get your name into the newspaper for shooting a tremendous bag. Even better, for shooting more birds than your neighbour.

The country gentleman was now expected to keep stables of English Thoroughbreds, carriages, packs of hounds, hundreds of game cocks out at walk, and kennels of fighting dogs, fox hounds, and pointers or setters all matched for type and colour. This was life with style. To keep up with his neighbours, he strove to keep better dogs, to acquire a better shotgun, and to shoot more birds.

The acquebus had been fired by applying a piece of smouldering tow to the touch-hole as its long and heavy barrel was rested on a forked stick. It was an almost impossible weapon to kill game with and to carry it in the field was a penance. The flintlock was provided with flint and steel and a neat mechanism to send a shower of sparks at a touch of the trigger into the pan leading to the breech. The improvement was huge. Powder was improved so it burnt faster, cleaner, sending the charge of shot out through the barrel with more power. Barrels could now be shortened and still contain the full force of the explosion. Innovations in steel-making allowed gun barrels to be made lighter and stronger, witness the beautifully patterned Damascus steel barrels still in use today on old guns made by forging red-hot plaited steel bands onto a mandrel. My own gun, used by my grandfather sixty or seventy years ago, is of this type and still in use. Two barrels, three barrels, even more to the point of absurdity, were brazed together to provide greater firepower. No doubt the traditionalists protested that it was all so unsporting but fashions had to change in the face of such progress. Double barrelled guns proved the most practical and, although declared unsporting when first introduced, remain the most common form right to the present day.

Around the middle of the nineteenth century, breech loading guns began to come into favour. The transition was gradual, aided by regular innovations and improvements prompted by various conflicts around the world and the continual demand for better weapons of mass destruction, whether of man, beast, or bird. Black powder which left a great pall of dark smoke after each shot was replaced by smokeless propellants. Someone came up with the idea of incorporating the percussion cap next to the charge itself, all packaged together in what we know as the shotgun cartridge. The hammer gun was replaced with the hammerless shotgun and a mechanism was invented to eject the discharged cartridge after firing. The hammerless ejector double barrelled sporting shotgun had reached the pinnacle of evolution nearly a century ago and no one has yet come up with a better design for game shooting.

Up until the Victorian era nearly all game shooting had been over pointers and setters. Hutchinson's *Dog Breaking,* first published in 1848 and one of the first books on psychological dog training, provides an intriguing insight into this period and by 1898 it had run to ten editions. It is still a work of reference for many modern dog trainers. The book was written before the modern epidemic of 'pedigree-itus' (the enthusiast's obsession for paper pedigrees). A dog was judged on what it could do, not on what the registration certificate claimed it might do, and if a man wanted a dog to do a particular task and there wasn't one available, he created one by cross-breeding, amalgamating pure-bred strains to produce the ideal compromise. There is nothing new in that idea. The farmer creates a cross-bred ewe from hill and lowland breeds combining hardiness with prolificacy and milking ability, finally crossing this with a meat breed to produce the ideal butcher's lamb. The only novelty in today's situation is that the modern breeder has thrown out a perfectly practical solution for some supposed value in paper pedigrees. Could there be a better true life version of the story of the Emperor's magic suit of clothes? It was by such judicial crossing that the modern Flat Coat Retrievers and Labradors were created. The Irish shooting men, ever more practical than their English counterparts, cross a pointing breed with a flushing or retrieving breed to produce a dog capable of doing both jobs. The only problem with such a hybrid is that it might take several generations of careful selective inbreeding to establish type. But if one just wants a dog for shooting, why bother?

So popular did the sport of deer stalking and shooting over dogs become during the Victorian era that the railway meandered and wove its way through the Scottish Highlands from one shooting lodge to the next and from one sporting estate to another.

The evolution of the gundog followed a parallel course to that of the sporting shotgun. It is no accident that the top gunmakers also owned the top kennels of working pointers and setters. Thomas Bland, Joseph Lang, T Page, and W R Pape are just a few of these dog-owning gunmakers.

Our European friends are, today, often surprised that British dogs are seldom trained to retrieve. The same dogs (bred originally from identical stock) on the Continent would be expected to do a wide variety of tasks in special field trials including retrieving brailed duck from water, following a blood spore, even retrieving a dead fox over a distance of 1,000 metres! Details of these trials and training the traditional British pointer and setter breeds for them were published in a book, *Der Feld- und Wald-gebrauchshund,* by Hofmann, now sadly a rare collector's item. We British lamely mumble that it is difficult to achieve top class style and retain steadiness in a dog required to retrieve as well. The truth is that the eighteenth century gentleman sportsman had no need of a pointing dog that would retrieve. His desire was for a pointing dog which would find birds fast, quartering in a mathematical fashion with such precision that the maximum amount of ground was covered as the shooter walked forward up the centre-line of the beat at a steady pace. Find one covey, fire, load, fire, load, and then get on to find the next covey as quickly as possible. The gathering of the slain could easily be delegated to a couple of servants hired to do the job, or to specialist retrieving breeds. In such times, men were cheaper than dogs and the dogs usually ate and lived a lot better. The ordinary shooter might expect his pointer or setter to retrieve, but generally the gentleman did not. And so the Flat Earth Syndrome persists! 'They don't retrieve', they say. And of course they don't, because they are never trained to do it! Very often, all these breeds need is the opportunity and some slight encouragement. If one hundred per cent steadiness is to be retained, commonsense, too, needs to be applied. But then the same is true in spaniel training.

Two pointers painted by T. Blinks around 1890. (Derry Argue)

The country gentlemen owning kennels of pointers or setters were relatively isolated and there is no doubt that their dogs were inbred by modern standards. Herbert Atkinson, writing in *Cock Fighting and Game Fowl,* quotes Richard Stamp, a famous breeder of game cocks in the early nineteenth century, as advising, 'Mother and son, aunt and nephew, half-brother and half-sister, grandmother and grandson, the more crosses in that way the better' as being the way to breed these birds. No doubt, dogs were bred just as close. Indeed, they had to be because transport was so difficult, often near impossible at the time a bitch might come into season, and the best kennels were jealously guarded. Today, we are apt to forget just how bad disease was amongst dogs even a few decades ago before inoculations were available against the great killers of distemper, hepatitis, and leptospirosis. So local breeds and strains developed in greater profusion than The Kennel Club, established in 1873, would ever acknowledge. Edward Laverack, writing of English setters in his book *The Setter* in

1872, mentions the Naworth and Featherstone Castle breed, Lord Lovat's breed, Earl of Southesk's breed, the Earl of Seafield's breed, Lord Ossulton's breed, Mr Lort's breed, Llanidloes, and his own, The Laveracks. All 'English setters' in the eyes of the Kennel Club and all, except the last, now sadly extinct or crossed out of existence. Laverack remarked (in 1872), 'A great controversy has been going on of late years as to whether our breed of setters are *better* or equal to those of the olden time. I am decidedly of opinion *they are not* .... With the exception of a few kennels of choice blood, and which have been most carefully guarded, I fear, nay I am sure, the setter has been greatly *degenerated* and *mongrelised*'. So by the latter half of the nineteenth century the rot had already set in.

The demise of the general popularity of shooting over pointers and setters came about through many small factors. Changes in feed formulation permitted the artificial rearing of game birds on a scale hitherto only dreamt of. The Continental fashion for 'battu', i.e. driven shooting, was gaining in popularity and was given the seal of royal approval by Prince Albert, Queen Victoria's German husband, who was keen on this type of sport. Who would dare to condemned the practice as ungentlemanly or unsporting now? More traditional British sportsmen had condemn this style of shooting for generations, now it was dogging that was decried as 'old fashioned'. The fertility of the hills, built up through centuries of natural afforestation, had been made available by burning the trees and replacing the Highland crofters with sheep. The sheep in turn manured the heather and the grouse increased in huge numbers, protected as they were by ruthless gamekeeping which brought death and violent destruction to every wild thing with a hooked beak or sharp claw. Grouse could now be driven to waiting Guns in undiminishing hordes. And later in the season, droves of pheasants and partridges would be driven over standing Guns on the low ground. Sportsmen could shoot faster, too, thanks to the perfection of the sporting shotgun.

Perhaps the low ground could produce pheasants and partridges but the ground cover beloved by game birds had disappeared. Hand reaping left knee high stubbles. The new reaping machines shaved stubbles to ground level and the straw was carted off. Improved fodder conservation, and most of all the turnip, allowed greater numbers of livestock to be kept over the winter and the rough pastures so loved by game on the hitherto understocked fields were nibbled down just when cover was needed most. Dogging simply does not work if there is no ground cover in which game birds feel secure enough to lie to a dog's point. Strangely, things go full circle; the latest harvesting machines strip the grain and leave the straw standing. Farmers are paid to leave fields uncultivated. Dogging fell out of fashion in every area except where there was no other way of coming to terms with game. Shooting over dogs has always continued in the far north where grouse stocks are too low and the topography is unsuitable to permit driving. Driving works best where there are hills and gullies to channel grouse. It is less efficient on flat rolling ground such as the traditional dogging counties of the north of Scotland.

Shows and Field Trials
While all this was happening there was a considerable export market for the best dogs to British colonies around the world. Amongst the good dogs there were even more

bad ones and some sort of quality control was called for. It was in an effort to redeem a deteriorating situation that the first dog show, for pointers and setters only, was held at Newcastle-on-Tyne in 1859. The show was organised by a well-known gamekeeper and trainer, Mr R Brailsford, who had charge of Mr Haywood Lonsdale's Ightfield Kennels. Yet it soon became obvious that the dogs also ought to be tested for work. Dogs were winning on the bench that had never been near a grouse moor or a partridge manor. So the first field trial ever, again for pointers and setters, was organized by Mr William Brailsford (a son of Mr R Brailsford) at Southill, near Bedford in 1865 in connection with the Islington show. Sixteen pointers and setters competed and the stake was won by Fleming's Gordon setter champion 'Dandy'. The experiment led to a repeat the following year when a field trial was held on the 1 and 2 May at Cannock Chase, near Stafford, with stakes for both pointers and setters, of course. But at that time no one would have dreamt of keeping a bird dog that would not work.

The interest in shows increased at a tremendous pace, all initially for pointers and setters though other gundog classes were soon to follow. This alone demonstrates how numerous and important these breeds of pointing dogs were at that time. Everything was tried to 'improve' bird dogs for shows and trials, so great were the rewards, and, then as now, fanciers soon discovered there were greater rewards to be had from breeding dogs for the bench where everyone could see one's successes, than breeding dogs for work which was more expensive and less open to public acclamation. We are still reaping the dubious 'benefits' of this experimental outcrossing today.

One such early cross was that made by Colonel Thornton (1757–1823) of a foxhound onto a well-bred pointer bitch which produced the celebrated 'Dash'. This dog had, by all accounts, tremendous nose and was an excellent backer of other dogs. He seems to have caught the imagination of many sportsmen of the time because of his style of working. He was sold to Sir Richard Symons for what was considered to be an immense price, that is 'one hundred and sixty pounds' worth of champagne and burgundy, a hogshead of claret, an elegant gun, and a pointer . . .'. Dash was used widely at stud but left not a single pup worth keeping. There is no doubt that many others followed this lead with similarly disastrous results. Thornton's dogs were some of the first dual purpose pointers; they are said to have coursed and killed a stag as readily as they would point a grouse or partridge! Later foxhound blood was again introduced into the pointer to 'improve' its appearance for shows as contempory authorities suggested that the pointer should be modelled on the foxhound, a travesty of the truth if ever there was one.

Having introduced The Kennel Club, we ought perhaps to go off on a red herring, or rather a black one, to demonstrate just how extreme these competitions had become. Arkwright, a founder member of The Kennel Club which was established to be the canine equivalent of the Jockey Club, wrote vehemently against the way field trials and shows were organised by this body. It was clear from the start that The Kennel Club was mainly interested in the show element as that is where the numerical superiority was concentrated and where the greatest income from registrations and licences could be gathered. Such organisations seem to attract those interested in the business and politics of dogs rather than the sport of training, working, and shooting over them which requires few rules and is largely a solitary activity. My own view is that the main attraction of field sports is that there are so few rules, though these days it is sadly becoming more correct to talk of this in the past tense. Arkwright made the mistake, if that is the correct word for outspokenness and directness, of openly criticising The Kennel Club.

To get to the other side of the story it is worth reading Waldermar Marr's little book *Pointers and Setters* (1969 – republished in 1979) and his discussion of William Arkwright. There is no doubt that Marr's book is a valuable reference source on the recent history of British working pointers and setters world-wide. But he is unhesitatingly scathing about William Arkwright as a breeder and personality. Arkwright, he explains, achieved some success with his pointers until, in Marr's opinion, he introduced whole or self coloured pointers into his kennel around 1898. Marr tells us that Arkwright got some of these pointers from Mr W R Pape, the famous Newcastle gunmaker, who had them for forty years. From this Marr concludes that as some trial people introduced greyhound blood into their dogs around the 1850s (actually field trials were not started until the mid 1860s!) these whole coloured pointers of Pape's must have had greyhound blood in them. That appears to be the sum of Marr's logic on the point. Some might conclude this diagnosis to be rather tentative to say the least but since Arkwright had been dead some forty years when this defamation was published he was on safe ground. But it begins to make sense when we remember Arkwright's attack on The Kennel Club and the fact that Marr was very much an Establishment figure.

An elementary study of genetics will reveal that even if the whole-colour had been introduced by an outcross to a greyhound in 1850 it would make little difference to the dogs produced from that line forty or fifty years later! After all there have been plenty of other outcrosses. If we accept a generation interval of three years, that would allow for about fourteen generations in the same period. Gregor Mendel discovered in the earliest experiments in heredity that characteristics are inherited separately though today this is considered too great a generality. Modern geneticists suggest that an outcross makes little difference after just five generations and twenty generations is all that is required to produce a genetically pure strain in mice for experimental purposes. At even ten generations, the ancestors contributing to a puppy's make-up total over two thousand individuals! The whole-colour is controlled by a single dominant gene (*Inheritance in Dogs,* by Winge, 1950) and the genetics involved is quite straight-forward. That apart, Marr produces not one single grain of proof that Pape used the greyhound cross.

As a matter of interest, I researched the back pedigree of my own dogs which go back to Marr's Blackfield breeding. I found this Blackfield line contained a number of whole coloured dogs which Marr claims to have taken 'all of ten years to wash out'. Clearly, he did not succeed as this same breeding has produced some of today's top field trial dogs. Of course, we are dealing with the old belief that inheritance is 'by blood' when it has been known for very many years that inheritance is controlled by genetic material and the blood of mother and foetus never mixes.

Perhaps even more interesting was an unsolicited letter from a descendant of another gunmaker of the period, Joseph Lang, who carried on business in Cockspur Street, London. As was quite usual in those days, this gentleman also bred top class pointers, and, as chance would have it, black ones. My informant wrote that his ancestor had been plagued by young field trialers ever in search of more speed in their dogs for

Top: Two setters painted by Miss Maud Earl in 1908. (*T. Ishibashi*)

Bottom: Two pointers painted by Thomas Blinks. (*T. Ishibashi*)

Top: The very famous orange and while male pointer champion Idstone of Mr Arkwright, painted by Mrs Elena Marisaldi in 1954. (*T. Ishibashi*)

Bottom: Lemon and white English male setter Waygood Bruce owned by Mr L. Zavattero and bred by Mrs Maurice. Painted by Elena Marisaldi in 1957. (*T. Ishibashi*)

Top: F.T.Ch. Mina di Suno Pointer, painted by Mrs Elena Marisaldi in 1948. (*T. Ishibashi*)

Bottom: A famous blue belton English female setter – F.T.Ch. Quercia delle Morene. Painted by Mrs Elena Marisaldi in 1956. (*T. Ishibashi*)

Top: A very famous orange and white female pointer – Ch. Seabreeze of Mr Arkwright. Painted by Mrs Elena Marisaldi in 1954. (*T. Ishibashi*)

Bottom: English setter Ch. Gil della Spina, painted by Mrs Elena Marisaldi in 1937. (*T. Ishibashi*)

competition. So being of a mischievous disposition he decided to give them something to suit their desires. My correspondent told that Mr Lang put one of his black bitches to a greyhound and sold the progeny as pure-bred pointers. Of course, the nonsense of this story is that the greyhound could have been any colour as there were black pointers in Britain at least one hundred years before that and Mr Lang certainly owned some whole coloured dogs of excellent quality and impeccable breeding. But he clearly had no intention of letting some of his best dogs go to what he probably considered to be 'Yuppies'. The Flat Earth Syndrome at work again!

During the late nineteenth century, many other crosses were tried with the intention of producing better dogs for field trials or shows. The Kennel Club registration of canine pedigrees did bring order to a situation which could have got totally out of control. Gradually, dog shows became even more popular as the manufacture of proprietary dog foods made dog keeping even easier. There were still the wealthy landed families who kept pointers and setters for shooting because they had always kept them and many of these were probably never registered. But their numbers gradually decreased up to the First World War. Driving grouse requires more organisation than shooting over dogs but there is no need to keep a kennel of bird dogs twelve months of the year for, perhaps, six weeks sport during the grouse season. Even so, shooting was still very popular and several establishments bred and trained gundogs commercially, the hiring of dogs during the shooting season and the renting of shootings to young sportsmen from the south being a viable business.

One entrepreneur of this type was Isaak Sharpe (1867-1938) who ran a knackery at Keith, Banffshire. Sharpe was able to keep a large number of dogs at minimal cost by feeding them on fallen stock from neighbouring farms. Clydesdale horses which fell victim to the epidemic of grass sickness at that period or became redundant because of the introduction of the agricultural tractor provided excellent feeding for his dogs. These he is rumoured to have moored in nearby lochs, like so many partially submerged whales, to keep the flies at bay. At the outbreak of the 1914-1918 war, Highland gamekeepers and stalkers volunteered en masse and Sharpe was able to buy up redundant kennels at bargain prices. He is credited with having had over seven hundred and fifty dogs in his kennels at one time. Sharpe took over a large distillery warehouse and converted it to kennels. Local stories, as would be expected of the Scottish Highlands, abound. Isaak Sharpe was obviously a pretty shrewd operator who dealt in dogs in a fairly big way and would demonstrate a dog to a prospective purchaser, inviting his victim in for a whisky to clinch the deal while his kennel boys swapped the animal for an inferior specimen. In fact, no dog behaves as well in strange hands and the defamation may well have been unjust. But there was no doubt that Isaac Sharpe knew a good dog when he saw one and was well able to make a deal. He made his name in field trials and exported world-wide. He even sold dogs to the Emperor of Japan and there is a delightful story of how some emissary telegraphed ahead that he would be arriving at Keith station at such-and-such a time and could be recognised because he would be wearing a red carnation in his button hole. Just how many Japanese gentlemen might have been found on a remote rural railway station in the Scottish Highlands at that period to warrant such a form of identification I cannot imagine! On the outbreak of war in 1939, Sharpe, by local repute, is said to have destroyed over four hundred and fifty dogs in one day on the orders of the government 'to conserve food supplies'. Later the kennel changed to training labradors and spaniels and more-or-less gave up the pointers and setters due to the decline in demand.

Competitors and spectators at a field trial. (Derry Argue)

After the Second World War British pointers and setters were in a very bad state indeed, partly because of this policy of destruction and partly because of the ravages of disease and almost complete depletion of experienced trainers. The show pointers and setters had taken a different direction from the working dogs and they are now almost completely separate strains though still registered on the same Kennel Club register without any means of separate identification as to ability in the field. But that was not the end because pre-war there had been a fair international trade in bird dogs. Some enthusiasts retained the knowledge to gather together the best of this breeding and start again.

Of course, Ireland had remained neutral during the war and 'free' shooting was a legacy of the reforms following independence from Britain. Ireland has always been a great country for sport and famous for the excellence of its livestock breeding. The Irish mountains held a few grouse, the bogs plentiful snipe, and the rushy fields enough pheasants to make things interesting and there was a relatively low rural population, farming being at a subsistence level. Pointers and setters were the preferred gundogs and the countryside was in many ways similar to the British scene a century earlier with large badly drained and under-grazed fields ideal for dogging. Ireland kept an interest in pointers and setters alive in these islands during the war years and helped to revive and maintain the standard after the war. British sportsmen owe a huge debt to the Irish bird dog enthusiasts that they would be wise not to forget. In Britain, the wealthy patron of the sport gradually disappeared until the present day when he is almost totally absent, barring the very few still able to afford to employ the professional gamekeeper who doubles as a dogman.

In the last twenty years the scene has changed yet again. As might be expected, British pointers and setters today are almost as diverse in type as they are in origins. I don't mean just external appearance but in temperament and mental characteristics which are of so much importance to the trainer of a breed which has to work at extreme range. If, at the end of the eighteenth century, 'every family of position had its own breed of pointers' that alone would indicate that there cannot realistically be any 'standard of the breed' for such dogs. What suits one district might not suit another. Then there are the violent outcrosses introduced to 'improve' the breeds for shows and trials. To complicate matters further, there have always been further imports from abroad often carried out for no other reason then 'that is what has worked in the past'. The selective inbreeding which created the breeds in the first place is almost totally lacking and I have seen strains vanish in my own lifetime due to this silly policy of breeding out at every generation.

Angie McLaughlin, the late Lady Auckland's dog trainer/handler at Cromlix, and the late Mrs Patience Badenach-Nicholson judging a field trial.
(Derry Argue)

Today's British pointers and setters are almost all owned by enthusiastic amateurs who keep their dogs as family pets for most of the year and then trial them during the summer and, sometimes, hire themselves and dogs out for the shooting during August and September. Increasingly, the entrants to field trialing come into the sport from an interest in showing dogs rather than an interest in shooting. There is nothing wrong in that so long as field trialing does not lose sight of the original purpose. The changes could herald the dawn of a new era, or it could be the end of the fast, stylish, specialist bird-finder produced by the Industrial Revolution alongside the English hammerless ejector sporting shotgun; both have long been the envy of sportsmen the world over.

The traditional British pointer or setter is the supreme specialist, finding game for the sportsman under conditions where no other breed can compete on equal terms. When that high ideal goes out of sight, these dogs are finished. There will always be those who believe that they can improve on perfection but the unique history of these dogs clearly demonstrates just what circumstances allow such breeds to evolve. Perhaps it is the wealth and virtual dictatorship of a man like Louis XIII or perhaps it is the combination of events which went to make up the Industrial Revolution. If our fine English sporting shotguns disappeared tomorrow, they could be recreated from the plans and blueprints drawn up by gunsmiths long since dead. If our working dogs are allowed to degenerate, they are gone forever along with the knowledge to train and handle them. There is nothing more certain than that.

Chapter 3
The Llewellin Setter

There is a breed of setter which originated in Britain and became famous the world over, yet is scarcely known in its country of origin. The breed is considered to be so important that it has been given separate breed registration by working gundog societies in many countries but never by The Kennel Club in London.

Edward Laverack

The story of the Llewellin setter began in 1790 but the records start at 1825 when Edward Laverack, then about twenty-six years old, procured a dog and a bitch called 'Old Moll' and 'Ponto' from the Reverend A Harrison of Carlisle, Cumbria, in the North of England. One story is that Laverack was a shoe maker's apprentice who inherited a legacy from a rich relative which enabled him to follow a love of dogs and shooting all his life. Laverack was unable to explain the origins of these dogs except to say that Harrison had kept the strain pure-bred for the previous thirty-five years which takes us back to 1790. In the previous chapter the significance of the setters sent over from France by Louis XIII was mentioned. There is also a painting of Louis XIV's dogs in the Louvre showing setters similar to some of today's Llewellins. The evidence is circumstantial, but the time span between Hay's death in 1688 and the first reports of Harrison's setters in 1790 is only 102 years, a gap of less significance in seventeenth century rural England than in more modern times.

Two pedigrees published in Edward Laverack's book, *The Setter*, one of Fred II and the other of Dash, show how Laverack bred brother to sister for at least four generations, then continued this close breeding up to his death in 1877. He claimed to have introduced no outside blood to his strain in nearly fifty years. This was often challenged for Laverack writes of crossing his dogs with Irish setters and other breeds. But he also stated that these outcrosses were unsuccessful and that he always returned to his pure-bred stock. Those breeders who linebreed may indeed outcross but they are usually wise enough to retain the original line in case the experiment fails.

At the time, the announcement of such a close system of inbreeding caused consternation amongst less successful breeders. It was against all the recognized principles, yet here was the proof: big, strong, healthy dogs which not only looked good but performed to perfection with none of the congenital faults usually blamed on inbreeding. We now know that most of the great agricultural improvers created the modern breeds of farm livestock by following this same system of selective inbreeding.

His 'Fred I', 'Belle', and 'Jet' were the first he registered with the newly-formed Kennel Club and showed on the bench. 'Fred' was 1st at the London Show in 1863 and 1865, with 'Belle' and 'Jet' 2nd and 3rd at the same shows. 'Fred II', whelped 1862, was Champion at Birmingham in 1866, 1867, and 1868. All were lemon and white. From then on the list of wins at shows and field trials reads like a catalogue. 'Dash II', born 1862, was blue mottled and got the nickname 'Old Blue Dash'. He was champion at Birmingham 1869 and Crystal Palace 1870; then again at Crystal Palace in 1874 when twelve years old. This dog is said to have contributed more to setter breeding than any other single dog and breeders were advised to obtain as many lines to 'Old Blue Dash' as possible. Hence references to 'True Blue', 'Blue Blooded', and so on which are now part of every day English. Between 1863 and 1881 these Laverack setters won one Champion Stake and thirteen firsts at field trials, also thirty Championships on the bench in Britain.

Such success was based on Laverack's system of carefully selecting his dogs for work and that was only possible because of the very low cost and ready availability of shooting at that time. For example, Laverack told a friend that he rented a huge tract of grouse shooting on one estate in the north for £40 a year. In a few years, the same area was to be broken up into half-a-dozen shootings each let for £400 to £600. These days between 10,000 and 15,000 acres would be considered a reasonable dogging moor so we can guess that Laverack got around 75,000 acres for his £40! Mr Laverack's £40 might be just enough for the right to shoot one brace of grouse over dogs on a moor in Britain today, and perhaps double that would be asked if the birds are driven!

Laverack shot all over the country on all sorts of ground, from the grouse moors of Perthshire to the blanket bogs of Caithness. He rented partridge shooting near my home at Tain, Easter Ross, and woodcock shooting in the coppiced oak woods of Argyllshire where his dogs were run with bells around their necks so they could be followed in close cover. He shot in Northern Ireland and he shot grouse and woodcock on the Isle of Islay, everywhere, it seems, there was game that would lie to a dog's point.

In response to this unparalleled programme of work and selective inbreeding, Laverack developed a long, low dog, with relatively short legs, unusually bent hocks and stifles, which was described as having a crouching cat-like stance, with hindquarters that showed great power of leverage. Laverack mentions the appearance of his dogs as being that of 'a strongly built spaniel'. What fun a show judge might have attempting to interpret that standard today! Fortunately, two of Laverack's setters, 'Dash' and 'Fred 4th', are illustrated in his book *The Setter,* and they do not look unlike some working setters today. The direct descendants of these dogs are in my own kennel as I write. The coat and feather were profuse, colour black-and-white, usually with tan and ticking, or similarly coloured with lemon (actually a pale orange) replacing the black. Heavily ticked dogs are blue and lemon beltons respectively. They were fast and keen rangers with indomitable spirit, what American hunters would recognize as having an exceptional desire for birds. Yet they had the reputation with some critics of being difficult, headstrong, and even practically unbreakable. This contrasts with Laverack's comments in *The Setter,* where he devotes approximately fifteen lines to 'breaking', stating that his breed 'hunt, range, point, and back intuitively at six months, and require little or no breaking'. He goes on to tell how he broke eight setters in six days on the Cabrach in Banffshire which denies the truth of the headstrong criticism. Probably both views were correct. It is now known that periods of training ought to coincide with critical periods in the dog's development. Miss these, and the best of dogs may appear 'headstrong and wilful'. Also, a shooting dog ought not to require handling; a factor which was to have relevance for the Laverack as a field trial dog later.

Close breeding, as I can testify from personal experience, gives the owner a unique insight into his selected strain of dogs. The majority of working dogs are today bred 'out-and-out'. At each generation, new genes are introduced and excellence is a chance product, predictably vague to the point of non-existence. Close breeding allows the development of uniformity of type and character so that each individual, almost a clone of previous generations, is seen through the eyes of experience. The breeder, wise to the development and education of genetically similar individuals in previous seasons, can make rapid progress in training. Training techniques which will work well with nearly all individuals of that particular strain can be refined and perfected.

Yet the controversy over the inbred nature of the Laverack setters raged on and on until, after his death, the Kennel Club carried out an exhaustive enquiry. The verdict was inconclusive. Winge in *Inheritance in Dogs* (1950) picks up a couple of inaccuracies in Laverack's pedigrees. One concerns the description of a dog and whether it was blue belton or blue mottled. Since there is no clear distinction between the two types this seems to be nit-picking in the extreme. The other concerns discrepancies between the pedigree of Fred II published on page 20 of *The Setter* and the pedigree of the same dog published in the Kennel Club Stud Book. As can be clearly seen from the book, if this pedigree is compared with the pedigree of Dash on the opposite page, the mistake is a typographical error. The printers have listed only one side of Fred's supposed pedigree and then have taken the parents in each generation from the top and bottom line, missing out all other names. Poor Mr Laverack has been pilloried in the press for this mistake right up to the present day! That there was some confusion how colours should be described is clear from the references in these pedigrees to 'black grey', 'blue grey', 'blue', and 'blue mottled', all apparently referring to blue beltons! And so what? Such trivia are scarcely important when one thinks of all the many characteristics which go to make up a good dog.

Laverack did not claim that his dogs were unique in being excellent working setters yet there is no doubt about their worth as shooting dogs. These days no one would seriously consider going out for a full day's grouse shooting on the Scottish hills with just one dog. Yet Laverack worked his dogs from 9 am to 7 pm daily for a three week shooting season and others owning them did the same. It was their 'indomitable, enduring, hard-working properties' that he seemed most proud of which contrasts markedly with today's field trial dogs trained to run for a two minute heat at trials or a twenty minute relay out shooting. The dogs were taken up by sporting estates and shooting men very widely throughout the country at a time when the demand for good dogs was growing apace with the fashion and popularity of shooting sports.

Laverack's dogs were taken up by the most prominent sportsmen of the day including the Marquis of Breadalbane at Taymouth Castle, Perthshire; the Duke of Argyll at Inveraray Castle, Argyllshire; the Marquis of Bute, Rothesay Castle; and the Duke of Northumberland. He introduced the breed into Perthshire, Badenoch, Lochaber, Strathspey, Caithness, the Isle of Islay, and Northern Ireland.

Laverack established his kennels at just the right time. Industrial Britain was booming. The pink of the British Empire extended around the globe. Profits from exports to the colonies were ploughed into developing sporting estates. Grouse shooting and deer stalking were fashionable pursuits and by 1840 the railway had been extended to the far north, meandering its way from sporting estate to sporting estate, from one shooting lodge to the next. In 1844 Queen Victoria travelled north and stayed at Inveraray where she undoubtedly saw dogs bred from Laverack's strain. That was enough to set the course of fashion.

Grouse populations flourished on moors fertilised by sheep which had followed when crofters were removed from the land during The Clearances. Laverack mentions shooting over 800 brace of grouse (1,654 head) in four days with three other companions. One Gun shot 127 brace in one day over two setters. Laverack mentioned that relays of dogs were not used to obtain these prestigious bags and none of the Guns possessed more than two brace of dogs. From 12 August to 11 September Laverack shot 1,533 brace of grouse with his three companions, adding 'One gentleman killed within seven head, to his own gun, as much as the whole party, solely by having superior dogs, and in addition, he lent a brace of dogs several times to his friends'. He does not give the name of this gentleman but we can hazard a guess that it was the modest man himself.

Laverack admitted that there were many other excellent strains of working pointers and setters extant in his youth but he believed that such strains had deteriorated during his lifetime by being out-crossed and mongrelised.

Awakening the instincts: Llewellin puppies pointing 'the wing'. (Derry Argue)

Llewellin setters, bred from The Laveracks, were later to prove in competition just how much stamina they possessed. Contests for endurance were held in the USA where dog was matched against dog, running anything from a three hour heat to tests lasting days, with the dogs running from sunrise to sunset, the score being the number of points each dog had made on wild bob white quail. In 1876, a black-and-white dog called 'Drake', bred by Purcel Llewellin and imported by Luther Adams, won the stake, probably on a three hour heat. 'Drake' was by Mr Llewellin's Laverack Champion 'Prince' and out of his 'Dora', litter sister to his celebrated 'Dan'. In 1877 'Joe Jrn', a native Irish setter owned by Campbell, won a similar contest. Native dogs were those bred locally from American stock. The imported Llewellins were referred to as the 'blue-bloods' and there was great but friendly rivalry between enthusiasts of the two types. 'Joe Jrn' was actually a cross-bred between an Irish setter dog, 'Elcho', and an English setter bitch, 'Buck Jrn'. It was something of a tradition that the English did not outcross but bred pure; the American sportsmen of the period believed in crossing. The following year, 1878, 'Drake' and 'Joe Jrn' locked horns again for another three hour ordeal but the contest was declared a draw.

In 1879 the greatest test of endurance took place between 'Joe Jrn' and Bryson's imported Llewellin dog 'Gladstone'. 'Gladstone' was bred by Mr Purcel Llewellin by his Champion 'Dan', out of Laverack bitch 'Petrol'. The stake was $500 a side and this time the dogs were to hunt from sunrise to sunset, only the number of points on bob white quail to count, the highest score to decide the winner. After two days, 'Joe Jrn' had scored sixty-one and 'Gladstone', who was handicapped by having a recently broken tail, got fifty-two points. 'Gladstone's' tail was bound up with layers of canvas stuck together with varnish so it might be argued that the trial was a trifle uneven!

In December 1883 another great test of stamina took place. This time it was a native English setter 'Grousedale'' matched against the Llewellin setter bitch 'Lit' for one thousand dollars a side for a three day test. By the afternoon of the second day, during appalling weather with high winds, sleet and snow, the Llewellin had beaten the native-bred dog into the ground and gave every indication of being able to continue and run for double the period.

What was probably the longest heat at a field trial in Britain was run for The Kennel Club Champion Cup for Best Setter or Pointer in 1877. The contest was between Armstrong's Llewellin champion 'Dash II', owned by Mr Brewis, and MacDona's English setter champion 'Ranger'. 'Dash II' had won four All-Aged Stakes out of five and came Second to 'Ranger' in the fifth. In the first run in the Champion Cup the dogs were down for a full hour. The following day the judges ran the brace on for three hours and twenty minutes. 'Ranger' was reported to be the faster of the two but 'Dash' was the better worker; going to his game with more method and being so beautifully broken that it was a pleasure to watch him working for his owner. 'Dash' was given credit for also being the best looking dog that had ever been brought out to a field trial. This dog was sired by Edward Laverack's 'Blue Prince' and a grandson of 'Kate', sister of Barclay Field's 'Duke' which sired Mr Llewellin's famous 'Dan'. Mr Llewellin later purchased 'Dash' from Mr Brewis for an immense sum and it was this dog mated to his 'Countess Bear' (which won the Kennel Club Derby in 1875) that founded the Bondhu family of Llewellins. But we are getting ahead of ourselves.

Edward Laverack died in 1877 aged seventy-nine years and is buried in Ash Churchyard, near his former home at Broughall Cottage, Whitchurch, Shropshire, under a monument erected by his American friends. All his dogs were taken over by his friend and fellow breeder, Purcel Llewellin. Laverack's book, *The Setter*, is dedicated to 'R Ll Purcell Llewellin Esq, of Tregwynt, Letterstone, Pembrokeshire, South Wales, who has endeavoured, and is still endeavouring, by sparing neither expense nor trouble, to bring to perfection the 'setter', this little volume is dedicated by his sincere friend and admirer, Edward Laverack'.

Richard Llewellin Purcel Llewellin

For the sport of field trialing, the Laverack setter was considered far from the ideal. Although it was probably the perfect shooting dog, it did not *handle*. It was difficult to train to perform the minor, and comparatively useless, embellishments required for trials. A good dog ought to have the intelligence to vary its range according to the country in which it is hunted. It should vary its mathematical quartering to more thoroughly search out cover that its experience tells it are likely to hold birds. So long as it does not chase, this is steadiness enough, but for field trials a dog ought to drop to wing and to shot and respond to the whistle and directions of the handler quickly and willingly. The Laveracks were bred to find birds and fill the bag. They were not bred for fancy work at trials. Laverack's boast was that he used no whistle, whip, or word to work his dogs. Consequently, they failed to achieve great success at trials (if one Champion Stake and thirteen wins of First can be considered failure!).

Towards the end of the nineteenth century an ardent field trialer emerged in the shape of Mr Purcel Llewellin. Laverack had been a comparatively poor man but Llewellin was a country gentleman from a family of sportsmen with a passionate interest in breeding better field trial setters. First, he tried Gordon setters with moderate success. He got dogs from 'Idstone', the editor of *The Field*, and they did well for him. But he wanted better and he got more Gordon setters from 'Sixty-One' (Reverend Hely Hutchinson), a popular sporting columnist, but still he was not satisfied. Then, he tried Irish setters, purchasing 'Plunkett', the winner of The National field trials, from the Reverend Cumming Macdona from which he bred further winners. At last he seemed to be achieving the desired result.

Then Llewellin discovered the Laveracks and he soon acquired some of these dogs. Breeding or acquiring pure Laveracks 'Countess', 'Lill', 'Rock', 'Phantom', 'Peeress', 'Puzzle', and others he was at last headed in the right direction and he gave up his Gordons and Irish to concentrate on the Laveracks.

At that time it appears that Laverack came under considerable criticism in the sporting press, the chief tormentor being 'Idstone' (the Reverend T Pearce) who bred a strain of fashionable Gordons. Perhaps Pearce realized that Laverack was not a trialer. But Llewellin challenged 'Idstone' to a match, a brace of Laveracks against a brace of the Idstone Gordons, to be run on a test of endurance. The challenge was not taken up and that silenced the opposition.

But Llewellin was experienced enough as a breeder to realize that great as the Laveracks were, they lacked the qualities required for trials. Llewellin won with them but it was an uphill struggle putting on the polish. Then, in 1871, he saw a brace of setters, owned by Thomas Statter, named 'Dick' and 'Dan'. Walter Baxendale, writing in *The Gun at Home and Abroad* in 1913, states that 'Dan' stood at twenty-nine inches at the shoulder which, by modern standards, is a very big dog indeed, comparable with a reasonably sized Scottish deerhound. But if the measurement was in fact to the top of the dog's head, this is a reasonable height for a working setter. Llewellin judged these dogs as possessing all the best qualities the Laveracks lacked. They were solid, calm dogs, possessing a trainability and ease of control where the Laveracks had independence and fire.

Llewellin purchased the brace for £300, the highest price ever paid for such dogs at the time, and promptly disposed of 'Dick'. In his place he purchased a litter sister, 'Dora', and a half-sister 'Ruby'. These dogs were bred out of Thomas Statter's 'Rhoebe' and sired by Barclay Field's 'Duke'. 'Rhoebe' was by Paul Hackett's 'Rake' and out of Statter's 'Psyche'. Barclay Field's 'Duke' was by Sir Frederick Graham's

'Duke', out of Sir Vincent Corbet's 'Slutt', the latter described as being 'from the old Shropshire strain'. 'Psyche' was described as being 'South Esk and Gordon', the latter being the old tri-coloured Gordon breeding from Gordon Castle and not the later black-and-tan 'Gordons' (which were actually self-coloured English setters) recognised by the Kennel Club.

The cross was an unmitigated success producing big bold dogs which were easier to train and handle but had all the guts and fire of The Laveracks. Llewellin obtained many more dogs of similar breeding but confined all his experiments to crosses between Barclay Field's 'Duke' and the Laveracks, Armstrong's 'Kate' and the Laveracks, Statter's 'Rhoebe' and the Laveracks, and the pure Laveracks, and the progeny of these. 'Kate' and 'Duke' were brother and sister. Although 'Rhoebe' never won in trials, she was considered the greatest *producing* bitch ever known. She bred three winners of the National field trial in succession and was grand dam of the winner the following year.

From then on followed a great succession of wins by the Llewellin setters, as they were to become known, both in this country and abroad. To list these achievements would take the rest of the book. Llewellin expanded his breeding programme to take in any combination of the above dogs he could procure. It was well known at that period that anyone hoping to win at trials, both in Britain and the USA, had first to beat the Llewellins.

Even so, Llewellin was reluctant to sell dogs to his competitors and the export trade was a slow struggle. Sportsmen are always slow to take up anything new and would rather sit back and see how their friends and neighbours get on before taking the plunge themselves. Then, in 1868, a Mr L H Smith of Strathray, Ontario, Canada, was the first to import. Smith imported 'Petrel', bred in England, which soon after arrival produced a litter. A pup from this litter became the famous 'Gladstone' which became a celebrated field trial winner in his own right and the sire of many more. Luther Adams of Boston imported two dogs. By 1879 Mr Llewellin made a breakthrough when these dogs won eight places out of ten at the Memphis trials beating all contenders of whatever breed or breeding. I was sent a clipping from *The American Field* (undated) telling of an importer, Mr Bevan, who had established a breeding kennel of Llewellins when in their hey-day with thirty-two brood bitches. The article reported that Mr Bevan had over forty puppies, all Llewellins, ranging from three to six months, all to be trained on the premises. Since Llewellin refused to give this breeding to his competitors in Britain some took the extreme measure of re-importing his products from America, by no means an easy business in the days of the steamers.

Llewellin got the right combination to achieve success just as Laverack had done before him. But this time it was the tremendous international interest in field trialing and a thriving export market which financed the success. Throughout the history of bird dogs, it has always needed some impetus for the great breeders to succeed. In recognition of this success and of its contribution to field trials the Llewellin setter was accorded separate breed registration by *The American Field Dog Stud Book,* the first canine registry in the USA and the one now devoted entirely to working bird dogs in that country. It was becoming fashionable to call any useful setter a 'Llewellin' and the situation required regulating. The Llewellin setter is defined as a descendant, without outcross, of the dogs mentioned above which Llewellin used to create his great strain. The new breed is also registered as such by the Kennel Club Belge and the South African Field Trial Club and there are still kennels of pure Llewellin setters in many countries including Britain, Europe, South Africa, and the USA.

Llewellin continued to linebreed as Laverack had done, developing families which were 'intercrossed and interbred' as Laverack had described and his Countess, Wind 'Em, and Dashing Bondhu lines still appear on the pedigrees of many setters today. In Britain, these affixes are still protected by the Kennel Club but they are used by other canine registries internationally so that the family system has somewhat broken down and the Llewellin is now only a distinct type in character and working ability.

Purcel Llewellin died in 1925, aged eighty-five years, and is buried at Stapleton, Dorrington, Shropshire. On his death, all his dogs went to William Humphrey, another famous dog breeder and field trialer. Another breeder of Llewellin setters, Mr H C Hartley, started breeding these setters in 1876 and had, according to Mr Humphrey, 'the finest kennel of both Laverack and Llewellin blood in the world'. He was not interested in field trials or dog shows and bred purely for his own use in the shooting field. He died in 1941 and all his dogs went to Mr Humphrey. Another breeder, Mr Laws Turner, also bred pure Laveracks and Llewellins and these dogs were taken over by Mr Humphrey in 1932.

Mr Purcel Llewellin's success was founded on producing the right dog at the right time, just when field trialing as a sport was taken up by countries all over the world. There is no doubt that the dogs were, and in the right hands still are, unbeatable, but it is doubtful if the conditions for producing such a unique strain will ever occur again.

William Humphrey

The late William Humphrey was a controversial character who not only continued to breed the Llewellin-Laveracks but participated in the sport of falconry all his life. He described how he met Purcel Llewellin in the following manner:

> 'My first meeting with Mr Llewellin was at The National field trials in 1892, and I well remember seeing the final between his 'Satin Bondhu' and the great setter field trial champion 'Fred V'. I went with my father who was running one of his pointers, I noticed a tall upright man, always alone and standing away from other people; this aroused my sympathy. I made my way to this lonesome, and I believed poor, person and entered into conversation with him. To my surprise he knew my name and said how pleased he was that I had come along to talk to him. During our chat I enquired if he could sell me a setter puppy cheaply, and if he had any luck, pointing out how important it was that both he and my father should win, as the money would be much more useful to them than the better-off competitors. With this he agreed. He told me that the dogs that he and his breakers were holding were 'Belle Bondhu', 'Cocquet Bondhu', and 'Satin Bondhu'. Until he told me that I was not aware that I was talking to the great Mr Llewellin that I had heard so much about . . . . From that period to the time of his death we enjoyed each other's friendship and trust . . . . Even as a boy of nine years of age I knew a good dog when I saw it in action, and I was greatly

interested in the final between these two dogs, 'Fred V' and 'Satin Bondhu'. I had heard so much praise of the former who was the ultimate winner. They were a grand brace, and possessed immense boldness and independence, with that true setter merry style'.

That was in 1892 and two years later William Humphrey was back to win his first field trial at eleven years of age. Humphrey continued to win right up to 1948, a period of fifty-four years.

Humphrey was considered controversial by some amateur sportsmen of his time because he was not coy in stating what he had achieved. Further more, he achieved what others could not, and that never goes down too well. It was considered ungentlemanly to sell dogs, and immodest to quote one's successes in sport. Humphrey made something of a specialty of winning Puppy Stakes and there were some who said his records must have been falsified because no dog could win at the young age they were claimed to be. Yet I have descendants of his dogs in my own kennel which hunt and point with style at under four months, so naturally precocious are the Llewellins. Laverack's statement confirming the point is quoted above.

William Humphrey continued the field trial successes of Llewellin and took a team of dogs to the USA where he won against the native dogs. In 1924 the American sportsmen presented him with a gold watch as a memento of the work done by his dogs in American field trials. But like many kennels, the Llewellins in Britain suffered a great reduction during World War II and Humphrey was to import thirty-three Llewellins from the USA to rejuvenate his strain in Britain after the war.

William Humphrey was openly critical of field trials under the British system which did nothing to endear him to the Establishment although he was himself an ardent field trialer and a founder of The English Setter Club. He objected to people judging trials who had never owned, let alone trained, a successful shooting dog. People without this experience, he maintained:

'Do not know a high quality bold ranging game searching dog from a common meat dog, as the Americans would term such a dog. All such persons know are the mistakes a dog may make and are lacking the experience to recognize the essential sterling qualities. There is no question that the present day dogs are over broken and that their natural hunting and self reliance abilities have been curtailed, and they are afraid of making mistakes. That they range too close and keep cutting in and back to their handlers, and far too much attention is paid to quartering, that is expecting a dog to quarter and range over ground that the dog's experience should have taught it does not hold game. An experienced natural game hunting dog should know whether the ground it is hunting is holding game or not. The dog's natural instinct should be to cast out with its head high, searching with nose in the air, feeling for any body scent, and go to the game. As long as a dog leaves no game behind, and will ever respond to its handler, no dog can be going too wide, neither can it be out of hand. The ideal dog is the one that possesses a choke bore nose; the dog that finds game at a great distance, which is most important when hunting wild game; the dog that willingly acknowledges its brace mate's points; that is steady to wing and fur and shot, and ever hunting in front and for its master. A great field trial and shooting dog should require but little handling'.

Such remarks hit home, then as they do today. All too often, field trial judges are appointed because they are 'good chaps' rather than because they possess first hand knowledge.

These are the specifications Humphrey put into being. Owning five of the best setters he believed he had ever owned, he killed thirty-seven brace of grouse in one day with one tiercel and two peregrine falcons. He killed three hundred and nine brace in five weeks with these falcons. He killed foxes with golden eagles on the Welsh mountains, reputedly using a trained Llewellin setter to find foxes as they lay out in the thick hillside bracken with the eagle waiting on high above. Other falconers and gamekeepers have confirmed the eagles preference for tackling foxes which might seem extraordinary to the uninitiated. And my own dogs have on occasion pointed foxes as staunchly as they would point a bird. (I used several of my dogs to find ground nesting merlins which I ringed for the British Trust for Ornithology. So many birds were ringed by me in this way that a special note had to be included in *Bird Study* to explain the apparent population explosion in the species!). William Humphrey was said to have killed over a hundred foxes with his eagles, no mean feat in any context. Ronald Stevens, a personal friend of William Humphrey, was my host in Ireland and he was able to confirm these facts and Geoffrey Pollard has achieved equivalent success with his own falcons in Caithness (preferring to use Llewellin setters) proving what is still possible with good dogs.

Not being a man for facts and figures, I cannot list the numbers of stakes William Humphrey won but he has always been held up as the standard to beat for as long as I can remember, both in field trials and in falconry. It is comparatively rare for a man to be both an expert falconer and an expert with dogs. William Humphrey was highly proficient at both. Even when in his seventies he was training and flying a golden eagle.

William Humphrey made a reasonable living breeding and training Llewellin setters which were exported in considerable numbers as 'started dogs' to the USA and other parts of the world. But some said he lost uniformity of type which was inevitable when he absorbed the remnants of so many other breeders into his own kennels and suffered the losses he did from disease and two World Wars. Humphrey continued to breed under the 'Wind 'Em' and 'Dashing Bondhu' prefixes inherited from Llewellin, also under his own 'Horsford' prefix. Others bred Llewellins under other prefixes or with no prefix at all so it is becoming increasingly difficult to track down pure Llewellin setters and the breed is in danger of being crossed out of existence. But for the *American Field Dog Stud Book* registering the breed it would undoubtedly by now be extinct. An extraordinary situation when one considers that The Kennel Club was set up by sportsmen to look after the interests of working gundogs and their owners.

William Humphrey died at his home at Lakeside Cottage, Lydbury North, Shropshire, on 22 November 1963 at the age of eighty years. Before his death he gave most of his dogs away to his friends.

Chapter 4
Choices

Do You Need a Bird Dog?

A little care in the choice of a dog can save a lot of unnecessary expense and trouble. That, of course, assumes you really do need to own a dog and can do one justice.

Buying a working dog of any breed just because it appeals to your sense of romance or the image you would like to see of yourself is probably the worst possible reason you can have. Owning a dog of any breed is a real responsibility; owning a working dog bred to hunt birds with an all consuming passion, and to run all day, can quickly turn into a liability rather than an asset. Buying a young puppy on whim is the action of a fool and when it has grown into a large, hyperactive delinquent it may have irreversibly wormed its way into the family's affections. By then, it may mean a very serious upheaval to make a change and no one who knows anything about these dogs will willingly take on a subject that is at best going to be a long repair job and at worst end up with the dog having to be destroyed. Acquiring a working pointer or setter is a serious step requiring very careful consideration.

Owning a dog from show stock of your chosen breed can give you all the joys of dog ownership with fewer of the frustrations. These dogs are superficially similar to the working strains but lack the passionate hunting zeal of the true worker. And you never know, you may be one of those who get far more pleasure out of showing their dogs than working them. I am sure it must be less frustrating! Frankly, because so many essential instincts required for work have been lost along the way, no trainer of any experience will consider a dog from show breeding for serious work in the field though many make acceptable shooting dogs if one's standards are not high. The temperament required to pose unconcerned on the show bench, impervious to the distractions of the on-looking crowds, is about as far removed from the sensitivity needed in the working dog, which has to respond to commands and gestures at extreme range, as it is possible to get.

A working bird dog not only needs regular exercise but also access to hundreds of acres of training ground if it is to make a success in trials or as a shooting dog. Its owner will need time to devote long hours to its training and *regular* exercise. A working dog that is not allowed to express its hunting instincts in the field will quickly find other outlets for its energies and these may turn out to be extremely anti-social. When not working under the direct and continual supervision of its owner, working bird dogs should be kennelled or on the lead. There are no 'ifs' and 'buts' about it. Later in life, some dogs certainly settle and can make wonderful pets but that may be years ahead. Elsewhere, I have mentioned the famous pointer from a shooting kennel pensioned off to a farmer in old age. Although considered too senile for serious work, the dog took to sheep killing presumably to alleviate the boredom of enforced retirement. Not many pet owners are prepared to subject their dogs to such long period of incarceration and, not having access to suitable training ground, such people should think very carefully about taking on a dog that they may never be able to use. And if you still want a working pointing dog but cannot justify acquiring one of the specialists, turn to the section on crossbreds and do not let the lack of a pedigree prejudice your judgement.

Against my advice, my sister decided she would like to own a working pointer. For a while things went well. Then, as the pup got older, the inherent hunting instincts began to surface. In the absence of game birds the pup took to hunting moles. Having harassed the mole population of my sister's suburban garden to extinction, she turned to pastures new . . . this time to the neighbours' lawns. My sister was lucky. It could have been someone's sheep. Other dogs learn there is game beyond the picket fence and go Absent Without Leave whenever a door or gate is inadvertently left open. By the time I got my sister's dog, she was completely out of control, but, fortunately, not irredeemably so. She became my first field trial champion. It was an uphill struggle and I would never contemplate taking on such a problem dog again. Humane destruction is generally the sensible solution, repugnant though that is to all responsible owners. And that scenario is easily avoided by not taking on a dog totally unsuited to the home in the first place. Fortunately, few responsible breeders of these dogs will sell to pet homes for reasons which I hope are now quite clear.

Even though everything seems to rule against owning a working pointer or setter, genuine enthusiasm and determination can overcome the very real difficulties involved. Top labrador retriever trainer Ron Montgomery tells of the postman living in the centre of Glasgow in a high rise flat who not only trained his dog, a German Short Haired pointer, but successfully competed and won with it in trials! Not that I recommend this as the route to success, but it shows what can be done. I hand-trained an Irish setter in Hyde Park in the middle of London; teaching her to quarter, to point or ignore the many feral pigeons in the park as ordered, and drop to wing on my word of command, much to the amusement of commuting office workers.

All right, so you have been warned, but you are still determined to embark on the perilous journey into bird dog ownership. You ought to consider carefully when and where you are going to work the dog. A pointing dog can only point birds that will lie to a point. It sounds so obvious as to be scarcely worth mentioning but you would be surprised how many fail to consider this essential element. Access to a few thousand acres of farmland may sound the ideal set-up for training and working pointers and setters. But there is a lot more to it than that. Permissions can be withdrawn. Modern agriculture may make practical work on birds difficult if not impossible for much of the year because no ground cover is left when the birds are naturally inclined to lie to a dog's point. Sheep farmers are naturally suspicious of dogs; sheep panic without any reason whatsoever when they see a strange dog. Reared birds do not necessarily lie to a dog although they may proliferate in large numbers. Pheasants particularly often prefer to 'leg it' to the nearest wood or covert, especially if they are used to being disturbed, frustrating a dog beyond endurance. Access to a grouse moor might sound like heaven but gamekeepers can be notoriously fickle and access may be denied when it is needed most, even to the moor's owners! Gamekeepers are notoriously authoritarian where their birds are concerned and with prices for driven birds around £80 a brace they are quite right to be so.

What next? First, take a long critical look at your own character and temperament. If you have difficulties in arriving at an honest appraisal, there will be someone close to you who can give a frank assessment. Some people just cannot get used to the idea of a dog working at long range, let alone control one at a distance. A man who cannot train and control a Labrador or a spaniel is certainly not going to be able to manage a hot blooded pointer or setter. Those who lack the mental concentration to give one hundred per cent of their attention to a dog when it is working ought to consider a less demanding pastime.

The chapter on the origins of the pointers and setters underlines the extraordinary mix that has produced today's bird dogs. First, the way each landowner developed his own strain in virtual isolation, then the inter-breeding of these different inbred lines as transport improved. The experimental crossing with other strains of pointing dogs, that is crossing pointers with setters and vice versa, and the various crosses with other breeds (foxhounds, bull-terriers, greyhounds, etc.) tried with the aim of 'improving' the dogs for shows or trials. Last but not least, the current trend of fashion that dictates which breed or strain will be the popular choice at any particular point in time. All these elements mean it is impossible to define what the temperament of a breed will be; there is so much variation between strains, families, even individuals from the same litter. Having said all this, it should not be forgotten that there are still some strains that have been kept relatively pure. But this variation in type is how things should be. Owners and their temperaments vary as much as the dogs; some thought and care will match the dog to the owner and the breeder's advice is often the best source of such information.

The English Setter

This is the oldest pointing breed in Britain and when The Kennel Club was founded in 1873 all multicoloured setters were lumped together under the general nomenclature of 'English setters'. The object was apparently to bring some order to a very confused scene but to categorize dogs on mere external physical appearance seems a rather extreme remedy. The shooting owner is usually more concerned with what his dog will do than what the colour or shape may be.

It is dangerous to generalize about the English setter. This was the dog used by the falconers and by the professional fowlers. The character of the modern English setter is therefore highly instinctive and generally soft in nature. What I mean by this is that they are usually very sensitive to a good handler. Given the opportunity most come to hunt and point without special training. After a correct introduction, most are extremely keen on hunting. These dogs are usually easily inhibited to the extent that the breed has a reputation for becoming sticky on point or even blinking (both faults caused by too strict control in training and discussed elsewhere). English setters usually need to be allowed to chase a few birds before settling down to serious training. Work them long and hard and even the wildest will eventually settle down to point enthusiastically especially when things begin to fall into place and they are rewarded by having game killed to their points. Rough handling is fatal and the best are easily spoilt. English setters become fixed in their ideas at an early age which has given rise to the defamation that some are hard headed and difficult to break. They can be very precocious. Tackled the right way, training an English setter ought to be relatively easy and straight forward but it does take time and they need more game than pointers. Once the instincts are aroused, setters generally need less game than pointers to encourage them to continue to hunt, hence their popularity in areas where game is not plentiful. Being long coated, they are not suitable for work in the heat or where water is scarce. In some parts of the USA they cannot be used because burrs get entangled in their coats. Many English setters make excellent retrievers given half a chance.

English setters can develop a fanaticism for game. They require a close relationship with their handlers and if this is upset a 'bolter' or 'self-hunter' may result. There is also evidence that this is a genetic fault particularly prevalent in American strains bred for field trials. Bolters, and self-hunters, which just go off hunting on their own, are very annoying and I know of no cure for the vice. Some English setters are also incessant barkers which is also an inherited problem very difficult to cure.

Seven-month-old English (Llewellin) setter puppies pointing game without training. (Derry Argue)

A majority of today's working and field trial English setters are bred from Llewellin origins. The famous Sharnberry kennel owned by the late Captain W Parlour was, at one time, made up of pure Llewellins but they were outcrossed and, I believe, have recently been dispersed. I ran my own dogs with many of these at field trials on the moors at Blanchland, Northumberland, when they were handled by Parlour's keeper, Tommy Sparks. Another breeder with predominantly Llewellin stock was the late Dr J B Maurice. Some of Dr Maurice's 'Downsman' setters were very small but they made up for lack of size with tremendous speed. Dr Maurice was rumoured to have X-rayed all the pups he bred, keeping only those with the largest hearts; hence the pace his setters were noted for.

Not all working English setters were bred from the Llewellins, nor were they all field trial dogs. Some of the old landowning families in the far north of Scotland kept their dogs on because there are not sufficient numbers of grouse on the moors to drive, nor is the terrain suitable. As country to show off a good dog, the counties of Caithness and Sutherland can have few equals. I particularly remember very large setters at some of the north trials owned by Marcus Kimball, now Lord Kimball, of Altnaharra, Sutherland. But sheep ruined the moors and the dogs were outcrossed and lost size. The late Sir John Brooke of Midfearn, Easter Ross, had another kennel of setters, also defunct. Incidentally, the kennel can still be seen from the main A9 road north, complete with the first corrugated iron roof ever built in Scotland and as good as the day it was installed!

The English setter is invariably coloured white with varying shades of lemon (the same colour would be called orange in pointers), red, brown (liver in pointers), or black markings, with or without ticking, and with or without tan markings around the head, muzzle, and throat, and legs. The coat is long, fine, and wavy, and can be profuse with feathering down the legs and on the tail. The length of coat makes the ticking merge with the white so creating the marbled effect known as 'belton'. The tail carriage on point ought to be somewhere near forty-five degrees to show off the 'flag' to best advantage. My own preference is for a straight tail, or perhaps slightly curved upwards. Tail carriage can only be assessed when the dog is confidently and firmly on point. This last applies to all bird dogs.

The show English setter is now almost a distinct breed having, according to Marr, been mostly bred from the Maesydd kennel of Thomas Steadman, and is considered useless for field work by serious sportsmen. Originally, I believe these dogs descended from the Laveracks. The show dog makes an ideal family pet and would certainly be more appropriate to a non-working home than the potentially hyperactive worker.

The Irish Setter

This is said to be the oldest breed of setter. The claim could have some foundation as Ireland had stable links with the Continent long before the English patched up their differences with the Europeans. There were as many red-and-white setters in Ireland as the solid red sort before the show craze took a hold when any Irish setter outside its homeland was condemned if it had white markings. In fact, the Irish setter standard published by Irish and English Kennel Clubs allows white on chest, feet, tail tip, face (as a blaze), and muzzle. International Field Trial Champion Patricia of Killone was of this colouring. These white markings are due to an inherited factor called 'Irish spotting'; nothing to do with Irish setters, incidentally (except in the above context) but so named because the same colour pattern occurred in tame rats of Irish origin used in genetic experiments! The red-and-white Irish setter is, as the name implies, red and white without ticking and is now bred and registered separately. When this variation became popular a few years ago many were highly strung and nervous but I believe this fault has to a large extent been bred out. Unfortunately, it has found favour as a show dog with predictable results.

The show Irish setter became very popular and was exported in large numbers around the turn of the century. They were mostly descended from a single very successful show family and are characterised by big, slab-sided dogs, notorious for having very little brain and no field sense. It is these dogs most people think of when

The late John Nash with three field trial champion Irish setters. Patricia of Killone, with white markings, is on the right. (Derry Argue)

Irish setters are mentioned which is a pity because the *real* Irish are hard to beat. The American red setter is a different thing again and has very little in common with this useful gundog in its native land. But the real Irish setter is a first rate gundog and I have seen and owned some excellent ones. If I wanted an Irish setter again I would go to Ireland to get one but there are of course many excellent imported lines in this country of good type.

It would be difficult to write anything about the Irish setter without mentioning the late Mr John Nash (kennel prefix 'Moanruad') who was tragically killed in a freak accident in 1990 when a tree fell on his car in a storm. I met John in 1962 and spent many summers with him training dogs, mostly Irish setters and the occasional pointer, on the Irish mountains. I learnt a lot from John, and possibly as much from Dinney Fitzgerald, very much the unsung hero, who took on any dog John had problems with but who never received due credit so far as I am aware. Dinny and I would sit on some high point with half a dozen setters while John gave a prospect a turn. All the while Dinney would give me a running commentary of what John was doing, what the dog was thinking, and what would happen next. Generally, he was right. But there are also other excellent working Irish setters in Ireland containing little of Mr Nash's breeding.

The Irish setter is a rougher, tougher working dog than the gentlemanly English setter. Its dark colour betrays its ancestry because it is well known that a dark dog will get closer to wild birds than a light one. Also, many Irish setters carry their tails pointing slightly downwards, below the level of their backs, and on point many lie down naturally. This, then, was surely the dog used on the Irish bogs and mountains for netting game, the net being pulled up behind the dog by two men, over the dog and onto the birds, otherwise the breed never would have survived the terrible Irish famines. For this reason, the Irish setter lacks nothing in sagacity, getting cleverer with age, and it develops a tremendously close relationship with its handler, too much so in my case as running a professional kennels I had to give them up. I found it difficult to get them to change owners. An Irish setter will laugh at treatment that would have an English setter cowed and broken.

Harry Nash (son of the late John Nash), in the sixties, with F.T. Ch. Moanruad Dan, a large, powerful Irish setter not untypical at that period. (Derry Argue)

Several of my Irish setters were excellent retrievers. One I was attempting to train to retrieve was giving problems when I shot a pigeon across the other side of a frozen river. I badly needed that pigeon to feed a falcon but there was no way I could cross the river. My setter, apparently correctly assessing the situation, plunged in and retrieved perfectly to hand. I shot another pigeon on the way home which fell in plain view out in the field on my side of the river. This the dog absolutely refused to retrieve and I could only assume that she realized I could get that one for myself! This dog would crouch down and crawl beside me when I stalked duck on the Scottish burns. Several other Irish setters of mine were first class retrievers, putting the specialist breeds to shame.

The chief criticism of the Irish setter is that it lacks sufficiency of point. It shares the English setter's passion for game but not the Englishman's style and attitude. The trainer has to be something of a psychologist to succeed with an Irish setter; the iron fist in the velvet glove might be the best description of what is required! I suspect most problems encountered in training Irish setters arise from faulty technique. All setters ought to be started early rather than late and that is undoubtedly the cause of many problems.

I saw some very beautiful Irish setters in the sixties of good size but they seem to have been replaced by the small, wiry type at trials in recent years though I am advised they are still available in Ireland. There is nothing intrinsically wrong with a small dog, but it would be a pity if the large animal were completely ousted. Presumably the small type, which looks faster and more exciting, has replaced it as the more successful field trial dog. The coat of the Irish setter is generally less profuse than the English setter and harder in texture. Again, they are very variable in type. But, more than anywhere, the Irish setter in its native land was and is a dog of the people, used for generations (certainly as long as its English counterpart) for hunting the wide barren bogs and heather moorlands. The Irish setter is particularly noted for its stamina and ability to shrug off wet and cold conditions. In the Outer Hebrides, my own Irish setters took their morning swim in the loch as any other dog might take a run in the park, summer or winter.

The Gordon Setter

The Gordon Setter has long been associated with Alexander, the 4th Duke of Gordon, who is said to have established the kennel of black-and-tan setters at Gordon Castle, Fochabers, Banffshire, near the mouth of the River Spey, during the nineteenth century. The exact date when this kennel was established is not known. Colonel Thornton visited the area in 1786 and made no mention of the Gordon Castle setters yet G St G Gompertz (in *The Gordon Setter; History and Character*) quotes Thornton as follows, 'The Duke of Gordon still keeps up the diversion of falconry . . .' If that was so, what dogs did he use to find and point the game if not setters? The Duke was at that date forty-three years of age. 'The Druid', a popular sporting writer of the period, is quoted by Laverack as hearing Judd (the Duke's kennelman) say, 'better to put up half a dozen birds than make a false point'. This is a real falconer's remark as there is no greater sin in this sport than a false pointing dog which disappoints the falcon. It is probable that the black-and-tans were present at Gordon Castle a long time before that date. The dark colour, again, would have been thought useful when the birds became wild later in the season. In practice, the colour is no disadvantage because a sportsman seldom takes his eye off his dogs when they are working.

The predominant colour in the breed is the characteristic black-and-tan. Tri-colours, due to their 'English' ancestry, are also possible though today are considered suspect. Occasionally, reds are also produced. But there were black-and-tan setters in other

George Burgess with his Gordon Setters, F.T.Ch. Dipper of Crafnant and F.T.Ch. Crafnant Ruff.
(Farmers Weekly)

kennels, well distributed all over Britain. And by Laverack's time, the Gordon Castle dogs had already been crossed out and were predominantly tri-coloured. These dogs were large and coarse and reputed to be nervy, sullen-tempered, and hard to break. Many were heavy and lacking in stamina. Those, at least, were the comments of early writers and not necessarily true. But if they had been used for falconry for generations, as is probable, they would have been selected for long noses and strong working instincts. I have certainly met Gordon setters which were too sensitive, but others more-or-less trained themselves. That is my experience of the Gordon setter. Perhaps not the best trials dog because they are not inclined to subject themselves to the regimentation required for these competitions but a very wise and natural hunter with a lot of character. Again, many are excellent natural retrievers. The coat of the Gordon is long, as in all the setters, but tending to the coarseness of the Irish rather than the softness of the English, sometimes quite curly which is also correct (at least in the working strains).

At shows and trials, the dogs were originally referred to as black-and-tans. When the Kennel Club was established, the dogs were again classified as black-and-tans. No doubt it carried a certain status to be able to claim that your black-tans were 'Duke of Gordon's dogs', so 'Gordon setters' became a mark of distinction as the Llewellins did in the USA. By 1924, the Kennel Club had decided to register all black-and-tans as Gordon setters although the majority could probably lay no claim to such illustrious ancestry.

The working Gordon today is in a minority but what the breed lacks in numbers it makes up for in the enthusiasm of its supporters. The Gordon setter has undoubtedly been outcrossed as much as any other breed and Laverack mentions crosses with Irish setters. They have certainly been crossed with English setters but the alleged cross, by the Duke, with a working collie is almost certainly nonsense.

Isaak Sharpe, owner of the 'Stylish' prefix, kept a big commercial kennel of pointers and setters at Keith, Banffshire, and was something of a specialist with Gordon setters. The dogs were hired out during the shooting season to visiting sportsmen and exported all over the world. That about sums up the character of the breed. Once trained, they are excellent workers and are said to change owners easily. The show strains, which are very similar in external appearance, are said to be useless in the field but I have no experience of this never having been tempted from the straight and narrow.

Because the breed is so numerically small there is some incidence of congenital heart defect which would not be impossible to breed out if owners had the commitment to do so. Some of the show strains also have an incidence of hip problems.

The Pointer

This breed is universal. Although the breed is sometimes referred to as the 'English pointer' the name is not really correct and is used to distinguish the breed from other more recent imports. While the English setter really can be credited to English origins, why ignore the influence of Scotland on the formation of the pointer which arrived on the scene a hundred years after the setter? And what about the imports after the 1939-1945 war when British pointers were virtually extinct? There is probably more variation in the pointer than in any of the setter breeds due to individual owners developing their own strains and the nature of the original imports which clearly came from several different sources. The situation is still more confused because of later crosses for shows and trials.

Generally, the pointer is less exacting than the setters. If things go wrong in training a pointer, the situation is seldom irredeemable. Training can also be delayed to an age when it would be very difficult to mould the mind of a setter. But this is a two edged sword. It may well be that a setter's behaviour becomes fixed early in life. That will inevitably make it very difficult to correct faults later on (giving rise to accusations of 'hard-headedness') but pointers, because they are more easily influenced at a later age, often require some maintenance training. My setters will generally ignore the poultry which wander around my yard but I would not trust every pointer.

As has already been said, the pointer handler needs to be something of an authoritarian. But much depends on the individual temperament of the dog. A word will keep one dog under control, another needs stronger tactics. Pointers are said to require more game to keep their spirits up than setters. But many point the first time they encounter game and they take training for field trials, in my opinion, better than any of the setters though this has to be a generalization. Pointers usually have to be taught to quarter and to hunt – something seldom necessary in any of the setters.

Some pointers are extremely hard and impersonal characters. Sometimes this is due to lack of early socialization, but sometimes it is just their nature. I once heard John Nash describe the setter as looking into your very soul while the pointer has his eyes on the mountains (for game) behind you. It is an apt comparison. My own pointers are very soft indeed and I prefer them this way. There is a joke amongst dogmen that explains the difference. A professional trainer told his son how dogs were trained with kindness. Then one day the son sees his father flogging a dog. 'Father, why are you

The late Jack Stewart with pointer F.T. Ch. Glenburn Don. The spots around the dog's head are flies, a curse of training in the summer.
(Derry Argue)

beating that dog? You told me they were trained with kindness'. Father replies, 'Yes, son, you are right. But first you have to get the dog's attention'. No doubt much blame must be laid at the door of early breeders who are said to have introduced bull terrier to increase aggression for trials, the theory being that a more aggressive dog wants to beat his brace mate to the birds. The foxhound cross was also tried to 'improve' conformation and stamina with obvious influence on temperament. I see no point in keeping a dog that needs harsh treatment when a dog that will respond to a word costs the same to keep, is easier to train, and generally handles better than the hard sort.

Some trainers, of course, have so little command of temper that they need this type of dog which will 'take a kick in the ribs and come back and lick your hand' or 'retrieve the stick after a good flogging'. There is really no further comment I can make on the subject.

Pointers come in all colours except tri-colour. Whole- or self-coloured pointers were extinct in Britain until the last year or so because of the prejudices outlined in a previous chapter. Lemon, orange, liver, and black patches with white ground, with or without ticking is usual. Orange- or lemon-and-white dogs may have dark or flesh coloured noses – both are correct though, I think, the former more attractive. Self-coloured dogs will often have variable amounts of white 'Irish spotting' on face, nose, throat, chest, feet, and tail. Of course, these self-coloured dogs can be lemon, orange, liver, and black but should not have tan. The coat of the pointer ought to be dense, hard, and short, so much so that it is almost impossible to expose the skin by separating the hairs. Generally, pointers do better in the heat than setters. I have seen pointer puppies with a paling factor, so they appear grey and white. Arkwright mentions that Lord Sefton had some. But the eye pigmentation is also affected and they are pink eyed, like an albino ferret. Humane destruction is, I fear, the only answer as the dogs so obviously suffer in bright light.

Buying Dogs

Having chosen the particular breed, the next decision concerns the choice of the individual dog. Prospective purchasers of working pointers and setters are encouraged to attend a few field trials so that they can see the dogs in action, talk to other enthusiasts, and get to know what it is all about. Better still, offer to lead dogs at training time or invest in a few days shooting over dogs. Both areas are given more coverage elsewhere in the book.

Buying a dog is not the same as buying a new washing machine or a car. When buying a dog, the purchaser is acquiring a potential partner. For the working relationship to succeed, the partnership must succeed. The success of that partnership depends on the contribution of *both* sides. If the partnership does not work out, too bad, or in legal terms, *caveat emptor*, which loosely translated means, 'Let the purchaser beware'. In very few circumstances will the purchaser have any redress against the vendor when things go wrong because of the psychological factors involved. Mostly, the established breeder *wants* the purchaser to do well with his dog. There is no good publicity to be had from selling bad dogs. On the other hand, many people these days expect to get a machine when they buy a dog. They do not realize the complexities of dog training or how easy it is to ruin a potentially first class working dog by, literally, 'doing nothing'. The unscrupulous will hide behind these facts while selling a 'dud'; the purchaser incapable of forming any relationship with a dog will blame the vendor for his own shortcomings. When things do go wrong (and we all occasionally experience problems in dog training), the breeder is the first person to contact as a source of informed advice. As the saying goes, the purchaser has 'bought the horse, not the jockey'. Acquiring a well-bred, or well-trained, dog does not necessarily equip the purchaser with the knowledge and experience to work it! No one who has never ridden before would expect to be able to ride a racehorse he has just purchased because he paid a big price for it, yet the same man will expect a dog to work impeccably for him even though he has never trained or worked a bird dog before.

Buying Pups

Buying an untrained pup can seem a tempting proposition. The price is lower and the purchaser is usually aware that a youngster will adjust to a new home easier than an older dog. But a pup is also easier to ruin and top breeders will be reluctant to part with a youngster that could have potential way beyond its face value. There is also the possibility of purchasing a dud! Of course, the purchaser ought to see both parents or at least close relatives in the same kennel. An experienced person can judge conformation easier at six to eight weeks than at the age of a few months when pups, like teenage children, start to grow in all directions at once! I am never put off by the seemingly nervous pup at six to eight weeks unless it is a very extreme case. Here, of course, I refer to pointers and setters. In the case of bird dogs, such puppies sometimes turn out the best. Individual attention will often cure the shyness with dramatic rapidity, especially if the strain is noted for intelligence.

Puppies are cheaper than older dogs because the risk of things not working out is greater. The best bred pups, from a good breeder, are obviously worth more because of the increased chance of obtaining a good worker. This particularly applies to closely bred strains with a proven track record where successive generations are generally excellent. Fifty pounds extra paid for a well bred pup is only ten pence a week when costed out over the dog's life; a negligible amount when set against other costs. The best age to acquire a pup is between six and eight weeks but any age up to several months *provided the upbringing has been correct* could be a good investment.

The Started Dog

What is a 'started' dog? I suspect the title hides a multitude of sins! Not so long ago, I read an advertisement in a sporting paper offering an eighteen month old Gordon setter 'ready to start training'. Experience would suggest that such a dog would probably be beyond redemption! The same dog from a professional kennel might be worth almost as much as a fully trained dog. It all depends what has been going on over those critical eighteen months as will become clear if you read the chapter on 'Training'.

A started dog, aged anything from a few months to about a year and a half, ought to show a keen inclination to hunt and to point and be under reasonable control. It ought to be dropping to hand, whistle, and voice, perhaps not with any great reliability but the foundations ought to be there. A started dog, by definition, ought to be hunting and pointing, perhaps not with one hundred per cent reliability but well enough to demonstrate the potential. The pup should not show any undue nervousness, especially to loud noises which might indicate a potential for gun-shyness, but, speaking personally, I would not expect a youngster to be impervious to the sound of a gunshot at close quarters. I would worry less about flushing and chasing due to youthful exuberance than excessive pointing and caution which could indicate too much restraint and the seeds of stickiness and blinking. Running up game by a pup that is showing signs that it *will* point can be cured in minutes whereas stickiness (sometimes considered by the inexperienced to be desirable 'staunchness') may be so firmly engrained that it can never be eradicated. The definition of a started dog presumes that further training is needed. There is no redress if you buy a started dog which never finishes – unless of course the vendor has been so unwise as to give a warranty (hopefully, for the purchaser, in writing) about the dog's future performance.

Trained Dogs

Buying a fully trained dog has advantages in that you can see what the dog is capable of doing at the time of purchase. I am assuming here that the purchaser either buys from a reputable source or sees the dog working. Dog training continues right up to about three years of age, formal training gradually being replaced with practical experience in the shooting field. Even so, any newly acquired dog should be allowed at least a month to settle down and probably a course of re-training by the new handler to make sure it responds to all the various commands. It is very important to establish the man-dog bond between the dog and his new owner and as important to make sure that communications are working as they should. Having said that I hope I have stressed that the man-dog relationship is a partnership. Some owners never succeed in cementing that relationship and even if the dog is a field trial champion there will be owners who will never be able to handle such an animal simply because the rapport is missing. The purchase of a fully trained experienced dog is undoubtedly the best way for the novice to get into bird dogs. An old experienced dog, perhaps a pensioner, will teach the beginner far more than a library of books and, in the end, it is probably the cheapest way to get into the sport.

Trained dogs at the beginning of their working lives, if they are any good at all, generally cost a lot of money. They need to if they are any good. Add up the cost of a well-bred pup, the cost of rearing, those trips to the vet, kennelling, hand training, those hours on the hill, possible attendance at field trials, etc., etc. and you begin to understand what it is all about. If you wonder how to cost out all this time and boot leather I suggest you get a quotation from your friendly local plumber for a weekend call out and apply this hourly rate to the months, nay years, of patient breeding and training to produce these dogs. True, trained dogs can be purchased from amateurs for knock-down prices (especially if you are in the right place at the right time!) but the old saying that no one sells a good dog is probably applicable. Professional trainers generally charge a proper commercial price for a dog; but then it is in their own interests to sell *good* dogs so that clients come back.

Some purchasers talk themselves into thinking they are buying what they want when in reality all anyone can hope to do is to buy the dog that is for sale. That may seem a trite statement. Let me explain. The purchaser has a picture in his mind of the dog he would like to own. Let's face it, it is probably the dog we would all like to own. On the other hand, the seller may wish to part with his dog for some reason best known only to himself. Maybe he needs the money. Most professional dogmen are poor people (and I would have my suspicions about one who wasn't!) There may be a gap between what the seller has for sale and what the buyer would like to purchase. The proper way to go about the purchase is to fix in one's mind the value of the ideal dog and then deduct from that figure for the deficiencies in the dog offered for sale. It is not reasonable to suggest that the seller should in some way change what he has for sale to bring it up to the purchaser's ideal by further training. It is a principle in buying a dog that you buy what you see and there are few exceptions.

A really top-class dog of good breeding will often recoup the initial investment from its value at stud or from puppies sold. Occasionally, breeders will let good dogs go cheaper on the understanding that they will not be exported, bred from, or that the breeder gets first refusal on sale. These conditions may be imposed to protect the seller's sales of related dogs still in his kennel in the future. A dog could still be a real bargain even with these restrictions written into the agreement.

Dog or Bitch?

Personally, I prefer dogs but the current vogue is for bitches. 'They are easier to handle and, anyway, I may want to breed a litter' is commonly heard. I learnt the hard way. I took five of my best dogs off to trials and a few days later the only bitch came into season. There was nothing for it but to cancel my holiday and return home. As for the difference in temperament, it is really scarcely noticeable. A good dog is a good dog but, for choice, I would prefer the male. The experts tell me bitches are more aggressive than dogs leading to more problems when kennelled together. But it is six of one and half a dozen of the other.

Prices

Well bred pointer and setter pups can be purchased for prices of £100 or so up to four figures with around £200 – £400 (in the UK) being usual. 'Started' dogs, if they can be found (most amateurs will want to retain anything that shows promise), are probably worth anything from £500 (which would barely cover costs) to £1,500 and more, depending on potential. Trained dogs can sometimes be obtained for a few hundred pounds . . . but the reader probably would not want to own them if he has taken the trouble to buy this book! The best dogs are, quite literally, priceless because of their breeding potential and the pleasure they give. And that is how it should be. Over the last twenty years or so I have bred perhaps half a dozen I would categorize as 'the best' and seen fewer that I would have liked to buy. Britain is still capable of producing the best pointers and setters in the world which is why they have been sought out and purchased by other nations for so long. Unfortunately, among the great dogs there are far more also-rans. A good shooting dog, on today's market, ought to be worth £1,000–£2,000 upwards. And if you think this is expensive for an animal capable of giving its owner many hours of pleasure, just look at the prices for some of the top racehorses . . . or what it would cost to purchase a Van Gogh! Neither, for all their worth, will find a grouse or point a pheasant, let alone give the trust and companionship of a dog.

Dogs and puppies can be purchased through advertisements in the sporting press and from established breeders. Field trial schedules usually list details of dogs and their owners. Inevitably, there is an excellent 'grapevine' in gundog circles and many dogs are sold through word of mouth though it is probably wise to consult several sources as professional jealousy and personal prejudice is not unknown. 'Kennel blindness', where an owner cannot see beyond his own dogs, is a common affliction amongst enthusiasts and I count myself fortunate that for many years, as a full-time student, I was unable to take on a dog and so had a long time to consider what others owned and how they performed.

Selling Dogs

The prospective purchaser of a trained dog may reasonably require a demonstration and, out of fairness, any faults or deficiencies ought to be declared by the seller. It is a criminal offence to conceal defects which are the subject of specific enquiry by the purchaser. It is also a criminal offence to knowingly make misrepresentations about the animal one is selling. It is most unwise to sell a dog 'on approval' or 'guaranteed'. I have no doubt your dog is a perfect example of its breed but the prospective purchaser may not be. No matter how good your dog may be, there are too many charming, plausible characters out there who will do stupid things which could at worst irredeemably ruined your dog or at least make it necessary for you to put your pet through a complete course of re-training . . . if you are lucky. Make it clear that the dog does not leave your possession until you are in receipt of the cheque for the full amount of the price and do not part with the registration papers until the cheque has been cleared. The gentleman's agreement only works if both parties are gentlemen. In the absence of a written guarantee on that point, strict commercial practice ought to be followed. Better still, make sure the contract is evidenced in writing adding, if possible, that the dog is sold 'as seen'. That will effectively counter any later problems if the purchaser is unable to supply the other side of the man-dog partnership. All this may sound very cynical but the advice is given in the light of cold experience over many years. My own dogs are sold fully guaranteed . . . as far as the gate.

Exporting Dogs

Sadly, the main market for working pointers and setters these days is for export because, in many ways, bird dog training and handling is almost a lost art in Britain. Assuming a dog is sold to an overseas buyer, transport will usually have to be arranged by the seller. The international transport of live animals is now a very complex affair hedged around with draconian rules and regulations and rightly so too. Many will prefer to engage the services of a professional shipping agent but it can be done by the ordinary owner.

Entry requirements vary around the world and the various embassies will provide details. The Export Division (Dogs) of the Ministry of Agriculture, Fisheries, and Food, Hook Rise South, Tolworth, Surrey, telephone 081 330 4411, will usually be able to provide information sheets on the export of live dogs to various countries.

This office will also supply application forms for the Export Certificate required by most countries stating that there has been no recent outbreak of rabies in the locality. Some countries require dogs to be inoculated against rabies, some have age restrictions on imports, others require imported dogs to go into quarantine, etc. It should be emphasized that the export of live dogs is quite complicated and not for the faint of heart. The airline transporting dogs will also have its own rules and regulations.

The shipment of dogs is regulated by the Transit of Animals Order and the International Air Transport Association mandatory requirements. Travelling crate dimensions required, for example, by British Rail are different to those required by airlines most of which are now members of IATA. Travelling boxes must conform to these rules and although they can be made up by any competent handyman, they are best made to measure for the individual dog. Generally, dogs must travel individually. Invariably the airline will also require a veterinary certificate stating that the dog is free from signs and symptoms of disease and is fit to travel. The standard health certificate also requires a note of the dimensions of the dog (measured by the veterinary surgeon) so that the suitability of the box can be easily checked by airline staff. As may be expected, this is anything but an exhaustive list of the complicated rules and regulations for shipping dogs but, generally, the Ministry, the airlines, and your veterinary surgeon will help with the relevant details. Having said that, some documents must be obtained, and returned completed, within strict time limits and it can be a nightmare getting everything together for a successful export. Murphy's Law ('anything t hat can go wrong, will go wrong') definitely applies! Another book would be needed to list my own frustrations and experiences, including the day I got a full apology from what was then British Overseas Airways Corporation and was taken home in the chairman's chauffeur driven Daimler! This illustrious company had copied the wrong diagram into their shipping manual from the original IATA source!

When things do go wrong through the fault of others, I believe every dog owner has the duty to complain in very vocal terms to the highest authority. Live animals are involved here and some agencies definitely feel that they are just cargo, perishable cargo it is true, but simply cargo that will begin to smell and cause offence only if it is delayed too long. It is now a criminal offence for the carrier to neglect livestock and that is a point well worth pursuing. It is no use arguing with the man at the counter, get all the facts and take them direct to the chairman or at least to the senior cargo officer. If possible, he should be approached by letter marked 'Private and Personal' and full name and title can be obtained from the company's head office. Usually there will be an attempt to short circuit complaints with a request from some underling as to the nature of your call. That is not his/her business. Politely insist that you need the information for a purpose which need not concern them. Once the chairman has your complaint, every tier of officialdom will be required to report and everyone down the line will have to account for what went wrong. I have seldom found this to fail and I am sure it has resulted in a better time for dogs in transit and a smoother system all the way through. Unfortunately, these changes are seldom made unless someone takes a stand and makes a fuss. There is still an almost total lack of concern about the psychological damage done to working dogs delayed in transit, damage which may render them virtually useless for work in the field regardless of how luxuriously fitted out the 'animal hostels' they are delayed in may be. It is all the same to a dog.

Puppies should not be shipped by air or rail under the age of ten weeks. I have found it dangerous to ship pups aged around twelve weeks because this is one of the critical periods. Ideally, dogs ought to be collected by, or personally delivered to, their new owners. But commonsense should apply. One Italian purchaser drove from Italy to collect his dog. I did not like to break it to him that the dog could have gone back and forth to Tokyo, twice, in the time it took to drive the dog home. My own practice, where ever possible, is to get someone else to take a dog out of its shipping crate. I have no proof but I believe a dog may blame the person who takes it out of the box for the traumas experienced while in transit. Of course, no dog should be taken out of a travelling box except in a secure area.

The Newly Acquired Dog

It goes without saying that a dog ought to be allowed a period of adjustment when it changes ownership. I allow at least a month during which time I get to know the dog, let it get to know me, try to establish a rapport with it, and gently take it through the actions and commands it is used to. Initially, the dog ought to be given restricted freedom, never taken out unless on the lead, and then run only on a long check cord until it knows its new owner and has settled down. Hopefully, I have a whistle similar to the one used by its previous owner and a list of the signals it is used to. Better still, a tape of the calls the dog is used to. Even so, I treat even the most confiding dog as if it will bolt at the slightest opportunity. It truly amazes me to hear of people purchasing dogs and then 'trying them out' within twenty-four hours of arrival. Do these people think they have purchased something on a par with a new washing machine?

Ideally, a new dog ought to be fed on the feed it is used to. Alternatively, be prepared for a period in which the dog will have to get used to a change of diet. A couple of days without eating will do a healthy adult dog no harm. In any event, some bowel upset is usual and there is seldom cause for undue alarm. A visit to the vet, unless there are glaring symptoms, is more likely to expose the dog to infection at a vulnerable time than prevent any serious problems. The vet's surgery is the perfect exchange for every disease under the sun. Routine worming and treatment for ear mites can be done cheaply and easily by the new owner without trauma.

When the dog has settled down and shows signs of eagerly responding to the commands and signals the previous owner has sent with it, it can be cautiously tried on some safe ground. But it is far more important to spend time creating that bond between man and dog than getting the dog out there to discover all those imperfections (real or imaginary) the seller has neglected to tell you about. Make that change of ownership carefully and cautiously and you may be pleasantly surprised to find the dog every bit as good as it was described, perhaps even better.

Dog Trainers

Experienced and knowledgeable professional trainers who will take in pointers and setters from the general public for training are now very scarce. Some professionals specializing in retrievers and spaniels will also take on the pointing breeds but they are few and far between. Generally, the pointer or setter man trains his own dogs because that is the most profitable way to do it. Personally, I found I could train twenty of my own breeding while I was trying to correct the faults in the 'untouched' pup brought to me by some amateur. Generally, it would be wise to obtain several references from satisfied clients before using a professional trainer, and then to see the results of this training at first hand if possible. Some people's standards are very low.

Chapter 5
How Dogs Learn

There are few things which give a trainer more pleasure than to bring on a promising young dog. And there are few processes that sometimes cause so much confusion to the mind of the novice trainer. Dog training is easy; the problem is to train the trainer!

In dog training there are times when progress is rapid; other times when nothing seems to go right. A pedigree should provide a guarantee that the dog *will* (eventually) work and, assuming good working ancestry, the fault must lie fairly and squarely with the trainer if things go badly wrong. Occasionally, even the best trainer ruins a pup. To quote the late Frank Gillan, 'The man who has not spoilt a pointer or setter pup has never trained one'.

The late Frank Gillan, gamekeeper at Cromlix, Tokujiro Ishibashi, a Japanese enthusiast, and the late Angie McLaughlin at a field trial. (Derry Argue)

It is a fact that many trainers spend more time trying to correct faults which should not have arisen in the first place than they ever spend constructively training the dog. It is truly amazing how quickly dogs learn if given the correct opportunity. My Llewellin bitch, Nirevale Ghost, probably took less than thirty minutes of formal training, made up of a number of brief periods, to bring to pointing game, steadiness, and dropping to wing. It took over three months of two or three hour daily training sessions to bring my first dog, an Irish setter, to the same stage! This lack of progress was because I started with a spoilt dog and then set about correcting faults in the wrong way.

Humans continue to learn throughout their lives; dogs cram most of their learning into a few frantic months; other animals and birds may learn almost as much in a few hours, even minutes. These periods are called 'critical periods' of learning and they are very, very important. Once these periods are passed, learning slows down. 'You cannot teach an old dog new tricks', goes the saying. In many situations, dogs are very much quicker to learn than humans. In others, they may appear to be inordinately stupid. It is really a question of understanding how dogs think and learn.

Some day soon, someone is going to ask if batteries are included when they enquire the price of a dog. In previous generations, almost everyone relied on horses for transport and at least an elementary knowledge of animal psychology was taken for granted. The ploughman was not considered odd because he talked to his horses and a dog was a working partner, not kept for purposes of status or amusement. It is a sad fact that more and more people consider dogs to be either machines or child substitutes. All too often, if a dog 'doesn't work' the purchaser feels he has a right to return it, like a faulty washing machine, on the presumption that some defect must have arisen during manufacture! Dogs are far more complex than that which is half the fascination. There are no short cuts to arriving at the fully trained, well-balanced, experienced shooting dog.

Obviously, dogs cannot talk. In fact, the barks, whines, growls, and howls a dog makes are designed to convey emotion rather than meaning. Dogs communicate with body language which at times may seem extremely subtle to their human partners. But dogs certainly understand each other's slightest movement or gesture. Each wag or positioning of the tail, movement of facial muscles, tenseness of muscles, stance and gait, all contribute to canine language. Our own body language is scarcely less subtle and although we may not be aware of it, we are just as quick to read the signs. How often do we decide we do not like a person, or take to another, on the experience of some brief few moments? How often is this 'feeling' due to nothing more than that person's failure to transmit the right signals through body language, dress, or even accent or skin colour? We expect people to conform to the stereotype we have learnt to expect, outsiders are recognized by differences in body posture, turn of phrase, or more subtle signals we may not even be conscious of. It is no different for dogs which is why one man is a 'natural dogman' and another can achieve nothing.

It takes experience to understand many of the signs a dog makes which is where the professional dog trainer scores over the amateur. The professional often knows what a dog is going to do long before it knows itself. In almost every other aspect of dog training the amateur has the edge which is something worth thinking about. I was called in to solve problems an owner was having with a dog he had purchased from me as a pet and shooting companion. On the moor, the dog wandered about rather aimlessly, lifting its leg on every other rock or tuft of grass and generally giving the impression it was bored to tears. 'There, you see? The dog is not interested in hunting', said the owner in a tone which clearly meant he held me responsible.

Although I had not seen the dog for a couple of years, and then only as a small pup, I gave it a whistle and started to walk across the moor in a purposeful manner.

In two minutes the dog had started to hunt for me and in another ten it had found and pointed a covey. The difference was that I had acted out the role of the hunting partner, whereas the owner wandered about the moor waiting for the dog to take the initiative, which of course it had no incentive to do.

Do dogs think? Watch the family pet asleep in front of the fire and there can be no doubt about it. He growls, whines, and barks in his sleep; clearly he pursues imaginary prey, warns off dreamed of enemies, and fights battles with illusory foes. But he cannot think in words, only pictures, and in the sounds he knows. So training ought to take account of these limitations. The commands we give him are sounds only and convey no meaning in themselves. That is why it is so important for a dog to be put through a brief programme of re-training by a new owner, to explain to the dog what the new sounds mean. Would a phrase spoken in a broad Devonshire accent be comprehensible to an Aberdeenshire countryman, located as they are at opposite ends of the country? The written words might convey tbe same message but the accents are as dissimilar as it is possible for them to be. We cannot know *how* a dog hears sounds, only its reactions to them. How often does a novice owner call his dog; 'Come here', then 'Here boy', and again 'Here, will you?'; all quite different sounds to the poor confused dog and all possibly delivered in different tones and inflections according to the owners degree of frustration or impatience. Also, it is impossible to carry out abstract thought, to reason, without words. So dogs are generally assumed not to be able to reason. Try thinking in pictures and you soon realize the limitations imposed on a dog. Rational thought is impossible. Do not for one moment think that dogs are stupid. It is just that their intelligence has limitations as does our own. A brain surgeon might find difficulty in carrying out an elementary service on his car; a mechanic could not remove a brain tumour. A more complicated life style is unnecessary to the dog. Perhaps they are not so stupid after all.

The question most often asked is, When does dog training begin? Dog training starts sixty-three days before the pup is born! Sixty-three days is the gestation period, the time between the mating of dog and bitch and the birth of the puppies. Successful training depends on the correct choice of sire and dam. Without that, a great deal of effort can be wasted.

Planning when a bitch is mated and thus when pups will be born can help too. A pup born on 1 January will be four months old when the birds are paired in April and it will be eight months old in August, nine in September. The importance of these dates is that they coincide with two critical periods in a dog's life and two important stages in the life cycle of the game birds it is intended to hunt.

Most experienced trainers have encountered the situation where a pup, picked out for special attention, does not progress as quickly as another that is relatively neglected. It is known that the dog learns very quickly at certain stages of its life and so long as appropriate training corresponds with these periods, progress will be swift. But it is an area where research still needs to be done. So the 'neglected' pup which gets training at the correct time will turn out better than the one given most of the attention . . . but at the wrong times!

Once the pups are born, whenever they are born, training can begin as soon as they are capable of learning. It may not seem like training, yet if these early lessons are omitted the pup will never develop to its full potential. Regardless of the pedigree and the qualifications of sire and dam, your pup will grow up stunted emotionally and mentally.

This process is particularly evident in the early learning experiences of, say, a new born lamb. A great deal of learning has to be crammed into the first few hours of a lamb's life so that it can survive in a world full of predators. Unlike the pup, the lamb must be on its feet and sucking very quickly indeed it if is to gain strength and follow its mother and survive. It is fascinating to watch this process in action. As soon as the lamb is born, the ewe licks it clean, not only ingesting valuable protein as it does so, but also hormones which stimulate milk production. This licking stimulates the lamb to get on to its feet and starts it working its way to the teat, attracted by instinct and a scent produced by a gland near the udder. Every time the lamb falls over and gets up it is getting valuable practice in the action of rising to its feet! So, what appears to be the roughness of the mother in repeatedly knocking the new born lamb over has a practical function in training it to stand. That lamb may need to get on its feet very quickly in the future and it is one behaviour pattern which needs to be perfected. As the lamb feels for the udder, the ewe nudges its rear end, recognizing its own particular scent as it does so. All the while, the ewe keeps up a continual bleating which the lamb answers so mutual recognition is by sound as well as smell. A strong bond between the two is meantime being created.

As every shepherd knows, the whole sequence is vitally important and if the lamb is taken away, even for twenty minutes, during this short critical period before the bond is established, the ewe may fail to recognize her own lamb or let it suck when it is returned. And if the lamb fails to reach the teat and start sucking within a specific time, it may never learn to suck at all and it will die of starvation. The difficulty of getting a ewe to accept a lamb which is not her own is well known. The problems of getting a lamb to suck that has missed that vital moment of learning are so frustrating as to remain permanently engrained in the mind of those who have ever experienced it!

Imprinting is a process well known to falconers. The time span involved in imprinting, when the young forms that bond with its mother, is shortest in those breeds which are up and following their mothers quickest. Konrad Lorenz, an animal behaviourist working in the 1930s, experimented with geese and jackdaws which adopted him as 'mother'. Lorenz's books are utterly fascinating reading. When Lorenz's jackdaws became mature, their abnormal behaviour included trying to feed their surrogate 'mother' (Lorenz) by pushing worms into his ears!

Similar stages are present in the dog's development. But they take place over a much longer period. Knowing of these should help in training a dog and explains why one trainer succeeds (his dogs more or less 'training themselves') without apparent effort while another finds the same dogs 'headstrong and untrainable'.

Puppies are born deaf and blind. Soon after birth, instinct causes the pup to locate a nipple and to begin suckling. The puppy's senses at this age are very limited. Its powers of scent are restricted to a few centimetres. New born puppies apparently possess a good sense of taste and will suck any smooth warm object but give up if no milk is produced. They rely entirely on their mother to keep them warm, sleeping in a huddle against their dam's belly and whining piteously if their environment is too cold or too hot. They are unable even to defecate without their mother's assistance. This she does by licking the puppies' rear ends. Orphaned pups have to be massaged with cotton wool moistened with warm water to allow their normal functions to operate. New born pups are incapable of learning very much at all but even at this stage simple behaviour patterns must become established quickly if a pup is to survive.

The instinct to suck is awakened by the pup's hunger. This stimulates the pup to move towards scent from the teats. The warm, smooth, soft surface of the teat stimulates the pup to suck, finally to attach itself to a nipple. The reward of warm milk reinforces the pup's response to follow the sequence prompted originally by instinct and the motivation of hunger. Every time the pup is hungry it will now attempt to follow the same sequence. We will soon see how every action the dog performs follows a similar sequence and how important it is to understand this basic principle if training is to be successful. If the sequence is to be set in motion, the motivation must be correct; the dog must be permitted to follow the pattern of behaviour without distraction or inhibition. If the sequence is to be repeated and become established as a behaviour pattern in the dog's mind, some benefit must be derived from its performance. And it must be repeated until the pattern is firmly engrained. This simplified explanation of how a dog learns to perform some sequence of actions is enough for an understanding of many aspects of basic dog training.

Puppies' eyes open at about thirteen days but their ears are actually sealed so they cannot hear until the beginning of the fourth week. During the fourth week the pups start to walk rather than crawl and leave the nest to defecate. They begin to explore their nest and are attracted to anything strange which they approach and investigate. At the same time, the puppies start to play with each other. Incredibly, this is the earliest pups have shown any real inclination to learn.

The fourth week of life is the most important in the puppy's development and everything begins to happen at once. The change from relative inactivity to a period of rapid learning literally takes place overnight and by the end of the week they will have developed from obvious babies into small dogs. All the sensory functions are now working and the puppy is rapidly becoming aware of its environment. The puppy's intelligence and emotions start to come into action within this twenty-four hours. Scientists working on canine psychology conclude that to deprive a puppy of its mother's attention during the fourth week can cause permanent emotional damage. Just a week later and the adjustments have been made but a puppy still needs to associate with his litter mates up to the sixth or seventh week to make an emotionally stable dog. Pups weaned before this age were found to be noisy and nervous, a neurotic state which persisted for life.

I make a point of talking to all my pups, daily if possible, occasionally picking one up, from the third week at least. I believe this helps to create a strong bond later in training. Some human contact from now on is essential. Fortunately, this need be minimal; just a few moments of brief contact every day is enough. I do not understand people who do not talk to their dogs. The object is to create a partnership. How many human partnerships, business or personal, would last five minutes without communication? How do such people expect to forge that close link with man's best friend without such interchange? Almost every animal attempting to form a bond with its young during this important period indulges in vocalization. During this stage I make no attempt to be quiet around the pups; rather the reverse. Doors are banged and buckets rattled, consequently gunshyness is virtually unknown in my kennels.

From the fourth week, I try to find time to get right in amongst the pups every couple of days or so, sitting down in the straw of their bed, gently playing with them and letting them crawl all over me and tug my clothes. Now the bitch pays less attention to the puppies, attending to them more-or-less on a part-time basis as they become more active and start to annoy her.

Some provision ought to be made so the bitch can get out of the way of her pups. Either the lower half of the kennel gate can be boarded up, so mum can hop over but pups are kept back, or she ought to have access to a bed out of their reach. Failure to allow for this can, in my opinion, lead to the 'battered baby syndrome' similar to the problems encountered when human mothers are incarcerated with small children in high-rise flats with no means of escape.

As soon as they are able to follow, I like to take the puppies on short walks. These excursions are punctuated with periods of play. Older children enjoy this part of dog training particularly and, provided they are gentle, are very good at it. It is something to be encouraged in moderation, say once a day when the weather is fine but once a week is better than nothing. Pups will follow their mother, of course, but allowing the family free range can lead to problems as mum tries to get out of the way of the puppies and pups struggle to keep up. On one occasion I found one of my bitches accompanied by a single pup, the rest of the litter were eventually discovered asleep in a tussock of grass within a few feet of a busy main road where they had dropped exhausted after just such a chase. Such walks are again punctuated with periods of play so that pups learn to expect a fun time from their human companion when called.

The ideal is to allow pups free range in a controlled environment where they can learn about life without coming to harm. On my farm pups run free and the only hazards likely to be encountered are the post van and the odd ewe or hen protecting its young. Whenever possible, I run on every litter so that I can pick out and retain the best for future breeding. So I probably rear as many pups as anyone in the course of a year. A compromise between total liberty and permanent imprisonment seems about right and although they are learning at liberty, they also learn to expect to be kennelled for part of the day and accept this without fuss.

The pups gambol about, doing whatever they like, until they start to get into trouble. On the farm, this usually takes the form of more serious hen chasing or other destructive actions which have to be curbed from about four months of age. Some pups run on until they are six months old without trouble. Then, unless out at exercise under constant supervision, they are kennelled in a large earth floored run. But for a few brief weeks they get their freedom. They get called to the back door for titbits, bacon rinds and table scraps, or for play and petting whenever I have a moment. On walks around the fields they are rewarded for coming to call by my lying flat on the ground, my hands covering my face to protect myself from over-zealous licking, when, like all youngsters, they enjoy jumping on and generally ragging someone who is normally bigger and more powerful than they are! This role reversal occurs, too, between the pups and the older dogs. The mature dogs making complete fools of themselves as they play with the youngsters just as their human equivalents do with their own offspring! Such periods of play ensure that pups come running at full speed when called.

The call, incidentally, is what I call 'the play call'. This call means the chance of a rough-and-tumble in the grass, some choice food, or some other reason for the pups to come at a gallop. It is *never* used to call the pups to anything unpleasant, such as going back into their kennel, though this may well *follow* a brief petting or game before feeding in the kennel. The reasoning, I hope, will become clear as we proceed but from now on the pups are beginning to get some serious training without their ever realizing it.

I should perhaps stress here that a young working pointer or setter puppy requires no 'punishment' or 'correction'. Punishment is some unpleasant experience meted out to pups *after* the undesirable behaviour has taken place. Punishment has unpredictable results and seldom produces a permanent solution in preventing the undesirable actions. If a pup removes the washing from the line and tears your favourite shirt to ribbons, there is no one to blame but yourself. If a pup retrieves your child's pet rabbit or kills your neighbour's hens, it is a lot cheaper to make sure the pup is kennelled whenever you are unable to give it full-time supervision and replace what has been destroyed than to hit the dog and risk ruining it for life. Mild chastisement of a retaliatory nature is natural. If a pup bites me too hard I let him know it is not appreciated. A very soft slap and a rough word is enough. They soon learn what is allowed and what isn't but that is a straightforward hierarchical situation.

Contrary to what some erroneously believe, a bitch does *not* physically punish its puppies and it is anatomically impossible for the bitch to lift a pup up to eye level and shake it, as at least one writer suggested in a well-known shooting paper, whilst maintaining eye-to-eye contact!. What it does is to *threaten* a pup in a specific situation, i.e. when it has acted out of rank in the hierarchy. What we might call 'taking a liberty'. I have watched this time and again. As soon as the attack is over, both the bitch and the pup restore normal relations by mutual licking and tail wagging. But the immediate reaction of the pup is for it to roll over on its back in a typical submissive gesture, sometimes emitting blood-curdling screams that convince all concerned that murder most foul is being done! And that is something we'll make use of later . . . . Severe punishment from dog to dog has the effect of driving the weaker participant out of the dominant dog's territory or subordinating a weaker member in the pack hierarchy. Physically punishing a dog has therefore an undesirable and counter-productive effect. At worst, it might drive a dog away. At best, it alienates the dog's affections and damages that delicate bond between man and dog. Seldom does it achieve the desired effect. A rough word or two with a shake is all that most correctly bred dogs need. Later, I'll explain how the dog is inhibited from performing undesirable actions by arranging for the act itself to produce an undesirable result for the dog. And if that sounds complicated, all it means is that the action is so staged as to become an undesirable act to repeat, it is not the trainer who metes out this punishment.

The object of rearing a working pointer or setter puppy is to produce a confident and self-reliant hunting dog, not necessarily a family pet. And there is a difference. Pups destined to be working dogs should be allowed into the house under strict supervision but they also ought to have an outdoor kennel. Immediately pups are seen to be sniffing the floor they are whisked up and taken outside to do their business. Accidents do happen but they are rare if pups are allowed time to relieve themselves before being brought into the house. The signs of a pup looking for somewhere suitable to relieve himself are very easily recognized and accidents are easily prevented. A puppy intended to be the family pet ought to be trained appropriately and there are many good books on the subject. But even a pup intended as a working dog ought to receive some socialization amongst the family on a regular basis, not as a plaything to amuse the children but as a youngster intended to trust and respect its human partners.

Scientists have proved that pups deprived of human contact until they are fourteen weeks old are wild and unapproachable. That accounts for many a pup ruined by being left unattended in the gamekeeper's kennel. The best time for socialization with humans is from the sixth to eighth week which is also the best time for a pup to leave for its new home. Even though pups may be properly socialized at this age, they become wild and shy if left in the kennel from three or four months to six or eight months. Such puppies will give problems when training commences. I sold a very promising puppy to people who kennelled it in the middle of a wood. All it saw was the man who came to feed it and clean it out once a day. There was no attempt to socialise the dog and it gradually became more and more nervous of strangers and difficult to handle, even by the regular kennelman. I bought this dog back as a neurotic wreck at a year old and it took six months of careful daily socialization to partially restore the dog's faith in humanity. I would judge this dog to be one of the best I ever bred, brought to the edge of ruin by stupid owners.

These important phases of a dog's life, verified by carefully controlled scientific experiments and supported by the experiences of Guide Dogs for the Blind of America, worried me considerably. How could I continue to train dogs if they had to be socialized up to the age of eight months? The answer is that pointers and setters have been kept as kennel dogs since their origins and provided they are handled reasonably and sensibly these problems never arise. It is a different matter for dogs required to take charge of a blind person. If dogs are reared in comparative isolation the problems can be very real but normal day-to-day training, without periods of neglect, provides just the sort of socialization that is needed.

That is not to say that a working dog will be completely relaxed in a strange environment. By their nature, bird dogs are sensitive creatures which react to strange encounters in the same way a finely bred race horse might do, seeming to have nerves strung out like piano wires until given the chance to perform as they have been bred and trained to do. But this very nervousness is needed in bird dogs under British conditions, just as it is a prerequisite in finely bred horses so they will be responsive to the slightest sign or gesture from their handlers. A falcon trapped from the wild can still be trained and flown with success by an experienced falconer . . . and few dogs are ever as nervous as a wild falcon.

The hunting instinct begins to become active around nine weeks of age. Before this age, pups do not seem to notice small objects they might profitably attack for food. I have had pups hunting and pointing game at ten or eleven weeks (the youngest was nine-and-a-half weeks) and it is not so unusual as to be remarkable to have pups pointing wild game at three months. But a youngster is physically unable to do anything like serious work on the grouse moor until it is at least eighteen months of age, possibly a lot older than this, and it is all too easy to ruin a dog for life by trying to force the pace. Some of my best pointers may be 'working' at four months, but by twelve months they seem disappointingly slow, then at eighteen months or two years they begin to mature and get over that adolescent hesitancy; then, at maturity, they really begin to show just what they can do. I truly admire the field trial judge who can assess a dog in two minutes flat; many of mine will not show their true form until two or three *years* have passed and in the meantime keep me guessing. A sensitive dog is generally a cautious dog and young pups which flash around in a devil-may-care style become very serious when they first learn that they must not flush birds. Many a promising youngster has been dismissed as useless before it has had a chance and some breeds and strains are more precocious than others.

Before a pup will start to hunt, the hunting instinct has to be awakened. When I started to train dogs I sometimes encountered problems getting a dog interested in running and hunting game when serious field training started on the grouse moors at around a year old. Up until this age, my pups were kennelled with daily exercise in a grass paddock with other dogs and hand trained in a field devoid of game. When they were introduced to game country it sometimes took a while for them to realize that there were birds out there for them to find. And when they did find game, my natural reaction was to try to control their actions and to get them to point rather than allowing them to run birds up and chase.

The problem had me perplexed as it was similar to something I had experienced with falcons. A correctly trained bird which flew magnificently to the lure and returned the instant it was called simply showed no interest in hunting wild prey, or hunted so inefficiently it took ages to make a kill. The problem is that such a bird, or animal, rapidly becomes discouraged with repeated failure. The fact that the problem occurred in falcons confirmed to me that it had nothing to do with genetics although many amateur trainers will blame the breeder for such difficulties. Then again, other trainers insisted that the best dogs were the wildest as it was their keenness for game which conflicted with their willingness to respond to their handlers. I could not understand why there needed to be this conflict and I have since convinced myself, if no one else, that it is possible to have complete control over a dog whilst retaining all the fire and desire one could wish for. The difference is all a question of the correct breeding and the proper sequence of training which I shall attempt to explain here.

But I noticed that wild hawks took great pains to teach their young to kill by making them chase and 'catch' the food they brought them in their talons soon after they had learnt to fly and left the nest. Young birds taken during this period were also much easier to train as they were already learning to hunt but were still responsive and dependant on their parents. It was this I wanted to simulate in my young bird dogs.

It seemed to me that the failure to start to hunt was something similar to the lamb failing to suck. Perhaps these dogs had missed a vital part of their education. I now have dogs working, that is hunting and pointing, wild red grouse within a day or so of going to the moors so my theories, at least with my own dogs, have been proved correct.

Hunting for a pup should be fun. Training, too, ought to be fun. Formal training sessions for youngsters are against my philosophy of gundog training and are kept to a minimum. I try to let the pup train itself, without its ever being aware that it is being trained or that I am in charge of the situation.

Dogs have been around, living quite successfully in one form or another, for about forty million years. They have done so very well without man's help. In comparison, man, in recognizable form, arrived on the scene about one and a half million years ago. Man has selectively bred dogs for a mere ten to fourteen thousand years and in that time he has succeeded in suppressing some characteristics and enhancing others. This has been done through selective breeding; training being applied to modify the dog's responses to predicted situations. But many of the instincts found in those wild ancestors remain intact. These ancestors were almost certainly a small type of wolf originating in the east. So it seems not unreasonable that the best system of training would be that which makes use of the dog's natural instincts rather than some system which seeks to impose our own ideas of how the dog should behave.

By three months of age a pup's hunting instincts are ready to be awakened. This may happen by nothing more spectacular than the pup starting to chase a leaf blown by the wind. But it is an important stage. I was approached by BBC Radio for an interview on pointer and setter training. I agreed but wondered what I could say that would interest listeners. As usual, I had half a dozen pups running loose about the farm and as I contemplated the problem my eye lighted on a pup playing outside the window. A gust of wind blew a dead leaf and the pup, then aged about three months, chased in pursuit. I knew that I had the answer!

By the time the interviewer arrived my plans were made. I produced the fishing rod I use to play with the pups. It used to have a partridge wing tied on the end of a couple of yards of line attached to its tip but over the years this had been replaced with a small piece of plastic from the handle of a supermarket shopping bag. Not quite so romantic as a partridge wing, perhaps, but it does the job. As I gave a running commentary, the pup chased the 'wing' on the end of my fishing line. As the pup got close; I whisked the 'wing' out of the way, imitating a bird flying off. Then I dropped it to earth again for pup to chase. As the pup continued to play, it began to tire and then to change tactics. Chasing got it nowhere. Even small pups are anything but stupid. The pup was learning from its own experiences. It began to stalk. And then to point. The whole process had taken about five minutes. Each time the pup ran in to catch the 'wing', it flew off just as a bird would do. Each time the pup pointed with persistence, the bird stayed on the ground. Still, the pup was undecided what to do.

The next step was to show the pup one of my tame pigeons. I let it gently nuzzle the bird in my hand, then released my hold on the bird and, suddenly, it flew off. The pup was a little alarmed by the sudden motion and flapping of wings, but it soon recovered. I got another out of the loft. This time the pup chased the pigeon as I released it, then watched as it landed on the roof and strutted about. All the time I kept up a running commentary for the radio listeners, talking to the pup, talking through each stage of the lesson with the interviewer.

Next, I 'dizzied' a quail and placed it in some long grass. Most birds can be hypnotized for a short while by placing their heads under their wings and gently rocking them to and fro. We call this dizzying as it seems to confuse the bird and it will lie quietly wherever it is placed. Then the pup was brought up-wind to where the quail was hidden. I had put a light cord around the pup's neck as a precaution against it grabbing the bird. But I need not have worried; as the pup winded the quail, not knowing its exact location, it stopped on point. Dogs use their noses almost as much as they use their eyes. Their ability to detect odours is about ten thousand times better than our own. So the transition presented no problem. I gently prodded the quail out of its hypnotic trance with a bit of stick and allowed the pup to chase as it took off. Dogs seem to get a thrill out of chasing (it is certainly a very basic instinct) and at this stage it acts as a reward. Later, chasing will have to be controlled.

Not particularly put out by its experiences, the quail dropped back into the grass about a dozen yards ahead. I worked the pup up wind to this spot. Again, the pup pointed. It stayed firm for several moments until the quail flew off again. Later, I heard the broadcast had gone down extremely well. It is certainly hilarious to watch tiny pups working in this way and, provided it is not taken too seriously, it does no harm. But keep it a game. Small pups tend to remember these early experiences and restraint can make them sticky or even blink (see below for definitions).

Allowing a pup of three to five months to chase birds, or even the 'wing', will awaken those hunting instincts and save a great deal of work later on. But it should never be over-done. From now on that pup will look at all birds and flying things with new eyes and it will never be quite the same again. Butterflies and small birds will be hunted with great zeal.

Using the fishing rod and 'wing' alone will usually stimulate the pup to point, but it is pointing *by eye*. The pup is using its eyesight rather than its nose to locate the 'game'. Such a pup may not recognize bird scent when it encounters it, let alone search for scent. And that is the objective; to get our dog to hunt for the air scent of birds and then to remain on point until the Gun gets up. The reason for letting the pup nuzzle a pigeon in the hand and then releasing the bird, letting the pup chase, is to fix in its mind the connection between the scent of the bird and the bird itself.

One summer I spent every lunch time beside the estuary of the River Dart, in South Devon. Sea gulls shared my sandwiches and I enjoyed seeing how tame I could make them. Then one day they flew down to get the crumbs as usual but veered off, refusing to take the bread. For a while I was confused. I could not understand why hungry birds would refuse to eat. Then I realized that, for a change, I had got sandwiches made from brown bread, instead of the usual white, which the birds simply did not recognize as food. The thought struck me that no animal could know, except from inborn instinct, what was outside its own experience.

In the above sequence, each stage is linked to the next in a clear chain, instinct providing the driving force to get the dog to move from one stage to the next, each experience leading it on to the next stage.

What we have now established is the basic hunting sequence of a predator. This is made up of a number of individual stages which can be summarised as:

Hunt – Locate – Approach – Pause – Approach – Pounce – Chase – Catch – Kill – Carry – Eat

In the pointing dogs, the 'pause' has been refined into a point. The second 'approach' is inhibited and carried out, after training, under the strict supervision of the handler; and the 'pounce' has been replaced by the dog being trained (in Britain) to drop to wing. I believe the British way, of channelling the pounce into a positive action, the drop, makes more sense to the dog than just training it to stand steady. The chase and catch are omitted in the trained dog. The dog delegates the act of killing to another member of the 'pack', i.e. the Gun who fires the shot. This is really no different to a member of a pack of wild dogs leaving the final *coup de grace* to one or several other experienced pack members. If the dog has been trained to retrieve it would then go forward, pick up the dead bird, and bring it back to its handler, this being a perfectly natural part of the sequence modified by training. Later, it will be seen how shooting game over a pointing dog makes everything come together; so much so that careful shooting will greatly improve your dog. But we are getting ahead of ourselves.

Interestingly, Laverack describes how he trained his dogs by checking them and making them 'sit' at the moment before the pounce (*The Setter,* page 38). I can testify to the dramatic effect of this method.

Each action the dog goes through follows a similar sequence, the same simple behaviour pattern we discussed earlier. Usually, the dog will be driven to complete one of these patterns by some compulsion or incitement and the pattern will become fixed through the prospect of some reward and finally by constant repetition. The importance of establishing a behaviour pattern became clear to me when I trained falcons. I heard that a fellow falconer, a very experienced person, dispensed with the most frustrating part of the training and I could scarcely understand how this could be managed. What this falconer was doing was dispensing with that part of training which involved calling the hawk to the fist or lure out-of-doors over increasingly long distances. This stage is a problem because the bird has to be flown on a long line, or creance as it is called in the language of falconry, to prevent its flying off. It is a frustrating and worrying period because the line inevitably gets snagged in long grass or on some twig and the hawk is effectively 'punished', by being brought up short by the cord, for coming to call. I realized that this falconer had avoided the problem by very firmly engraining the response to his call by repeating the exercise over and over again over very short distances. In fact, this clever person had got his bird literally 'hooked' on coming to call over short distances in his living room! When he went outside, the bird responded immediately and without hesitation as it had been trained to do. I attempted the same method with my own hawks, dispensing with that annoying creance, and got instant success. But it had one unpredicted side effect. One evening I got an unexpected call at my door from the local minister of the church who I had not previously met. Opening the door just a crack so the bird could not escape into the night, I hesitated wondering how to explain that I had a wild bird in the sitting-room without creating the inevitable misunderstanding. As I pondered the problem the poor minister mumbled some inaudible apology and fled into the night, obviously convinced that I was an atheist!

The way dogs learn is not so difficult to understand. The stray dog runs away when it sees someone stoop to pick up a stone. It feels fear when it sees the man go through the actions which it knows from experience constitutes a threat. That fear is relieved when it runs away and is replaced by a feeling of pleasurable relief. The whole sequence takes only a few seconds yet it is a well-known scenario to every countryman.

A similar sequence is followed when a dog is hit with a stick by a stupid trainer. The dog sees the blow coming, knows from experience that it could be painful, tries to avoid it by dodging, and runs away so gaining relief. Next time the dog anticipates any similarly sudden movement as a threat and takes evasive action. And so the familiar nervous dog that jumps at any sudden movement or sound has been created. In reality, the dog which learns this quickly is often the easiest for the knowledgeable trainer to handle as it is inevitably the most quick to react. But suppose we *train* the dog to expect to experience relief, even pleasure, if it goes into the drop position in response to a mild threat? Now, instead of a neurotic dog we have a snappy obedient performer. So discipline and training actually makes a dog feel more secure because it knows exactly what to do to relieve stress in a given situation. Not only that, it begins to predict situations and never encounters the stressful point in the exercise at all. But first, let's take a look at how a pup is taught to drop.

In the wild, a pup would normally join the pack at a kill between three and five months of age and it must quickly learn the submissive gestures so as to avoid an attack from another dog higher on the social scale. The pup's teeth, at this age, are still immature and it cannot make much of a job of defending itself so submission is the normal response to a threat from an older individual.

Scientists recognized that a flock of hens develop a hierarchical structure which they called 'the pecking order'. The most dominant hen in the flock could peck all the other hens, the least dominant could peck no one! The hens in between could peck those below them in status but not those higher up on the social ladder. This is an over-simplification but it will serve. The same sort of hierarchical structure develops in a litter of pups kennelled together, or indeed in any close knit group of animals, including humans though the hierarchy is seldom as simple as it might appear. One pup becomes dominant and can take a bone away from any of the others. The least dominant pup can be robbed of his bone by any one of his litter mates!

In order to avoid being attacked by a more superior dog, the pup may cower, lower his head, expose the vulnerable side of his neck, roll over perhaps onto his back to expose his soft under belly, and probably expel a few drops of urine containing his unique body odour by way introduction. Or it may do only a few of these things according to its rank and the degree of the threat. The senior dog may stand stiffly on the tips of its toes and raise his hackles to increase height, arch his neck to protect the throat region, growl, show his teeth, and general give all the signals we know so well in a threatening dog according to the situation. But more likely, only a hint of these signals will be necessary. As relationships relax, the dominant dog smells the genitalia of the lower ranking dog and gradually establishes a more normal stance. Once rankings have been mutually established, peace is restored. Putting pup through this act of submission reinforces his rank in the pack, and strange to say he feels secure and more confident.

Owners often state that 'my dog knows when it has done wrong'. The owner has reached this conclusion because the dog 'has a guilty look'. The dog interprets the body language of its owner and realizes that an attack on its person is imminent. The reasons for this expected attack are irrelevant. The dog therefore assumes the correct body language needed to reassure another dog (or in this case the owner) that it (the dog being threatened) is no threat in return. This 'no threat' body posture typical of the cringing dog (for example, the fawning spaniel) is merely an attempt by the dog, which assumes it is being threatened, to placate a larger and more powerful pack member! So, those signals interpreted by the owner as 'guilt' are not guilt at all, but submission in response to his own subconsciously threatening actions and poses!

Training a pup to drop would therefore seem to be straightforward and free of trauma if we realize the processes involved. And so it is. Both well-bred pointers and setters of traditional British breeding are naturally submissive and not inclined to want to dominate other dogs or humans. Extremes in the hierarchy, i.e. very aggressive or subordinate dogs, are not usual in these breeds but are occasionally encountered. Generally, they are more difficult to train because of these extreme characteristics and are best avoided.

At this point it would seem to be appropriate to say something of the 'Pavlovian reflex', correctly called Classical Conditioning. Pavlov discovered that dogs began to salivate when they heard a dinner bell even before they smelt or saw their food. He recorded that a dog could become conditioned to respond involuntarily to some recognizable signal, a secondary inducement (the bell), which replaced the normal signal, the primary inducement (the sight or scent of food). That, simply, is the basis of most responses we seek to establish in dog training. The command acts as the secondary inducement causing the dog to carry out the trained response. Think about your own actions and there will be many instances in which you follow the same routine; the responses are often unconscious and completely automatic. Sometimes the actions involved became difficult or clumsy if we think about them or attempt to consciously follow them through. For example, the action of changing gear by an experienced driver in response to a change in the engine tone of his car is done without any conscious decision, without thinking, and completely automatically. Hitting a ball with a bat, or killing a bird with a gun, involves similar unconscious coordination which becomes more difficult the more we think about it.

Establishing these automatic responses to our commands is the basis for control in working dogs. Allowing natural instincts to develop whilst modifying how behaviour patterns become established is an essential part of educating the dog through experience. The next chapter describes how we assemble all these component parts to make the fully trained dog.

Top: F.T.Ch. Or, painted by 'Spartacus'. (*T. Ishibashi*)

Bottom: Orange and white male pointer Int.F.T.Ch. Barnabe de Valesia, winner of many field trials in France, Belgium, Switzerland, Italy and also the winner of many International Shows. Painted by 'Spartacus'. (*T. Ishibashi*)

Top: Black and white male pointer Int.F.T.Ch. Brio, a most stylish pointer. Painted by 'Spartacus'. (*T. Ishibashi*)

Bottom: Two pointers on point, painted by Mr Lallo. (*T. Ishibashi*)

Top: Pointer on point, with Irish setter backing. Painted by Mr Lallo. (*T. Ishibashi*)

Bottom: Pointer and English setter watching the game flying away. Painted by Mr Lallo. (*T. Ishibashi*)

Top: English setter watching pheasant flying away. Painted by Mr Lallo. (*T. Ishibashi*)

Bottom: Ch. Bang on point with English setter backing. Painted by Mr Lallo. (*T. Ishibashi*)

Chapter 6
Training

It has been said that bird dog training comprises only two items. These are the recall (calling the dog to you) and the drop (flat down), the rest being instinct and experience. There is a lot of sense in that. The trick is to give the dog the right sort of experience to allow these instincts to develop whilst retaining control with the recall and the drop.

Training usually takes place during daily exercise and anyone who claims he has no time to train his dog has no time to exercise one and in those circumstances he should not own one. The simple behaviour patterns we wish to implant in the dog's mind follow sequences similar to the hunt/kill pattern previously mentioned. Some of these behaviour patterns may be very brief. Each sequence is influenced by many extraneous factors easily overlooked. Every detail of the circumstances where, when, and how these responses occur can, and do, influence the completion of these behaviour patterns. Even though we may not always understand why a dog responds or acts in a particular way, understanding how these reactions occur will help us diagnose problems and decide effective action to correct faults. This may all seem terribly obscure, but hopefully all become clear as we proceed.

The response of a trained dog to the 'Sit' command illustrates how one simple behaviour pattern is accomplished. A puppy flattens itself on the ground in response to the threat of an older dog. This is a purely instinctive response. The trainer modifies this sequence to his own ends so when he gives the command, 'Sit!' the dog responds by dropping flat. The sequence can be further modified by training the dog to drop in response to a variety of stimuli – a word, a hand signal, a whistled signal, a gunshot, a bird flying off, etc. Training a dog to drop in the regular exercise field is one thing; getting the dog to perform the drop consistently under the infinitely variable circumstances of every working situation, and at long range, is another. Every trainer knows how things go wrong when he attempts to show his pupils off to visitors. The presence of the visitors introduces another variable into the formula and the completion of the behaviour pattern is disturbed. Put simply, the dog is distracted and fails to respond as he has been trained to do.

Substituting a command to cause a dog to drop rather than threatening it with a more dominating dog is the simple Pavlovian Reflex mentioned in the previous chapter. The dog should not have to think before completing the action. By 'thinking' I mean 'choose an option'. It is quite usual to see the partly trained dog trying to decide how he should respond to a command. Should he drop or run back to the kennel? The trained dog responds without hesitation. There are many actions in our own behaviour which follow a similar pattern. The experienced driver changes gear unconsciously in response to road conditions and engine tone. The accomplished shot kills the bird without conscious effort, the action being automatically programmed to the speed, height, and angle of travel of the bird. Conscious thought often causes failure. A trained dog responds automatically, without having to think.

My own method of teaching the drop is to physically place the pup in the 'dropped' position and hold it down whilst gently stroking it and rubbing its ears. Push the pup down with one hand whilst pulling the feet out in front with the other, then carefully position each leg so it is comfortable for the dog to stay in that position. Between three to five months is the best age to teach the drop for the reasons stated in the previous chapter. Initially there will be struggles, sometime quite violent struggles, as the pup suspects your motives. It may be helpful to kneel with one leg each side of the pup to steady it. But gradually it relaxes in response to gentle stroking. A dog will generally 'sell its soul' to have its ears scratched. At the same time I repeat the command, 'Sit, sit, sit . . .' in the tone I expect to use when ordering a dog to go down in the shooting field. (Hopefully, the same tone will be used for this command throughout the dog's life so confusion does not arise in it's mind.) No praise, no congratulatory phrases. This may seem illogical, but the object is to associate the word 'Sit' with the dog's position in which it now should feel secure. 'Sit' is used in preference to any other command because the hiss, 'Sssss . . .' (which is similar enough to 'Sit' to cause the dog to pause . . .) will later be used for fine control. For example, when controlling the speed the dog walks in to a point.

The photographs on the following pages illustrate 'The Drop'. (J. Rimell)

Pup is pushed down and restrained in the correct position, with the command 'Sit' being repeated.

The pup gradually relaxes as he is stroked and has his ears tickled. The command 'Sit' is repeated and he is pushed down if he attempts to rise.

The check cord supplements hand restraint; the cord being jerked with the command 'Sit' if pup attempts to rise.

The cord is used to extend contact with the pup, but a restraining hand is still within reach.

Pup remains down and the trainer now retains control solely with the cord and voice. The hand signal is introduced.

Quite confident now, pup remains dropped. The verbal commands and the hand signals continue, contact is maintained through the cord.

Lesson over, the pup should happily and confidently run to the trainer.

After the lesson, pup and trainer should resume a happy, confident relationship.

Once the pup has learnt that, contrary to something unpleasant happening when he is pushed down, he gets his ears scratched and is gently stroked, he begins to relax and feel secure. Just a few moments in the down position and pup is given the play call and a few moments of play as a reward. As in the situation when the young dog is dominated by an older dog, the pup very quickly reverts to its happy, normal mood. It will be clear that we are merely using the pup's natural instinct to drop down when confronted with a more dominant, threatening dog so there is nothing unnatural about teaching a dog to drop, rather the reverse. Incidentally, it is quite startling to see, for the first time, how quickly the mood of a pup changes from obvious apprehension when confronted by a strange, more dominant and therefore threatening dog to obvious ecstacy when it receives the signs of reassurance it looks for from the older individual.

These exercises are repeated several times each day, the pup being told to 'Sit' and, if necessary, being pushed down and held in that position. Initially it is enough that the pup accepts being pushed down and holds the 'Sit' position for a few moments until called to play.

The correct 'Sit' position for a bird dog is flat down, forearms flat on the ground, head in contact with the ground between the paws, and belly on the ground. We seldom bother with the intermediate position, with the rear end on the ground and the front upright as spaniels are taught to do. British bird dogs should go right down.

So far, the pup has had to be pushed down. Hopefully, it will begin to relax and stay down. Keeping the pup down is a matter of pushing it down with the word 'Sit' every time it attempts to rise. Gradually, the trainer should attempt to back off but as he does so the pup can no longer be stopped from getting up by hand because he is now out of reach. Control is extended by introducing the check cord.

A check cord is simply a strong piece of light cord with a slip knot on the end. It is used to extend the distance of contact between trainer and dog, *not* as a long lead. I use the orange polythene twine supplied by agricultural merchants for machine tying small bales of hay or straw. About £6 will buy about a mile of the stuff and part used rolls sell for pennies at farm sales. It is quite strong and so cheap it can be cut to any length and thrown away after use. Patent retractable check cords and other expensive training aids always get lost when I need them most but I can afford to leave a few lengths of this twine lying at strategic spots around the farm so it is handy whenever I need it.

A simple and cheap baler twine check-cord. (J. Rimell)

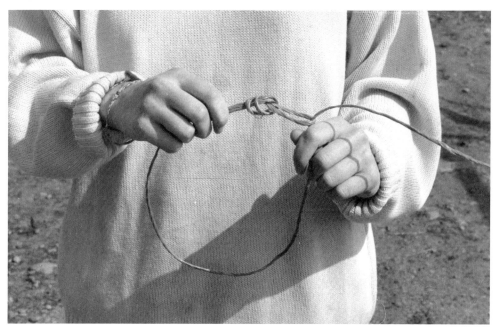

As the pup rushes up to you for one of those play sessions, slip the noose over his head. Ten to one it will never notice what you have done and that's the way it should be. Make sure there is plenty of slack and continue playing. Then, with the pup close to you, give the command 'Sit' in the usual snappy tone and push the pup down just as before. Now, instead of pushing the pup down as he tries to rise you can *gently but firmly* jerk the cord and say 'Sit' at the same instant. Correct timing is vital to success. 'Firm' is one of those annoying words writers of dog training books are rather fond of using. Unfortunately, there is no easy definition. One pup will require quite severe treatment, another the lightest touch. This is one area where trainer is on his own and it is a matter of judgement. Really, the best way is to watch an experienced trainer at work to see how this is done.

The mild unpleasantness of the cord's jerk should coincide, or slightly forestall, the pup's first movement to rise and the verbal command 'Sit' is given at exactly the same moment. Pup, never having known the cord before, believes it is you pushing him down again and he should stay down – but be ready to push him down if you have to. If he does get up, just push him down again and go back to the previous lesson.

Carefully used, pup need never be aware that the check cord exists. The movement of your hand can be concealed by carefully positioning your arm behind your leg as you kneel down. Some dexterity is needed in getting the timing right but there is no hurry. Getting this part of the training right is absolutely vital to success. Roughness and losing your temper can spoil the pup, or at least set training back for weeks. Excessive softness may convince the pup that the situation is anything but threatening and he can do what he likes.

Gradually, pup will learn he must stay down or he will experience a mildly unpleasant shock as the cord is jerked. He also knows that while he is down he is safe, that he will not be kept down for long, and that he will very soon be called for more play. So dropping becomes a mild inconvenience, a temporary interruption. If he attempts to run off, he is restrained by the cord. But if he is inclined to do that, the initial lessons have not been sufficiently firmly engrained so go back to stage one and start again.

You can now position yourself behind the pup and push him down whenever he attempts to get up. As he can't see you, his inclination is to look round or try to get up. The temptation is useful as you can train him to resist it. A light stick can be used to brush the top of his head or tap his nose to keep him down or from turning. Gradually, as he learns to stay down, the trainer can move around to the side, introducing the hand signal as he moves into the pup's line of vision and then to the front, and finally, walking around the prostrate dog, all the time keeping the cord taut and making sure he does not rise. Gradually, greater temptations are introduced until the drop is well implanted and the cord can be dispensed with.

First lessons are in the exercise field, then in strange and varied locations and at different distances. The trainer will talk, sing, throw his arms about, and generally tempt the pup to rise with anything but the command which releases him from the drop. When a dog has been dropped, it must stay in that position until released from it by the trainer. It is a useful trick to peg the dog down on a short tether, especially if pup attempts to bolt. After a few attempts to escape, the pup may well accept that once down he is there to stay. A short length of cord with a noose on the end that can be dropped over a peg makes it possible to drop and secure your pup, even several pups, anywhere you have had the foresight to put a peg or two.

The pup is released from the drop by calling him to you (something many trainers warn against) or giving the command 'Get on'. Get on means just that. It is used to encourage the pup to run (usefully given when letting a dog off the lead for a gallop, out of the kennel, etc.) and as a release from the drop.

The long drop over a longer distance is taught in the same way but with the pup on the cord he can be brought to submission by running at him, putting your feet on the cord as you approach, so he cannot run off. Feeling threatened, the pup should go down as he will feel secure in this position. Following this reasoning, no dog should ever be dropped so the trainer can give him a beating or do anything unpleasant to him. That merely teaches him that the 'Sit' position is anything but safe! To stop a pup creeping towards you from the drop, loop the cord around a post or peg. The creeper is just anticipating your call to conclude the drop. Keep this type guessing and do not let him take the initiative. The bolter, caused by the trainer's failure rather than the pup's disobedience, can be checked with the cord – but gently!

As soon as the drop is established it is best treated as part of a game. I play the old game of 'grandmother's footsteps' with a group of pups. I'll tempt them to rise, then rush at them with mock severity if they move. Then, the 'get on' signal and they all rush off again at the gallop. The more fun training can be the better it will succeed. Suddenly, I'll spin around, throw up my arm in the 'Sit' signal and shout the command. Every dog slaps itself down onto the ground; laggards are rushed at with mock severity, the 'attack' immediately being called off as soon as the pup is down.

Once the technique of training a pup to drop has been mastered, the 'Sit' can be taught in a very few minutes, even seconds. Dog training really is easy! I regularly train my own pointer pups to drop in a matter of seconds and the average time is three and a half minutes. This is not just getting pups to remain in the dropped position but getting them to recognize the signal and to go down themselves. But there are no prizes for rapid training. Setters are slower to learn and lessons over a few days may be required before 'the penny drops'. Irish and Gordon setters I have found learn quite quickly. English setters take more time, but the lessons stick. The softer type of pointers are generally very easy but some hard-headed types are the opposite and to get them to go down in the first lesson they almost have to be sat on! Dropping in response to a threat is an inherited characteristic and some imported breeds may be slow to respond. Trained to drop at four or five months, pups remember the exercise for life and seldom resent the experienced. After seven or eight months, expect lessons to take longer.

Overdo the drop, and pups will go down as soon as you look at them or make any unusual movement. This fault is called 'over training'. It is better to have pups slightly under-trained. You can always tighten up later on. Inhibit your pup and it will be very difficult to do anything with it at all, let alone get it to range out freely to hunt for birds. Things may get so bad that pup is fearful of leaving your heel. Keep everything happy and this situation need never arise.

A useful tip is to keep a handful of gravel or a light chain in your pocket. If a dog fails to drop, a suitable missile thrown when the dog is looking the other way *at the same moment the command is given* will shock him into thinking you have hidden powers. Just the noise as the gravel or chain lands is enough. If he sees you do it, or the correct response has not been properly ingrained, you may teach him to be nervous or to run off. The beer can filled with pebbles is recommended by some as a suitable missile to shock a dog into submission. But any loud noise associated with a shock can cause gun shyness for obvious reasons, so better forget this one.

These lessons take place completely separate from work on game. They can be started in the yard and continued at exercise. Once the pup is dropping and staying down, get rid of the check cord as quickly as you can. The longer you use it, the wiser the pup is getting. By all means, keep it in your pocket for emergencies, but use the check cord sparingly. It is nothing to call the pup to you and slip on the cord if it regresses. Gradually, pup will go down at any distance the moment he sees your raised hand or hears your command. Don't forget to scratch the dog's ears and stroke him occasionally as he lies in the 'Sit' position as a reward but do not modify your tone as you repeat the verbal command. If problems occur, keep cool and anticipate that the dog will likely repeat the behaviour when next in a similar situation. Anticipation is the trainer's secret weapon.

I find it difficult to understand why the novice has problems with dropping his dog at long range when I can take twenty dogs down the field and drop them all within a couple of hundred yards with a hand signal or a blast on the whistle. The difference is almost daily practice and insistence on compliance. As my dogs race out into the paddock and through into the next field, they generally turn three or four hundred yards out and start to gallop back. When they are running towards me I can throw up my hand and cause them to drop, one by one, as they realize I have given the appropriate hand signal. If any one fails to drop, I make a short run at it, perhaps emphasising the drop command by raising both hands and blowing the whistle, even shouting loudly. This the dog interprets as a threat. A threat, incidentally, that the trainer has to modify according to the dog's temperament and response. It is better to do this when the dog is headed towards you. If in retreat, the dog may decide escape is easier as the threat diminishes in proportion to the dog's distance from you. We want the threat to be strong enough to cause the dog to drop but not so strong as to drive it off into the next county. Once the dog is down I may go through the routine for teaching a puppy to sit even though I am dealing with an older dog. This reinforces the command. If this does not work, some individual tuition is called for going back over previous lessons.

I have deliberately spent some time going over teaching the drop because it is absolutely vital to the training of a pointer or setter. The drop is without doubt the cornerstone on which all other training is built. It *is* possible to work and shoot over a dog which has never been taught to drop but it is *not* possible to have such a dog under control. The Americans substitute the 'Whoa!' or halt, for the drop, but the effect is the same.

Once the drop is instilled, one can replace one command with another by the simple substitution. If you are not careful, this can happen without the trainer ever being aware of it, so the dog jumps a stage and takes the initiative upon himself. Verbal 'Sit!' quickly followed by the whistled command and the hand signal, will teach the dog to respond to the whistle or hand signal alone. Later, the verbal 'Sit' can be mixed with the shot, a bird flying off, etc. to prompt the correct response.

The recall has already been implanted. Our pup should come immediately it hears that call which so far has meant either a rough-and-tumble or some dainty morsel as a reward. But sooner or later pup is going to say 'Won't'. There will come a time when it seems more fun to be outside playing than back in the kennel. Dogs associate rewards and disincentives (I dislike the word 'punishment' as it implies guilt or deliberate wrong doing) with the most recent set of actions. It is an absolute rule that a dog must never be called to you for anything unpleasant, such as punishment (which should be avoided), going back on the lead after exercise, or back into the kennel. Call him to you for a pleasant experience, then wait a few moments before following this with whatever unpleasantness is necessary. The dog will associate its approach to you with the pleasant experience, not going back into the kennel, onto the lead, or whatever. Incidentally, calling a dog to you and then administering punishment has already failed in its objective. Whatever the fault, the dog associates the unpleasantness with its last action, i.e. coming to you, so the 'correction' is self-defeating. A very simple thing to remember and something which can save a great deal of trouble.

Let us imagine that pup has learnt, though your disregarding the last piece of advice, to run off, or avoid being caught, whenever he is called to go into his kennel or back onto the lead. (And *learning* that is. Don't ever be coerced into thinking that the pup is trying to annoy you or doing it out of wickedness. Such logic is beyond the mental capacities of a dog.) Get into the habit of calling the pup to you out at exercise and giving it a moment of petting or a tit-bit, and then immediately letting it off to run and play as before. The dog will associate coming to you as something pleasant. When it is time to conclude the exercise, call the dog to you, make a fuss of him and only then put him onto the lead. If this does not work, slip on the check cord before he is released and let him drag it. Ten to one, he won't even notice it is there. (Check cord shy dogs, which refuse to run or perhaps behave impeccably with the cord on, can be cured by having the dog wear a collar, or by letting it drag a shorter cord all the time until it ignores it.) Sweet talk him, as the Americans say, and keep it all happy. Just before you call him to you, catch hold of the end of the cord. If he will, let him go into the kennel by himself and praise him lavishly when he does so. If he dashes off, let him punish himself when he comes to the end of the cord. (*You* didn't punish him, did you? Better to keep this doubt in his mind if you want to retain his affection!).

If he will not come, apply gentle consistent pressure to your end of the cord. He cannot go backwards and his continual struggling merely causes further discomfort as the cord tightens cutting off his wind. Strangulation is not so dramatically swift and easy as it appears on the movie screen and although those struggles look dangerous, harden your heart and keep up the pressure. Keep calm and do not panic. Just keep the cord taut. It will do him no harm for all his antics and protestations. Call him to you with the play call and the offer of tit-bits if you can. Hopefully, he will at last head in your direction. If not, keep up your steady pressure. Eventually, he will come towards you and the pressure will immediately diminish. The realization of how easy it is to remove the annoyance comes to the dog like a bolt from the blue. Whatever you do, do not reel him in like a fish! Just keep up that steady pressure so he cannot go backwards but gets relief by moving in your direction. When he does come to you, make a tremendous fuss of him, lots of scratching of the ears, and any other bribery you can think of, repeating all the while 'Come here, come here'. Again, we want to create the association in his mind that 'Come here' means he will receive safety and reassurance near you. Once the pup gets the message, it is amazing how quickly a slight pull on the cord and the recall will bring him dashing up to you with tail wagging. Once pup has learnt to come on the cord, sharpen up his response to coming to call by doing a backward run and gently tugging on the cord to make him come in faster. Don't pull him in. The cord is merely there to allow you to apply momentary discomfort to the dog encouraging him to respond to the command 'Come here' and the sooner you get rid of it the better. Finally, avoid confrontations. The object is to persuade the pup that following the desired sequence of behaviour is best. It cannot be done with brute force, only mild coercion and gentle persuasion. And if a lesson isn't working within a few minutes, you are doing something wrong and ought to go back to the previous lesson. Alternating the drop with the 'Come here' will strengthen these responses and implant them firmly in the dog's mind.

So now we have the pup, hopefully, coming quickly to call and dropping to command. Coming to call can be reinforced out at exercise by calling and abruptly changing direction (giving the appropriate hand signal, of course), even hiding and letting pup come and find you. When pup does find you, although it may seem illogical, give the call, 'Come here', accompanied with lots of petting and possibly tit-bits. Again, the object is to establish the association between the command 'come here' and the reward of pleasure when near the trainer. Every time you change direction, give your call and then a hand signal. This is a great game and will encourage him to use the wind and his nose. He'll watch you in case you disappear again, and he will learn to respond quickly to your call knowing it may mean a change in your direction of travel, your disappearing, or just your invitation for a spot of petting. Leave these lessons or forget them altogether and pup gets too independent, too self-reliant. Why should he bother to maintain contact with his handler? The old fool will follow where ever the dog goes! Just because a dog has been taught to keep in contact with you, it does not mean he will continually watch you square on. Dog have excellent peripheral vision and can see you at the side whilst appearing to look straight ahead. They can also use their noses. These basics are consolidated over many weeks in various locations and during odd moments when at exercise so they become automatic and instant. They ought to take no effort to reinforce because every dog owner should exercise his dog daily. Later, maintaining contact may conflict with the dog's desire to hunt for game. Hopefully, we can maintain the correct balance which is what it is all about.

The theme of this book is that the dog teaches itself. So what better way to teach a pup to hunt than to put something out there for him to find? I explain my thoughts on this in the following manner. If you came onto my farm and found me crawling around in a field on my hands and knees you might reasonably conclude that I was at least slightly eccentric! But if you saw me picking up golden sovereigns by the handful you might very well join me in the hunt! This is the reasoning in training your dog to hunt. Many novices complain that their dogs will not hunt when in reality there is no motivation for them to do so.

Pups can be taught to hunt and to quarter by the same logic. Throw small pieces of meat or biscuit over a wide area of the exercise ground (my pups have to search nine acres to get their meal) and they will soon learn to hunt, use their noses, and understand how to use the wind to best advantage. You could go one better and feed a litter of pups like this, perhaps not every day but certainly every so often. Did you ever meet anyone from a large family who was a slow eater? The slight imperfections in quartering pattern caused by this type of training are of little consequence and can be corrected later. Nor will these exercises cause a dog to keep a low head as some fear; rather it will teach a dog to use its nose to best advantage and to increase pace.

Meantime, pup quickly learns to respond to your hand signals when he realizes that you are actively trying to assist him to find those choice morsels. By running out to the sides, using your hands to encourage him out in that direction, his quartering will start to cover the whole area he is to hunt. But there is no hurry. Let him learn to do this by the experience of hunting for and finding his grub. When they move on to wild game, dogs should quarter naturally after this introduction to hunting.

Chapter 7
Training in the Field

First time on the moor and your pup may not even want to run. It stands to reason that a pup ought to be strong enough to run before he is taken out for an encounter with wild birds. But assuming that, he may sink in behind your heels and stay there. Don't worry. Everything is strange to him and he doesn't understand what it is all about. Perhaps he has never had heather under his feet before. Perhaps travelling in the car to the moor has upset him. The harder you try to get him to run the less he is inclined to do so, like a shy child encouraged to join strange company when it just wants to run away and hide. Given his own time, he will come out of his shell and join in the fun. The best ruse is to awaken his curiosity and get him excited with the hunting. Small birds and butterflies present just the quarry to encourage him to run.

The traditional way to encourage a young dog to hunt is to bring the pup up behind a more experienced dog on point. The two dogs are then taken into the birds, the pup on the lead following in the wake of the older dog so he can smell the birds, see the attitude of the older dogs, and watch the birds as they get up out of the heather. Let the pup riot where the birds have lain. Very quickly, the pup realizes there are birds out there and things should start to fall into place especially if he is allowed to run in, flush, and chase once or twice. Running a young dog repeatedly and for long spells on bare ground will convince him there is no point in hunting and he may slow right down, even give up. But the occasional encounters with a pipit or lark will keep many keen ones going. Ignoring the pup completely may encourage him to wander off and explore but if has been soured against hunting it may take a lot to convince him it is worthwhile.

To get a youngster to run ahead, I may turn slightly down wind as I walk, which goes against the dog's instincts, hoping he will continue trying to get the wind in his nostrils. Sometimes it works. But patience is best. Best of all, make sure the youngster's instincts are aroused early on. Chasing will help and provided it does not become a habit, it will do no harm at all. A brood of young grouse fluttering in the heather will excite most dogs, but better make sure your pup is on the lead or the keeper will not be too pleased.

Next step is to get the pup to hunt out and find game by himself. Some do this straight away and the problem is to get them back. My own technique, then, is to hide and, although it may seem impossible at the time, get pup really worried. Blow the recall and show yourself; lots of petting when pup finally rushes up to you. By the way, a dog sees stationary objects with difficulty, so move at right angles to his line of vision to catch his attention, wave your arms, even jump up and down. Always run a young dog so he gets the benefit of the wind, i.e. head into the wind. Evening is best after a warm day. Two or three casts with some rough semblance of quartering is enough the first time out, especially if he contacts game, just to get his interest up and get him running. Running a youngster on too long is the worst possible mistake as it will tire him and next time he will reduce his pace. A dog should be put back on the lead when his tongue starts to hang out which is a sure sign he is getting tired. When a dog starts to falter, to occasionally trip over a tuft of grass or heather, it is past time to take him up as he is already tired. Put the pup back on the lead while he is still fresh and he will be keener to go tomorrow.

Pointing: here the 'wing' (bird's wing on a fishing line) has been used to bring out the pointing instinct in Advie White Smoke.
(Derry Argue)

Gradually, the pup will begin to extend his range. Occasional game contacts will keep his interest up. At first he may run into birds and chase. *This does not matter.* Chasing makes the pup keener and it is very unlikely that he will catch anything. Game birds are the prime choice of many predators and they have developed very effective mechanisms for escaping stupid bird dog pups. Provided the weather is fine, the broods strong on the wing, and the wind is not more than a mild breeze no harm will be done to the grouse. There is an old saying amongst shepherds that you can always take it out of a pup but seldom put it in. Pointers and setters have been bred to be easily inhibited so it should be relatively easy to stop a correctly bred youngster from chasing but it can be extraordinarily difficult to enthuse a pup for hunting if the instinct has not been aroused in the first place. Like the lamb that never learns to suck, some dogs really do never learn to hunt.

Marking down game birds in suitable cover and then working your pup up wind to where they lie is useful for getting a pup going but it should not be over done otherwise he will be expecting game every time he goes out. A game contact, say, every second time out would be about right. Psychologists have found that an animal learns to try harder when success is occasional rather than guaranteed at every attempt. Young pups may get only two or three casts, literally a minute or two only. Older dogs need to be worked longer to develop pace and persistence but field trial dogs need a special technique to attain maximum flash and style. Running a dog on too long without game contacts can cause it to alter pace to conserve energy, in other words it slows down. This is what separates the ordinary shooting dog from the field trialer.

The hunting instinct: chasing encourages a puppy to hunt – but it should not be over-done!
(Derry Argue)

Training the pup is a slow gradual process and the trainer will often be grateful that his pupil is still relatively unfit. That pup that pointed the hens so stylishly at home may seem to be a complete fool when he starts work on wild game. He can see the hens and get close to them. Wild game flies off if the dog gets too close and pups will chase out of sheer frustration. But learning is a trial and error process. The first priority is to get the pup hunting and quartering with some semblance of the finished pattern. But any correction of his course has to be done with subtlety, never upsetting him. Young dogs vary considerably in temperament according to age, breed, even strain, and it is better to err on the side of softness than be too hard and put the pup off. Sadly, today's trainer has little patience for the late developer which is a pity because these often make the best dogs in the long run. Some dogs run without knowing why they run. They are easy to get going and train for trials but, in my opinion, often lack intelligence. The intelligent dog hunts and learns to use the wind to the best advantage and this comes with experience; the dog that is drilled into it never achieves the same degree of excellence. A compromise is probably the ideal to aim for.

Sometimes a young dog gets lost on the moors. This can happen when a young dog chases a hare in a fit of youthful exuberance. If they have been taught to use their noses, the lost dog will generally cast downwind and then attempt to quarter to find the handler. Alternatively, a dog will follow ground scent. If you have gone to the moor by car, this ground scent stops at the vehicle. I hang an old coat on a nearby fence and, if the worst comes to the worst, the dog will often be found curled up near the coat the next morning. Obviously, the loss of a dog during lambing is a very serious matter.

The most frequent faults in quartering are not going wide enough and back casting. The dog should be encouraged to go wider by stopping him and sending him out at

Pointing: preocious Llewellin setter puppies, aged five and three months, start to point game after being allowed to run up and chase.
(Derry Argue)

the sides with a hand signal. Provided the pup is keen, it is an easy matter to show him that he must do it your way if he wants to run. Every time he tries to come back, drop him and signal him to go out, and run yourself in that direction. After a little while, if he has already learnt what hand signals mean, the penny will drop and it will take no more than a wave of the hand to get him out further. A dog can even be trained to back-cast by the same means, or to vary the angle of his cast out to the side. I got an award in the Champion Stake one year by sending my dog back for birds I knew lay slightly behind the correct line of the first cast. The other dog, quartering correctly, missed the birds by running upwind of them. But be careful not to upset the dog or he may decide it is easier not to run at all.

Back casting (see diagrams) is a fault when the dog turns down wind at the end of his cast. When he does this, he is going over ground he has hunted and wasting both your time and his energies. We are assuming here that our dog is inexperienced. A dog will back cast for a variety of reasons. An experienced dog may back cast to check some hint of ground scent that might indicate a bird tucked under cover and so giving off very little scent, too little scent to be picked up in normal quartering. Generally, faulty back casting is cured by running the dog where there are plenty of birds and interfering as little as possible. If the handler is slow and does not keep up with the dog, it will often cut back to keep in contact and this can become a habit. But if the dog has a brain, he will soon realize that he is missing ground and birds by back casting. It is a fault generally caused by attempting to drill a dog into a 'correct' quartering pattern rather than letting this develop through experience and the dog's natural instinct to reach out and search into the wind. It may also be caused by the over-use of planted birds. It is also probable that an anxious dog will run behind his handler to get his wind and gauge his mood, especially if the handler is showing signs of impatience or over-using whistled or verbal commands. A dog can undoubtedly assess the mood of his human companion from his scent. Rather than tampering with this type of dog, lots of work in gamey country is the answer. A tendency to back-cast can also be countered by blowing the turn as the dog is headed slightly into the wind, rather than headed downwind.

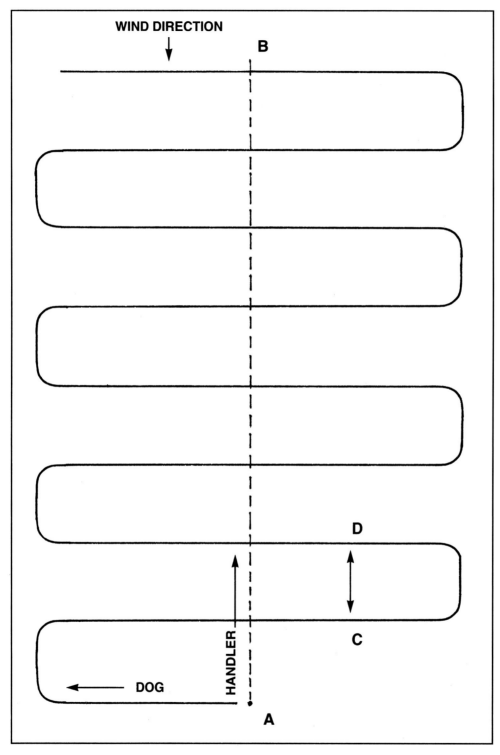

Figure 1.
Diagramatic
representation of
quartering into a
head-wind. Handler
and dog start at point
A. With the dog
crossing in front of
the handler at each
cast, the handler will
arrive at point B at
the same time as the
dog. C-D represents
upwind distance
searched by the dog's
nose.
(Important note: No
dog quarters with this
degree of precision!)

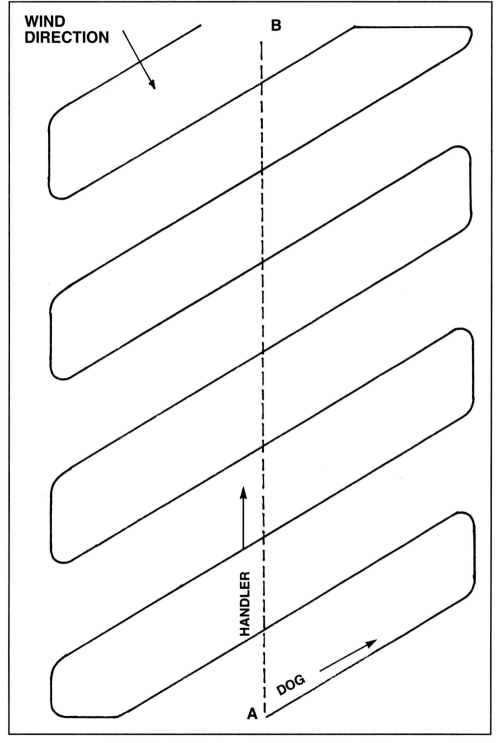

*Figure 2.
Quartering with a
cheek wind. The dog
works at right angles
to the wind,
regardless of the
direction the handler
walks.*

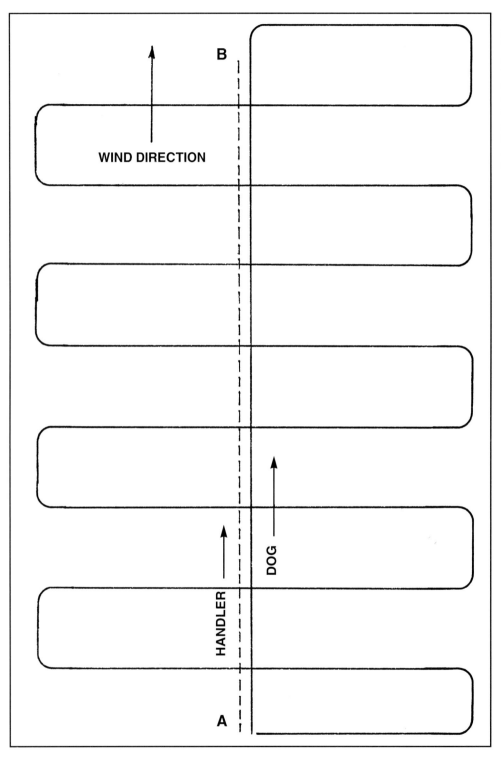

WIND DIRECTION

B

HANDLER

DOG

A

*Figure 3.
Quartering with a tail
wind. The handler
remains stationary
while the dog goes
straight out
downwind and
quarters back.
Handler and dog then
move forward to point
B and hunt the next
area downwind.*

Figure 4. Quartering with side wind. Handler remains stationary at A while the dog goes downwind and quarters upwind to left-front of the handler. Handler can move up to point B when the dog has covered the ground to his (the handler's) front. Dog then runs down-wind to search the second area, and so on.

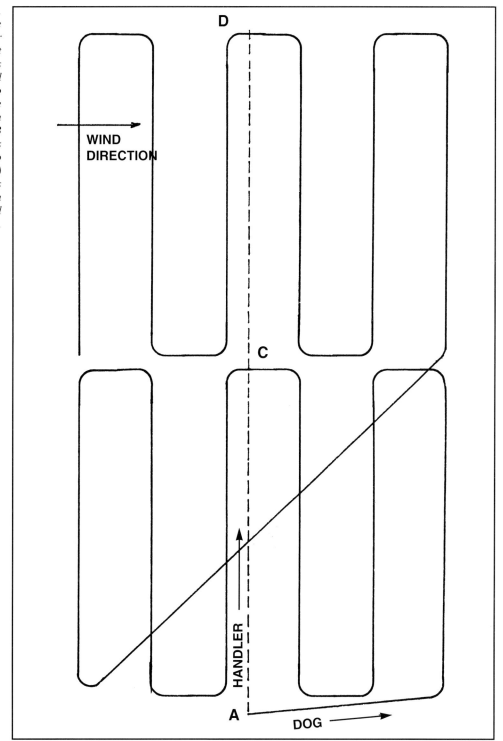

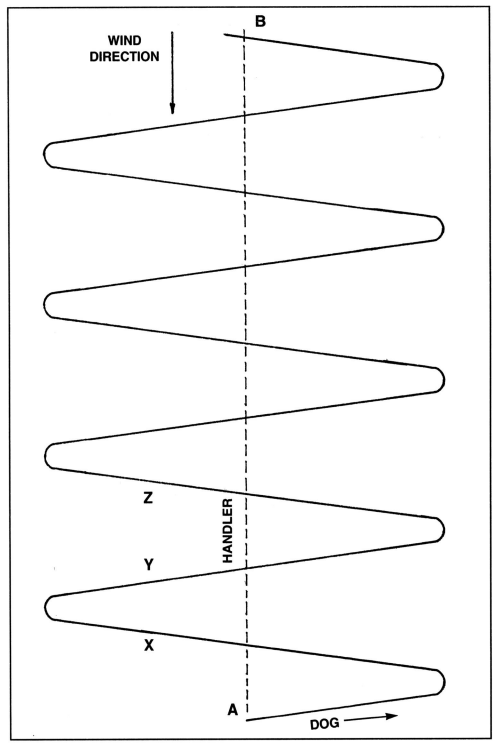

*Figure 5.
Incorrect ground
treatment caused by
over-training. Dog
turns too abruptly at
the extremity of each
cast. Casts are not
parallel. At X the
dog's search overlaps
the next forward cast.
At Y the dog's
olfactory powers
cannot reach Z,
alternately missing
ground and covering
ground twice.*

*Figure 6a.
Correct back-casting:
the dog starts
quartering correctly
from point A but
encounters ground
scent at X. Since the
dog winds nothing
upwind, it back-casts
at Y, double-checking
for air scent until Z.
Encountering no air
scent, the dog then
resumes normal
quartering.*

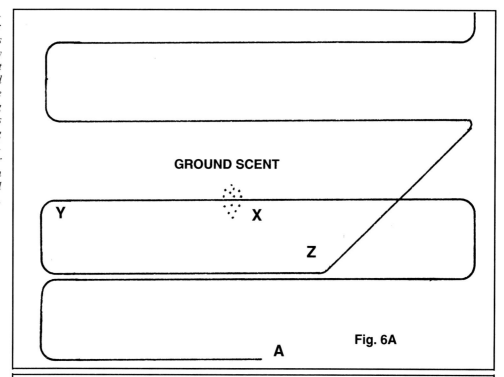

GROUND SCENT

Y   X

Z

A

Fig. 6A

WIND DIRECTION

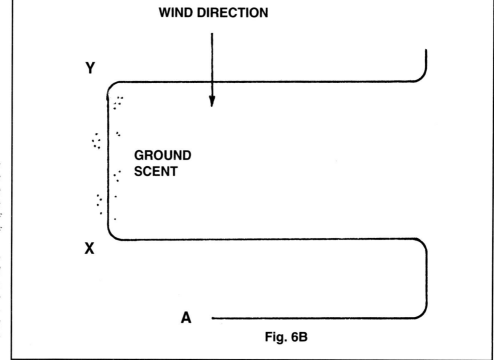

Y

**GROUND
SCENT**

X

*Figure 6b.
Faulty boring into the
wind: the dog start
working correctly at
point A but
encounters traces of
scent at X. Instead of
continuing to quarter,
the dog wrongly
bores into the wind
until Y, then
continues to quarter
correctly. But it has
missed ground
between parallels at
X and Y.*

A

Fig. 6B

Trio of six-month-old pointer puppies share a point down the fence-line. (Derry Argue)

A young dog may have a very ragged quartering pattern as it goes forward to investigate every strange scent. But it will all come right with experience as the dog learns to interpret what his nose tells him and becomes more confident. If a dog bores too far into the wind, call him back to you and send him out to the side again. This will teach him not to miss ground. Allowing a dog to resume quartering after boring merely convinces him that there is nothing left down wind. After all, you are the clever one, aren't you? So how could *you* leave birds behind? Running a dog down wind is said to extend his range.

In these days of field trialing, it is usual for many to train a dog to quarter on bare ground. The dog's natural enthusiasm for running is controlled so it will run back and forth according to a mathematical pattern rather than what its intelligence dictates. I have seen dogs drilled in this way quartering the same ground, back and forth, in a completely aimless fashion. In the early days I used this method myself and got quite irate one day when my dog, an Irish setter, would not quarter at right angles to the wind. So insistently was the dog in wanting to quarter at what seemed to me to be the wrong angle that I eventually got down to his level on hands and knees to find the dog was quite correct as the air currents at his level were running in a different direction to those at my height like an under-current out at sea.

The Gun

So far I have said nothing about the introduction of the gun. In my own kennel, shots will be fired off at the occasional rabbit or passing crow fairly regularly and when this is not happening, I will let off a blank pistol as the dogs are let out for a gallop down the fields. This is done as a matter of course and it is no 'big deal'. Of course, the young pups hear this too and catch the excitement as the adults are let out for exercise. Shooting in the fields around the kennels means the dogs accept gunfire as something quite usual from an early age. When pups hear a loud sound they look to the older dogs and if they seem relaxed they know there is nothing to fear. I have found that very young pups which have received no training at all stand the shock of a shot best. The reason is that they have (or should have) no unpleasant experiences to associate with the loud sound.

Using any loud noise as a corrective measure can sow the seeds of gun-shyness. The ubiquitous rolled up newspaper produces both a loud noise and a nasty shock when used to punish a pup, so gunshyness, a nervous reaction to a loud noise, is easily established. Introducing the gun, in cold-blood so to speak, as we start to train a pup to drop is equally fatal. In fact, the loudness and suddenness of the shot may easily be interpreted as some new and horrendous form of torture by a sensitive pup and the trainer ought to be aware of this danger.

Many young dogs will be nervous of the shot, yet it is overcome by sympathetic handling and a bit of intelligence. Cavalry horses were trained to look forward to the sound of gunfire by firing a cannon at feeding time. Similar logic ought to cure all but the worst case of gun-shyness. I have heard that a loop-tape, a continuous recording including the sound of a gunshot, played over and over in the kennel will cure the problem. Gradually, over a period, the volume is turned up. But better still not let the fault develop in the first place. It is a problem I seldom encounter and have, touch wood, never had to cure.

Birds

When training on broods (young game birds and their parents) in July (red grouse) and August (grey partridges) the young dogs ought to be brought close up behind the older dogs being worked so they can see them point, see the birds fly and get a whiff of scent. This will encourage them to point and back and drop to wing and it makes them very keen. Then, when shooting begins when the season opens, these dogs ought to be kept well back until it is quite certain that they do not fear the shooting. It used to be possible to do this sort of grooming at field trials but as more and more people (who increasingly seem to understand less and less about dogs) become involved in such competitions, restrictions are imposed to exclude all but the competing dogs. Provided dogs are on the lead it is difficult to see what harm they can do or how young dogs are to become accustomed to the atmosphere before they compete. (A dog owner was recently ejected from a trial for allowing his young dog, on the lead, to point some grouse droppings so farcical has the situation become.)

Gradually, the youngsters can be brought to associate the sound of gun-fire with the sight of birds falling and the occasional sniff of a freshly killed bird and everything should begin to fall into place. A good dog boy will have his charges half trained by putting them through routine of dropping and backing before they are even off the lead. Once again, it is a question of the association of ideas.

Every advantage should be given to a young dog. Is he being run into the wind? Is there plenty of ground cover to encourage the birds to lie to a point? Is it the correct season?

One way to teach a pup to point is to let him chase until he starts to point naturally. Some dogs will point the first time they encounter game and it is just a matter of encouraging staunchness. But I would prefer a young dog to go in, put birds up, and

At four months, this pointer pup is very positive on point.
(Derry Argue)

chase a few times first. The reason is this, as was mentioned in the previous chapter, an animal cannot know what is outside its experience and if a dog has never run in and chased it may be reluctant to approach game, be fearful of flushing it and to complete that part of the hunting sequence. Later, such ideas become fixed. I believe stickiness is caused through some traumatic shock (which may, in human perceptions, be very slight) in that hunting sequence causing a mental block. A dog has to flush a few birds to learn how close he can get to them. A dog learns to interpret scent through experience and that must include a fair percentage of mistakes. It needs to run into a few birds to learn the limits of what birds will take before they spring. Even an experienced dog will occasionally put birds up for the same reasons and such mistakes should be viewed with understanding and patience.

Some young pointers are prone to hesitate a bit on any hint of scent and it is best not to pay much attention to them. These dogs are very cautious and afraid of making a mistake. Take too much notice when they hesitate like this and they begin to false point, taking the initiative from the handler. I remember one young dog that was inclined to do this and I had started to cure the fault when clients arrived from overseas. The dog was very stylish and every time he hesitated my clients had the cameras out and wanted to photograph him. Of course, it made the fault worse. The dog began to pose at every opportunity. Fortunately, my clients were so impressed with the dog that they bought him which solved the problem. No doubt he is still posing away on some distant hillside, the perfect photographer's model and not a bird within miles.

The cure for this problem is just to walk up beside the dog and then fast forward putting up the birds if there are any there in the hope that it will inspire confidence. Such dogs are often fearful of flushing game and it has to be got across that this is no big deal but actually required. The dog should be made a fuss of and petted whenever birds are raised. That way it's fear of raising birds will diminish. This only becomes a serious problem when an ignorant trainer uses harsh methods to 'punish' the dog for its 'faults'.

False pointing, where there are no birds at all, is merely an extreme form of this fault often exacerbated by the handler attempting to interfere with the dog when he, the handler, erroneously judges the dog to be near birds. An unproductive point is where no birds are produced at a point and the reasons why there are no birds are legion. Repeated 'unproductive' points must eventually be interpreted as false pointing.

With the sort that rushes in, our objective is to slow down the hunting sequence so we can get up to the dog before it races in to chase the birds. A check cord, used to 'spin' the dog when it chases, can be used but it is rather an extreme measure. I like to use the cord to restrain the dog and then get up to it and gently stroke it and talk to it, hopefully encouraging it to point. It will help if the dog's response to dropping (back home in the exercise field) is sharpened up and time is spent teaching the dog to drop to wing. Ideally, this is done by following a friend training on a lot of birds, dropping the dog whilst it is on the lead every time birds are seen in the air. Or, as above, following at a field trial. After a while, the dog will point in preference to putting up birds which is arriving at our destination by another route. Any situation can be used to encourage the pointing instinct. Cats, hedgehogs, even mice, may be amongst these first points. Sooner or later, the pup will point; then it is a matter of reinforcing the instinct.

At six months, this 'started' pup shows his potential: Avie Shot. (Derry Argue)

Once a pup starts to point, get up beside him and caution him in a soft voice and stroke him all over. If it is a very definite point and the birds are not likely to run, I will sit down in the heather for ten minutes to teach the dog patience. When the dog understands that he gets pleasure from pointing, it should all begin to fall into place. Once a dog has started to point solidly enough to allow the handler time to get up beside him it is relatively simple to stop him chasing. Repeated dropping to wing is one method that has been mentioned, followed by a few minutes wait in that position after the birds have gone. Turning the dog over with the check cord as it is in the act of chasing is another. For the latter, use a braided nylon cord about 1/4 in diameter and put the noosed end around the dog's neck. Allow about fifteen yards slack and wrap the end of the cord several times around your *gloved* hand. When the dog starts to run, let the cord take the full shock as he gets to the end of the line. I have never heard of this causing the dog more than a rather nasty surprise and two or three experiences are usually enough to cure the problem. It is the dog's action that causes the discomfort and the handler should give no hint who is really to blame. The dog commits no fault by moving forward onto a point *until it prematurely raises birds*. It may be perfectly legitimately maintaining contact with running birds and we humans cannot know what the dog is winding.

Then, when the dog is doing it right, *everything right*, shoot a bird for him and bring it back to him as he remains in the dropped position. The answer to the problem of running up birds and chasing is generally to give the dog a lot of work and a lot of birds; then to kill birds to his points. The dog is only chasing because it believes this is the way to kill the birds. Of course, there is a conflict here. To obtain maximum style and speed we must not over-work the youngster. To get him to point may need tiring him a little. Sometimes just leaving the problem is the solution; dogs which chased like the devil one season seem to have grown out of it by the following spring. Maybe a few months in the kennel has given the dog time to work it all out in his own mind.

Backing

Once a dog is pointing consistently, it ought to back another dog's point. When one dog points, all other dogs which see that dog on point ought in turn to point it in acknowledgement of it's finding birds.

This ought to be an instinctive response and in well bred strains it is possible to see tiny puppies backing intuitively as others in the litter point small birds in the run by sight. Natural backing is an inherited characteristic, some having the propensity more strongly than others, but most dogs can be taught to back if they have the instinct to point.

The backing dog recognizes the other's point and the fact that he knows he might disturb game by moving. It has aptly be called 'pointing on trust'. It is generally accepted that the backing dog should not move until the pointing dog moves, and then only by an equal amount. Some accept that the backing dog may move up to share the point provided he does not go ahead of the pointing dog and this is my own opinion. Others would not allow the backing dog to move a single inch until ordered to do so. For trials, the latter is generally accepted to be correct though a dog will not be faulted if it drops on command instead of backing. The pointing dog might move to keep in contact with running birds and so get unsighted by the backing dog; in my view no harm is done so long as the backing dog does not do anything which might

Point: the far dog points, the nearer backs, both just seven months old.
(Derry Argue)

disturb the birds, but it is a matter of interpretation and field trial judges have their own ideas about such things. No dog can be expected to back a dog that consistently false points. That is against reason. And I personally would not fault a dog that went ahead of a hesitating dog however confidently its handler claimed 'point'.

Backing can be taught by letting all the dogs run in the usual exercise field and then quietly ordering one to drop. As the others in turn spot the dog in the dropped position they also should drop. With practice, it is quite easy to drop one dog out at exercise like this without the others noticing. Then, as another dog catches sight of it, drop that one too until they will all drop immediately they see one dog down. Initially, they may back in the dropped position, but they soon learn to back standing. It is not difficult to stop a dog in the standing position by giving what I can only describe as a half-hearted drop signal. The dog is unsure, so he stops. Hey presto! you have stopped the dog in the standing position!

The one-dog owner can achieve the same objective by using a plywood silhouette of a pointing dog, suitably painted, which is set up where the pupil will come on it suddenly, say a field where the pupil will see it when he comes around a corner. Or it can be set up on hinged springs with a radio controlled trigger. A pigeon in a trap is placed in front of the dummy and released to convince the pupil that the silhouette was, in fact, pointing. A few experiences and the dog will back every time it sees the pointing 'dog'. My own pups will often back bronze statues of setters on my sideboard when they catch sight of them for the first time; a trait I find rather endearing, as if they feared to disturb some bronze grouse lying to the statue's point!

Chasing is an annoying vice and dogs are occasionally guilty of chasing sheep, deer, game birds, even small birds and butterflies! Really, most of this is a frustrated hunting instinct and few properly bred bird dogs will bother with these diversions when they are regularly getting game shot to them. But if chasing gets to be a habit it requires some serious thought to cure the problem. The best solution is to get on top of it before it becomes engrained and then try to kill birds to the dog's points. Often curing the fault is a job for the professional though carefully setting the scene and using a check cord can solve most problems. Careful observation will tell you where hares lie and turning a dog over with a check cord will often stop the dog's interest in such vermin. I have heard that it also helps to shoot a hare or two to a dog's points but I fear it would also make the dog point them and that is *not* what I want. My own technique is to give a young dog a lot of experience on birds away from hares. Then, when a hare gets up, just call the dog and start to move in the opposite direction. If the dog can be dropped, order it down and then, after a pause, call it in for a petting. I realize this may sound all too simple. But it is what I do and it seems to work!

Most shepherds are only too delighted to help cure a dog of chasing sheep. And let's be honest about this, most young dogs of spirit will occasionally take a chase after a sheep. As I am a sheep farmer, this seldom presents a problem. Put the dog on the lead and, with the appropriate permissions, take it to the sheep, preferably where problems have occurred in the past or where problems are expected. When the dog shows any interest in sheep, a cut with a switch will generally be all that is required. Alternatively, bowl the dog over at the end of a check cord. If the shepherd/farmer is approached, arrangements can generally be made when sheep are being gathered for routine dosing, etc. Most shepherds are experienced in dealing with such problems and can often give useful advice. Deer chasing can be dealt with in the same way, especially where deer are being fed over winter or perhaps, if permission can be obtained, by visiting a deer farm. But the answer is really to kill a lot of birds over the dog when the problem will generally evaporate.

Point and back: the far pup points and is backed by a brother, aged seven months, and another, aged ten months. (Derry Argue)

Where game is scarce, even experienced dogs will occasionally chase just to relieve the monotony. Who can blame them? The late Jack Stewart was asked how he stopped his dogs chasing hares. He dryly replied, 'We train 'em'. And this, of course, is the answer. It is highly amusing to see a line of handlers at a field trial all in turn beating their dogs as a hare runs past. As the last dog on the line gets his beating you can almost hear him say, 'A beating? There must be a hare! Oh where? Where?'

Whistles

I seldom bother to use a whistle until I start training on game. But I whistle by mouth, shout, talk to dogs a lot, and use my hands continually when hand training on my own ground. The reason is that a dog thus trained will automatically look to you for instructions when it first hears the whistle . . .

Verbal commands come first, then hand signals are added, generally a wave to indicate a change of direction or hand and arm extended to indicate 'Sit' *with* the verbal command. The choice of whistle is very important. I prefer a straight whistle without a pea which produces a good range of tone. A sharp blast from a good whistle ought to be physically painful to the ears. Bells for falconry are expected to pass the same test. 'Silent' whistles are best kept for field trials, tuned to the lowest audible pitch, when they are less obtrusive to the judges but I sincerely believe many dogs cannot hear them either.

Commands

There is said to be a tribe in Africa whose members nod when they means 'no' and shake their heads when they mean 'yes'. Whether this is fact or fiction, I do not know, but it serves to illustrate a point. Your hand signals, whistles, shouted commands convey nothing until your pup learns what they mean. If your pup does not respond to a command, you have to assume that he ignores you because you, the trainer, have not instilled the correct response. It is not the dog's disobedience if you don't do your job properly! The correct thing to do is to go back to the previous lesson and make sure the dog knows what he should do. Dog training is a communications problem and very seldom anything to do with disobedience. Understand that and you are half-way home.

Commands should be consistent. Obviously, single word commands, or at least short phrases are best; conversational style commands confuse the dog. Occasionally check just what commands you have given when a dog is slow to respond.

Whistled commands are universal and it is generally agreed that a single long blast from a straight whistle is the signal for the dog to drop, or at least to stop. A series of short blasts, 'pip, pip, pip, pip . . .', is used to recall the dog with the abbreviated command of two or three quick pips being used for the turn. Incidentally, these pips are made by placing the tip of your tongue over the end of the whistle and using this to regulate the air flow. A manufactured whistle is essential. Try whistling by mouth when you have run up a hill after your dog and need to call him back urgently. It simply cannot be done. Nor can you pass your whistled commands by mouth to a new owner. There will be too much variation in the tone.

Fine Tuning

Generally, it is wise to try to get the wind in your face before casting off your dog and work it into the wind. Drop the dog and take a couple of steps back in the direction you want him to go, presumably across the wind. When you have his attention, cast him out with the command 'Get on' and signal with your hand that he is to run out on the side you have moved to.

As you now walk forward into the wind, watch the dog as he runs out. *If necessary*, give a brief whistle to turn him when you judge he has gone wide enough. When he is turned in your direction, give the hand signal for him to run across to complete the cast. Just incline your body slightly in the direction he is to travel so your back is towards the dog as if you were changing direction. Repeat the procedure for the opposite side. If you have put in the ground work as suggested above, the dog will anticipate your movement as a change of direction and run to get ahead of you. It may be necessary to run out in the direction you want your pupil to go to encourage him out.

With an experienced dog it should seldom be necessary to use the whistle at all and hand signals are quickly replaced with body language, that slight inclination of your body towards where you want the dog to go being enough to cause the dog to change direction. Most handlers use far too many hand signals and whistles which really should be unnecessary with an experienced dog. The less you use whistle and voice, the more inclined the dog will be to rely on signals made by your body language. Try talking softer and softer to a companion and you will notice how much more attentive he becomes as he strains to hear what you say. Dogs are no different.

Later, signalling the dog will be abbreviated to a form of shorthand. A pip on the whistle produces a glance from the dog who follows my hand signal or body language to change direction. The whole thing develops into a smooth rhythm as the handler walks forward into the wind at a steady pace with the dog quartering to and fro. Nag a dog and it will quickly learn to ignore you, as a hen-pecked husband learns to ignore and avoid a nagging wife.

Traditionalists may wonder why I have not mentioned the use of the check cord in training a dog to quarter. In this method the dog drags the cord which is given a sharp jerk when it has reached the extremity of its beat at the exact moment the 'Turn' command is given on the whistle. The dog learns to associate the sound of the whistle with the shock of the cord and turns to avoid the predicted unpleasant experience. It is forcing the dog to turn when ordered to do so and the result is a very abrupt turn. Training a dog to turn this way certainly gets it to 'turn on a sixpence' but, actually, that is not what is required though it may look very spectacular. A dog ought not to zig-zag up its beat but run in a series of parallels. A glance at the diagrams shows why; the area covered by the dog's nose lies upwind, and for a certain distance, parallel to its direction of travel. No dog can scent birds downwind; no matter how strong the scent. Assuming the dog's scenting powers do not vary and the scent carried in the breeze is constant, the dog's casts ought to be parallel. It is obvious that the zig-zagging dog does not cover some areas at all, and covers other areas with its nose twice. Plainly, this is inefficient and a waste of everyone's time and efforts. Far better to use the dog's natural affection for its handler and its sagacity for game finding to develop the correct pattern of ground treatment. Once the turn is

Manners: at twelve and fourteen months respectively, Advie Maedema and Annan are learning to share a point without jealousy. (Derry Argue)

established, reduce the recall whistle to just a hint, enough to turn the dog but not enough to inhibit it from travelling forward into the wind before starting across on the next parallel.

A lot of work on smartening up the discipline can be done at exercise. Indeed, it *should* be done at exercise. When working for birds, the dog ought to be tampered with as little as possible and if there is a problem in the dog's response to commands, go back to basic training in the exercise field and start that lesson again.

Once a dog is hunting and pointing, everything can be brought together by *carefully* killing a few birds to his points. I cannot emphasize too much that the way this is done in the first season is absolutely vital to success. The dog is a predator which will try various methods, as it perceives things, to 'kill' its prey. As a pack animal, it is quite prepared to hand over the act of killing to its human partner. I do not subscribe to the theories that a dog wants to please its owner. Maybe it does, but to presume this is bad psychology. Neither is there any reason to suppose that it ought to do certain things as if it had a duty, somehow, to repay its owner for food and lodging. That would be to completely disregard its near forty million year period of evolution without man's influence. Use what is there, rather than what you would like to think should be there, and progress should be rapid.

Killing those first birds over a young dog is an important ritual. Hopefully, you have someone who is a good shot and who you can trust. It is a warm day, sometime in the afternoon, and early in the season. Pup starts off, quartering acceptably, and works keenly. A grouse gets up wildly at the extremity of the dog's cast within shot of the Gun, but he has been well briefed and he lets the bird go. Pup gives a half hearted chase but turns to the recall whistle.

The pup is worked on and this time he comes to a confident point. There is no hurry. We have chosen the day well and the birds are lying like stones. After a pause of a minute or two, the check cord is gently slipped over his head and the pup is coaxed to stalk in alongside the handler with the Gun walking parallel to, but about 15 metres from, the dog. Taking our time, we work forward and a covey gets up out of the heather with that deceptive slowness as if annoyed at being awakened from their afternoon slumbers.

The handler should concentrate 100% on the dog which is now dropped, or at least gently but firmly pushed down as the birds rise. If there is a struggle to restrain the dog, early training is not yet complete. Get that right before doing anything else even if shooting a bird has to be postponed for a while. The Gun, concentrating 100% on his side of the task, takes a careful shot at a bird on the edge of the covey, taking care to select one well away from the dog, and, hopefully, drops it cleanly. He can now go forward and pick the bird and bring it back to the dog which has remained steady on the same spot. If the bird is dead but still fluttering, so much the better. The pup is allowed to mouth the bird while his trainer sweet talks him and joins in the handling of the bird. Young dogs are sometimes keen to eat a bird; older dogs seldom have this desire. Remove the bird after a minute or two and you can start off again looking for the next point. If the dog is trained to retrieve, the procedure is exactly the same, but after a decent interval of a minute or two the dog is urged to go forward to retrieve. The delay is essential so the two actions are separated. We don't want the dog to run in immediately a shot is fired.

It may well be that at the next point the pup runs in and chases. That does not matter. The object is to teach the dog what behaviour kills birds. After his brief chase and no birds killed he will be the more convinced that he made a mistake. Kill a bird to his next firm point as you did before and things will begin to fall into place. The individual steps involved in this procedure are absolutely vital and cannot be stressed too strongly. Anything less than this merely informs the dog that some other procedure, instead of the correct one, is what kills birds. Repetition will convince the dog of this opinion. How often do we see over-enthusiastic shooting people greedy to obtain more shots, completely disregarding the dog or dog work. What a surprise when they end up with a ruined dog!

If an experienced dog flushes birds he ought to have winded and pointed, he ought to be verbally admonished for doing so. I do this by shouting out my annoyance as the birds rise and by making the dog drop (which is in itself a subservient act) immediately. Take him back, on the lead, to where the birds rose and encourage him to point the ground scent. Naturally, one cannot do this on a shooting day and I refer here to training sessions. If you are too harsh on the dog you may cause stickiness, even blinking. If you are too lenient, the worst that can happen is that he will flush a few more birds and success will be delayed a day or two. It is obvious which is the more serious fault and careful shooting birds to his points when he gets things right will engrain the correct behaviour.

'Stickiness' and 'blinking' are closely related faults in bird dogs invariably caused by faulty training technique. Stickiness is a reluctance on behalf of the dog to go forward with the handler to raise the birds for the Gun to shoot. In the USA dogs are trained to stand as the hunter goes forward alone at the point to raise the birds. In

Britain game can often be a very long way ahead and the Gun would quickly discover that he is at a loss if he did not have the dog to lead him to the birds. Red Grouse, particularly, can run through the heather for long distances, and they do so at a fast walking pace, so a dog must follow quickly or the Guns will never get a shot. Pheasants and red legged partridges can do the same.

Blinking is a far more extreme problem than stickiness. In this condition a dog will apparently hunt keenly but when it winds game it either comes away or ignores the birds altogether. Sometimes the action is so subtle as to be barely noticeable to an inexperienced handler.

Both problems originate from a failure of the dog to complete the hunting behaviour pattern explained earlier. In stickiness, the sequence stops at the 'pause'. In blinking, the sequence stops at 'locate'. But what can be done?

Treating the dog roughly in any way will have the effect of inhibiting the completion of the sequence even further. Somehow we have to get the dog past these two mental obstructions. Various solutions can be tried, the effective ones will motivate the dog to complete the sequence itself. Blinking dogs are usually reluctant to have anything to do with game although they may appear to hunt for it keenly. This reluctance can be overcome by feeding them pieces of fresh dead game birds instead of their usual food. I have no doubt that game dealers would be delighted to sell the heads of game birds for a small consideration. Sometimes such dogs have to be very hungry indeed before they will eat game, so much do they fear it, but difficult problems demand hard solutions. This type of dog can sometimes be encouraged by allowing it to chase, even kill, game. One authority recommends shooting a bird and trying to excite the dog to grab it by acting the fool and waving it in front of the dog's face, throwing it in the air, etc. But the mere act of killing game in front of such a dog can have the reverse effect to what we require. I have cured such a dog by walking the moors with it, praising it every time birds were flushed so it eventually realized there was nothing to fear from putting birds on the wing. It *may* help to change to a different game species, say if the dog is blinking grouse, move onto pheasants or partridges. Any rough handling, even anxious glances from the handler, will convince such dogs to have even less to do with game. Some dogs can safely be left to run loose behind dogs which are experienced and pointing keenly. Seeing birds killed to these dogs' points may effect a solution.

Blinking and sticky dogs are usually sensitive types and if the problem can be overcome by encouraging chasing it is seldom difficult to get the dog back under control. *It is absolutely fatal to kill birds over a sticky dog* as it merely convinces the dog that it is acting correctly. Physically trying to force the dog forward is as bad in severe cases though gently encouraging an hesitant dog forward on the lead sometimes works. But some sticky or blinking dogs will chase enthusiastically once the bird is in the air. This is not inconsistent with the logic of the hunting sequence. One stage has merely been omitted.

I cured one very sensitive and sticky dog by crawling beside it in the grass and encouraging it forward to follow a bird by placing my hand under its nose every time it stopped (a hat or cap can be used to the same purpose). This cut off the scent from the bird to the dog and got it to move forward a few more inches until it re-encountered scent. Gradually, we got up to the bird (a young partridge) which I managed to catch right under the dog's nose. This I then killed on the spot and immediately fed to the dog. All stickiness disappeared very quickly and the pup is now one of my best dogs.

That, then, concludes training though it is really only the start. Every dog needs some maintenance training and, really, there is no such thing as a 'finished' dog. The important thing to remember is never to let a fault pass unnoticed so that such misdemeanors do not become ingrained through repetition. I do not mean that the dog has to be 'punished' for every fault; just that the dog ought to be aware of your disapproval (and, of course, approval). One last word; failure of the dog to comply with a command can be compounded by the trainer repeating the command over and over so the dog learns it can *ignore* that command. How many times does one hear the novice trainer shouting, 'Sit, sit, sit, sit . . .', to his dog which has learnt that the command means nothing, like a repeated threat that can safely be ignored. This, too, is training, though of the wrong sort. If a dog does not respond instantly to a command, go back to basics and make sure that the desired behaviour pattern is firmly ingrained. Don't blame the dog for disobedience when it is your own training that is at fault.

Chapter 8
Further Training

It is always best to train on wild birds. That's what your dog is intended to hunt. But we live an imperfect world and the 'best' is not always available when we need it.

During training, every detail involved contributes to the behaviour patterns we are attempting to implant but a lot of useful work can still be done using what can loosely be called 'planted birds'. Use such shortcuts sparingly or your dog will quickly become an expert at hunting these whilst not regarding wild game as something worth bothering about. However, much useful work can be done in training by contriving situations (hopefully simulating natural conditions as nearly as possible) and using these 'artificial aids'.

The wild red grouse (*Lagopus lagopus scoticus*) made British pointers and setters famous the world over and it is the preferred game bird for training dogs today. A dog that can handle grouse late in the season should be able to handle almost any other game bird species. Driving grouse, or any other game birds for that matter, makes them wild and grouse on regular driving moors will not lie to a dog's point once they are mature. Later in the season, when shooting is finished, they sometimes lie but seldom with any reliability. Grouse here in the North are never driven and unless over-shot will lie right through the season. The old keepers used to say that driving ruined a moor, which it did for dogging. Some clever fellow turned the story around and put it about that it was dogging that ruined the moor. This must have saved many keepers a lot of walking. Dogging certainly *can* ruin a moor if it is done in an unsportsmanlike way such as having too many Guns at each point (two is enough) and marking down each covey as it is disturbed and dogging it repeatedly. I have seen whole coveys shot out by such murderous behaviour. It is not dogging which ruins a moor but bad sportsmanship. Grouse can be artificially reared but only with difficulty and it is not economical to do so. Black grouse (*Lyrurus tetrix britannicus*) also lie to a dog and give off a strong scent but they are seldom so common that they can be regularly used for dog training. A point on black game is often very intense indeed with otherwise free moving dogs showing extreme excitement and stickiness from the novelty.

The Grey Partridge (*Perdix perdix*) is the next best game bird for training dogs. The partridge is my favourite game bird and I can hardly bear to shoot them! These birds lie quite well to a dog in the spring and early autumn but they do not have as much scent as the red grouse. The best cover to work partridges on is undoubtedly stubble under sown with a grass and clover mix. Dogs need to be more precise in locating partridges. They seem to have a strong scent close up but it disperses quickly. There is seldom the long draw (or approach) to a point on partridges as one gets with grouse and even experienced dogs can look awful fools on a single partridge that has just pitched in. Both grouse and partridge sometimes lie to a dog on bare ground so dogs have to quarter with mathematical precision to avoid missing them. It is said that wild birds lie better than reared birds. I rear a few grey partridges every year under bantams. The birds have to make the best of it amongst the domestic poultry on free range (which is against all the professional advice). Reared this way the birds are quite tame and a few pups can be brought up to point them whenever they are marked down in a likely piece of cover. As the birds get wilder, the pups get cleverer and the two progress quite nicely together until the partridges get fed up with being chased about and move to where life is more peaceful. A covey of young Grey partridges, purchased as six-week olds, can also be released leaving one or two caged as callers. That way, one always has birds available to train a young dog on, or several coveys if one cares to expand on the idea.

Wild partridges may be too wild to approach for a point after harvest in late September/October, the problem being that stubbles these days are left too short. Points can be obtained on both partridges and pheasants by dogging harvested fields before the straw is baled. I have heard that they can be approached by flying a kite shaped like a hawk but the practice is pretty murderous as the poor partridges are scared out of their wits. No doubt it would be worth trying to get a young dog going. The alternative is to watch where disturbed partridges land as they generally fly to cover where they feel secure, such as a root crop, and walk them up there with the bird dogs. The other morning I looked out of my window to see an adult partridge standing up in the hay field scolding two four month old setter pups that were pointing and backing him. No doubt this was one of my reared birds from the previous year but the thrill was no less.

Lessons should continue at exercise. Here, the older dogs are dropped with a hand signal. (Derry Argue)

Red-legged partridges (*Alectoris rufa*) were introduced into Suffolk around 1770 from Europe where the breed is strongest in Spain, Portugal, and Central France. Sensible British sportsmen regarded these foreigners as vermin and attempted to eradicate them at every opportunity. That, of course, was at a time when nearly all shooting was over dogs and these birds were found to have the infuriating habit of running in front of the dogs and not lying to a point. The criticism are probably a bit harsh but living as I do in the North of Britain I have no first hand experience of them and prefer to leave it that way. This year I refused 150 eggs offered free of charge. The price was still too dear.

Pheasants are too well known to need much description. The hens lie quite well later in the spring when they start to think about laying and young birds lie well in early autumn. Pheasants are not ideal to train young dogs on because they do tend to 'leg it'. One is often asked to demonstrate a dog for a prospective purchaser near a release point for reared pheasants, the idea being that the dog should get plenty of points. Generally, this is a disaster because the whole area will stink of pheasants and few will lie so well as to give a decisive point. Reared pheasants generally run as fast as they can for the nearest cover. Wild or well-released pheasants lying out in old grass, roots, or similar vegetation can provide excellent sport but if they run they can confuse a youngster just when it needs positive, firm points to encourage it to greater things. It ought to be mentioned that there are several different varieties of pheasants available to the British sportsman though most are simply mongrels. Willy Newlands, an expert on all game birds, suggests that the Japanese Green pheasant might have a future for stocking on rough grazing for shooting over dogs. I gather these birds tend to live in open country in their native habitat. I have enjoyed really excellent pheasant shooting over dogs in Ireland where game is found miles from woodland lying out in under-grazed rough grass and rushy fields. With so much land being taken out of agriculture, there must be possibilities in Britain, maybe in young forestry plantations, where even a few birds would provide training and a bit of sport later on.

Snipe is the favoured bird for training pointers and setters in Ireland. They keep the interest up and although not all will lie to a point there are usually enough young birds and residents to do some useful training on in some favoured spot. Without the snipe, few pointers or setters would ever be trained in Ireland because game is otherwise generally scarce. Snipe seem to have the effect of getting bird dogs to run faster and wider when they move onto grouse. Snipe do not have a strong scent so dogs worked on them regularly get to use their noses. Also, they are found in rushy grass fields which are easy for a dog to cover at speed. It is quite a different thing when these same dogs move onto grouse and after a little experience they get very confident and run like greyhounds. A dog attuned to snipe will think he has hit a brick wall when he encounters the stench from a covey of grouse! As soon as he realizes that's what he's meant to hunt and find, he learns to put his foot down. So, for some, Irish dogs are not too welcome at trials; they win too much!

That just about completes the picture of available wild game to train pointers and setters on in Britain. Woodcock are seldom plentiful enough for routine training. But in the absence of wild game, all is not lost. It really ought to be possible for most sportsmen to rear a few grey partridges under a broody hen in the back garden and find an obliging farmer who will provide a corner of a field to release them into. Perhaps gundog trainers and farmers should think a bit more about co-operating together. It would be to the gundog people's advantage to rear a few birds and release them onto farmland on the understanding that they could have the use of them up until, say, the end of the first or second month of the season. After that, the farmer and his friends might have the right to shoot them, possibly over dogs. I believe many partridges are shot over pointers under this system on the Continent and it works extremely well.

In the absence of game, both pointers and setters will point tame pigeons. The pigeons are usually 'dizzied' and gently placed in long grass. Dogs worked up to them from down wind will point them as staunchly as they would pheasants. But there are problems to using planted game. First, dogs are very clever and they will quickly learn to track the handler's ground scent to where the birds have been planted. Second, because the birds do not flush when approached, the dogs learn to point too close.

Most birds can be 'dizzied' by placing their heads under their wings and rocking them gently backwards and forwards. The birds are confused because they have three semi-circular canals on each side of the brain in the inner ear responsible for keeping the bird aware of its orientation. These canals are filled with fluid and arranged on each plane, one horizontally and two vertically, at right-angles to each other. The inner surfaces of these tubes are provided with hairs and the fluid has small granules floating in it. As the bird moves, the granules brush against the hairs which, through a system of nerves, send signals to the brain. These signals are interpreted by the brain to guide the body as to its orientation, roughly as a compass would do on a ship. Turn quickly and you will become dizzy. Exactly the same process takes place in the bird's ears and brain. So 'dizzied' birds will lie quite quiet where they are placed until they recover. By which time, we hope, you have got your dog on point!

It is a lot easier to train several young dogs on planted game in the same field because so much ground scent is left by the trainer's feet every time fresh birds are put out that the dogs have no option but to hunt for the air scent. Provided only a few planted birds are used (perhaps to implant some particular piece of training) close pointing need not become a problem. Some recommend stopping the dog as soon as he winds the birds but I prefer to interfere as little as possible. The answer is to switch to wild birds as soon as the dog has learnt to point. Getting planted birds to flush is an art. Birds can be dizzied so they recover fairly quickly. I do not like the proprietary wire traps designed to fling pigeons and other 'planted' birds into the air at the touch of a button. They certainly *seem* to provide the answer but many dogs are shy of the unnatural sound they make and I suspect they are clever enough to realize the deception. Of course, pigeons will return unharmed to the loft after use and can be re-used another day.

The bob white quail is a small but popular American game bird which is excellent for training puppies. Its use for training older dogs is, in my opinion, limited because it encourages dogs to point too close. Bob white can occasionally be purchased through dealers in fancy pheasants or quail. Young birds are best and they soon settle down to form a covey, or bevy as it is more properly called. The birds are strongly gregarious and it is an easy matter to train them to return to a 'call-back pen' by letting out a few each day and keeping the rest back as callers. The released birds readily learn to return home for food and shelter, entering their pen through funnels in the side like one of the old fashioned rat or sparrow traps. As the birds become fit they fly better and better.

Point and back:
pointer and Llewellin
setter. (Derry Argue)

The legal position regarding the use of such birds in Britain still has to be tested in court. Some authorities suggest that it is illegal to release exotic birds into the wild, others maintain that since the birds are trained to return so promptly they are never truly released anyway. It is, I believe, illegal to shoot quail in Britain anyway though not illegal, apparently, to kill domestic quail for the table. Naturally, I cannot recommend the use of quail for dog training in Britain for these reasons.

Assuming the birds have been trained to return to their flight pen, a few are driven into a wire mesh tube and this tube is transported to the training ground which should be within a couple of hundred yards of the home base, i.e. close enough for them to return home after use. The tube is gently placed in low cover (grass and clover is excellent) and the birds allowed to creep out into this cover in their own time. After a decent interval, say ten minutes, the wire tube is removed and the pup is worked up to the spot, into the wind, in the normal way and, hopefully, we get a classic point and flush, even though it is a scaled down version of the real thing.

The more the birds are worked the better they lie. To some extent, the concentration of scent can be varied by putting down more or less birds. But there is no doubt that the use of quail is an acquired art and some never get past the stage of teaching the quail to return to their home, let alone to using them. Quail can also be dizzied or dropped into grass where they generally settle before being pointed and flushed with a fair semblance to wild birds. Grey partridges can be used in the same way but they are generally smarter and go wilder quicker than quail. I once tried this and got back more partridges than I put out. Of course, once the birds reach maturity they pair up and lose the desire to return to the covey. The advantage of quail is that being smaller than pheasants or partridges they are relatively cheap to maintain, breed, and can be re-used. Handled properly, bob white behave as near to wild birds as it is possible to get. For starting puppies, they are ideal, but, like all planted game, they should not be over-used. The parallels to the quartering pattern of a dog trained on quail may be only a couple of metres (because the scent is so weak) and they keep cutting back to make sure they have not missed a bird.

Gadgets and Problems

Some trainers love training gadgetry. I do not. The more natural training can be the better and my only training aid is the baler twine I have mentioned previously. The old time trainers used such things as 'spiked collars' (to stop dogs running up game) and 'puzzle-pegs' (to force dogs to keep their heads up). Some of today's trainers use the chain choke collar which looks kinder but is just like the spiked collar to the dog. Old time trainers would tie a dog's leg up to slow it down, have them dragging a hundred yards of rope, and do on. The modern trainer would be better to spend his time breeding better dogs and eliminating the need for such nonsense. To quote Wright's *Book of Poultry,* 'Rottenness hath no cure but total eradication'.

The electric collar, or radio controlled remote electronic shocking collar, would *appear* to be the answer to the dog trainer's prayer. 'Punishment should be applied the instant the dog disobeys', we are told. And at last, it seems, we have the very instrument to do the job. There are problems to this philosophy; 'punishment' alienates the dog's affection for its handler and threatens that delicate man-dog relationship, and because a dog has no knowledge of fine moral judgements it does not 'disobey' in the accepted sense and such harsh treatment only creates problems for the future. No one can know how a dog will respond to such treatment until after the event, when it may be too late.

Punishment involves giving the dog some traumatic experience after the event and it is impossible to predict what the effect of such an experience will be; dogs are individuals and they vary considerably in their reactions to trauma. What we should be attempting to do is to modify behaviour patterns to suit our (man's) needs in a way that is predictable and has no dangerous side effects. The correct procedure when things go wrong is to analyze the problem and then go back one stage in the training process. Generally, dogs try out something new with some caution and trepidation before the experience becomes a habit. Catching them at the initial stage will stop undesirable behaviour dead in its tracks.

To illustrate the point, let me tell you of my setter pups which started to chase the hens. Each day I let out thirty or more dogs in a field for exercise next to where an equal number of Light Sussex bantams are kept on free range. Accidents are rare. But some of the pups on free range started to chase the hens. The situation is entirely predictable and I expect each batch of pups to go through this chasing stage. As usual, I simply caught one hen and the pups ran to me out of curiosity. As each pup tried to bite the hen I tapped it lightly on the nose with a small switch and stroked the hen whilst talking to it in endearing tones. On the other hand, I introduced these same pups to game and killed a couple of birds for them. The pups no longer chase the hens but are as keen as mustard to hunt game. Make sure the correct behavioural pattern is firmly ingrained at each stage before proceeding to the next lesson and it is truly amazing how easy dog training can be.

Radio controlled shocking collars include a collar which goes around the dog's neck incorporating a receiver and shocking mechanism. The outfit is completed by a hand-held transmitter through which it is possible to deliver a shock to the dog, via the collar unit, from a remote location, perhaps up to half a mile. I purchased one of these gadgets twenty years ago certain that it would cure all my training problems. In fact, it did nothing of the sort. I have had experience of four different makes since and my opinion remains unchanged.

You will read favourable reports in the press, but no one writes about the dog that was spoilt and had to be destroyed. In practice, the collar has to be tightened so tightly that the dog is scarcely unaware that it is wearing the collar. This is necessary so that the two electrical contacts are brought up tightly against the skin. Even so, dog's hair is an excellent insulator and in the natural motion of running, unless extremely tight, the contacts will come away from the skin, probably at just the moment the button is pressed and the shock needs to be administered. So, as often as not, the dog is shocked at some unpredictable moment rather than the split second needed to effect a cure. If a dog can so quickly become aware of the check-cord, how can he be unaware of the shocking collar?

I consulted a well-known animal behaviourist about the lavish testimonials given these instruments by an American colleague, an eminent doctor of canine psychology. As predicted, my contact not only knew the man personally but had visited his kennel in the States. My worst suspicions were confirmed. Later I learned that this person, too, had realized the harm these instruments could do in the wrong hands and all the advertising literature and hype put out by the leading manufacturers at that time had to be withdrawn and re-written.

Unfortunately, in Britain, the electric collar is now claimed to be the answer to every problem. We are at the stage the Americans grew out of twenty years ago. While the Americans now admit they were wrong, anecdotal evidence as to their usefulness appears in every other British sporting paper on the newsagent's shelves, presumably because the publishers are getting advertising revenue from the manufacturers. Sadly, there are more and more editors of shooting papers who know nothing about dogs and even less about the ethics of dog training and they publish any readable article no matter the source or experience of the writer. We never hear of the spoilt dogs. Or the hard-headed brutes that can only be trained by such methods. It only takes a few such dogs to win in trials to dramatically alter the temperament of our British working gundogs on a wide front so bad temperament becomes as common as hip dysplasia . . . but perhaps we are there already.

Earlier this week I was out training a very promising young pointer which was confused about hares. He had walked into a couple of coveys of grouse and I then spent five minutes grooming him up on another point only to find that he was pointing a hare. Next thing, not sure in his mind what he was meant to do, the dog was chasing hares. Then, the dog came to a brief point and started to march across the moor, pointing sporadically and then dashing on again, occasionally dropping his nose. He appeared to be on a classic hare line and I muttered something to the keeper about this being the only time I would consider using the electric collar. At the same moment a big covey of grouse which had been running ahead of the dog rose in front of his final point. Had I used the collar at the moment I considered correct, the dog would have associated the shock with the sight and scent of grouse with predictable results. Fortunately, I didn't use the collar and the next week the shooting season had opened. My pupil behaved perfectly once a few birds were killed to his points, even quartering and hunting for grouse right through a rabbit warren! Only use such extreme measures if it is the last resort and do so in the realisation that failure will mean the dog has to be destroyed.

The electric collar is as useful as the surgeon's scalpel. In skilled hands the knife can remove a tumour; in unskilled hands it can sever an artery. The electric collar *can* be used to good effect in dog training by someone who understand the complex nature of canine psychology; it can also ruin a dog when used by some well-meaning but untutored person. The trouble is, it is invariably the latter who purchases such things.

Nuisance barking and fighting in the kennel can be problems and the scientists have again come up with what they consider to be the answer in the form of an electronic bark limiting collar. The collar is activated by a pad pressing against the dog's vocal cords. When the vocal cords vibrate, which they do when the dog barks or growls, the wearer receives an electric shock through two steel prongs which maintain contact with the skin. These contacts inevitably set up an irritation which stimulate the skin to produce fluids in a vain attempt to wash away the foreign object. This material, kept warm by the animal's body heat, is the perfect breeding ground for bacteria. If left, infection could follow. Bark collars can solve an immediate problem. But they cannot be left on indefinitely, and when they are taken off the dog promptly starts barking or fighting again.

Recently another bark collar has come onto the market. This looks superficially like an electric collar unit but there are no prongs to bite into a dog's neck. The collar is activated by loud sounds, e.g. barking, and a brief spray of Oil of Citronella is squirted in the direction of the dog's muzzle. The unpleasant scent causes an unfavourable association in the dog's mind and it should stop barking. The idea is excellent and I am advised that the collar can be adjusted at the factory to work off a range of noises, loud to soft. In a large kennel, where several dogs might bark, the unit would seem to be of limited use but, being humane, it is a step in the right direction.

Collars and leads are not generally thought of as training aids but they are necessary items of equipment. There is a current vogue amongst some owners for the use of spiked force training collars, or pinch collars, to lead pointers and setters which, to me, indicates how dogs and attitudes have deteriorated. The type of collar used has a number of steel spikes which revolve inwards when tension is put on the lead. They are designed for 'force training' a dog (e.g. to retrieve) and were never designed to be used for leading a dog. The Kennel Club has banned their use at Cruft's but they have not been banned at field trials.

The fact is that bird dogs pull on the lead because they are keen to work and to see what is going on ahead. I generally use the traditional leather collar on my dogs, at least an inch wide and wide enough to cover two vertebra, and I am delighted if they pull as it is difficult enough giving working dogs enough exercise. Pulling on the lead will build up massive back and thigh muscle. If pulling cannot be tolerated (and I can understand this if there are several dogs to be led), the traditional solution is to couple two together. Obviously, slow dogs are coupled to faster dogs so the strain is shared. There is also a perfect solution in one of Dr Roger Mugford's haltis, the head collar specifically designed to allow strong dogs to be handled by ordinary owners. Some dogs have to be trained to accept these but this is no more difficult than getting a puppy to accept a collar and lead. Further details can be obtained from The Company of Animals, P.O. Box 23, Chertsey, Surrey KT16 OPU. The company has now produced a video on dog training with the haltis. I have used these collars and found them excellent. Some use a variety of rope or leather choke collars to discourage pulling which are certainly less severe than the steel sort.

Chapter 9
Home Life

Kennel Design

Every working dog ought to have its own kennel. Not only is a kennel a good training aid but a dog has a right to peace and quiet after the day's work is done.

In this context, I was asked by an estate to advise on problems they were having controlling their pointers on the moor. We solved the problems in the shooting field but my enquirer could not understand that his dogs also needed a quiet secluded kennel in which to relax after the day's sport. Instead, he thought he was being kind to the dogs by having them in the house where, after a hard day's work, they were then expected to amuse the children and ladies in their additional role as family pets. No wonder they sought peace away from their owners for a bit of quiet hunting when allowed to run free on the hill!

Kennelling a dog can have a beneficial effect on training. Dogs living in the house have the opportunity to learn more and become better socialized but there are also more opportunities for problems to develop. A kennelled dog is generally keen for exercise and work and that is an asset during training. I am also convinced that dogs re-live their experiences when they are in the kennel (through dreaming) and so it is an excellent way to make sure good experiences become ingrained in the dog's mind. A dog kept as a family pet has to learn so much more, some of which may be in conflict with its role as a hunting companion. It is sometimes inconvenient to have a dog in the house, perhaps there are visitors or bitches in season, and it is a great help to have a dog which will go into its kennel without protests. Perhaps a mix of home life and being kennelled outside is the ideal compromise.

The kennel for a single dog can be quite simple. I have individual kennels made from old oak whisky barrels set clear of the ground on a short post or a few blocks. The dog is secured on a ten foot chain which runs freely on a long steel wire. Whisky barrels are very solid and I recently purchased a dozen at £3 apiece which must be something of a record for a solid oak kennel. These were considered no longer suitable for their original purpose and were made of inch thick staves. The forty-five gallon size is ideal for a single dog. Bigger ones will accommodate several pups. Two battens are screwed across the boards at one end to hold the staves together and someone skilled with the use of a chain saw can cut out the doorway, say about 250mm by 350mm, in a few moments. A galvanized pressed steel canopy, easily made by any sheet metal worker, completes the kennel and stops rain blowing in. The opening should face due south, or away from the prevailing wind. Dogs seem to like the curved shape of the barrel and it is surprising how warm they become inside even in a Scottish winter. The barrels need a liberal painting outside with an asphalt based water-proofer which can be thinned with creosote. This will seal the cracks between the staves so that the structure is wind and water-tight.

Occasionally, after a dry spell, the hoops need to be hammered home and secured with screws to stop them working off.

Some dogs are very slow to learn to use these kennels. I have found the solution is to have a few barrels in the puppies' kennel so that they get used to them. Otherwise, the dog can be encouraged to go in by throwing a few tit-bits inside. After an initial protest, the dogs settle down very well and become very fond of them. Barrel kennels have found favour with military and civil police dog handlers.

My new barrel kennels are to be built on skids so they can be moved around as the ground becomes fouled. This type of kennel is not suitable for whelping but is ideal for a single working dog, especially as they are cheap and dogs can be kennelled individually. For obvious reasons, they are not suitable for bitches in season. There is something about being on a chain which changes the attitude of a working dog. It seems to realize that it is utterly dependent on you, the owner, for all food and water and, best of all, for getting released for exercise. For this reason, I would choose this type of kennel for a team of field trial or work dogs. Kennelling several dogs together in yards inevitably leads to a pecking order being created which is undesirable.

Kennels need not be elaborate. Old whisky barrels supported off the ground on railway sleepers provide cheap, dry, warm and daught-free kennels.
(Derry Argue)

Kennels built on traditional lines ought to include an inner sleeping compartment and an outside run. For a single dog, prefabricated commercial wooden structures are fine provided the floor is given a good covering of sawdust which is changed at regular intervals. I'm assuming here that the dog gets out for a daily run. Bird dogs are very active animals and need a lot of exercise. Access to a large run can partially solve the exercise problem.

Stone or concrete kennels are best. They ought to face south to get the benefit of the sun and ideally should give the dogs some interesting view, say a busy farmyard or road, to stop them becoming 'stir crazy'. Some kennel situations cause dogs to become neurotic barkers when they feel they should confront every passing stranger; more so when they get the feeling that they have 'won' as the intruder goes away. The dog-postman scenario is the classic situation.

When designing permanent kennels the first priority is drainage. If that sounds like a music hall joke I can only say that drains give more trouble than any other aspect of kennel design. First, the outfall. The river pollution authorities may object to what they consider foul drainage water being discharged into an open water course and one is usually advised to run such drainage into a soakaway. A soakaway is a drainage system designed to allow liquids to percolate into the soil below ground level and above the water table. Unfortunately, soakaways do not always work. Minute fragments of dog dirt very effectively block the pores of the system and the drainage water backs up and floods the kennel. A soakaway can work a little better if a sump is installed in the drainage system to catch the solids but this should be emptied regularly.

These days drains are easy to lay with 100mm plastic soil drainage pipes which fit together like Leggo. The only technical part is to make sure the fall is correct for the diameter of pipe and in the right direction. My own kennel drains are connected to the household septic tank which I believe to be the perfect set-up. The council will empty this free every three years, or more regularly for a nominal fee.

The sleeping area in old fashioned estate kennels were built like a domestic living room to full head height for the comfort of the owners, not the dogs. This is a mistake. Warm air rises and the stone floors, with no damp proof membrane, are always cold and damp so such kennels are usually dank, dark, draughty, and miserable in winter. All a dog needs is a dry, warm, draught-proof box to sleep in and a dry bed to rest on during the day. Both can be provided by what the well-known gundog writer Peter Moxon calls 'the fox box'. This is an insulated box measuring approximately 750mm x 750mm by 600mm high (size depends on the size of your dog) with a tunnel entrance down one side. The box can be constructed by any handyman by sandwiching 50mm expanded polystyrene insulation between 6mm ply sheets with 50mm x 50mm framing and using the resultant boards to build the box. The edges of the box may need to be protected from chewing by screwing on strips of light angle iron and the kennel needs to be supported clear of the floor to keep it dry. These boxes require no more bedding than a handful of wood shavings and a dry warm day time bench is provided on the top or by extending the floor and roof out to one side. Provided with a weatherproof roof, they are also suitable for use outside. But they really come into their own as whelping kennels, especially when installed in a garage or shed, as they are very warm and draught-free. Made to bolt together, they can be dismantled and stored or moved to a new location quite easily.

Top: Gordon setters, by Thomas Blinks. (*Hugh Blakeney*)

Bottom: Liver and white pointers in a landscape by Thomas Blinks. (*Richard Green Gallery*)

Top: Pointers in a landscape, by Thomas Blinks. (*Richard Green Gallery*)

Bottom: An illustration from Laverack's *The Setter,* showing a young lemon and white Laverack setter dog.

Top: Five-month-old lemon and white setter puppies; a shared point. (*Derry Argue*)

Bottom: Five-month-old Llewellin setter puppies; point and back. (*Derry Argue*)

Top: Starting them young. Irish setter and pointer puppies with a peregrine falcon. (*Derry Argue*)

Bottom: Steadiness to hares is essential. (*Derry Argue*)

Kennel runs, inside and out, ought to be concreted with a fall of about 1 in 30 to a channel down one side to a proper grilled drain outlet in one corner. If several kennels need to drain to a common gully, the channel should be placed underground or outside the kennels and the soiled water should reach this through individual apertures. All kennel drainage systems should allow plenty of rodding eyes in case of blockage. There ought to be a low wall around each run to about 600mm so that the dogs cannot urinate on the wire and cause it to rust. Chain link or weld mesh fencing can be secured to steel angle-iron or treated timber uprights. Timber is fine but keep the creosote brush handy in case chewing becomes a problem. Gates ought to be positioned in the *corner* of the run and open *inwards*. If the bolt is on the side towards the corner, it will be handier getting in and out without letting dogs escape. Bird dogs are not labradors or spaniels; they are extremely adept at slipping through half opened gates. Make sure the gateway is wide enough to take a wheel barrow. Self-filling water bowls, or patent drinkers as used by pig farms, save a lot of work but put them in a sheltered corner so they will be less likely to freeze in winter.

Concrete floors ought to be laid with an adequate fall and the surface ought to be very smooth with what is known in the trade as a steel float finish. The natural acids in dogs' urine will etch this surface and make the ideal slightly textured finish. Dogs, unlike cattle and sheep, are able to keep their footing on very smooth floors which are easier to keep clean than the tamp finish favoured by designers of farm livestock buildings. A good water pressure makes kennel cleaning easy with a hose; alternatively, use a forty-five gallon steel drum to collect water from the tap or roof guttering, then wash down with bucket and broom.

My own kennels have purpose built fox boxes for about seven dogs each with a heavy lid over the top made from 25mm ply which serves as a daytime bed. The fox boxes themselves are made of 100mm concrete block with floors insulated with 50mm expanded polystyrene and a cement skim over. These floors have a good fall to them so they can be hosed down in fine weather. Bedding is no more than a few handfuls of sawdust which keeps the dogs' coats clean. Visitors express reserve when they first see this design but the boxes are very warm in winter and the floor retains the heat because of the polystyrene. These kennels are ventilated in summer by wedging the hinged lids open slightly. The fox boxes are built into open front sheds which effectively keep out the wind and rain and face south to catch the sun.

Whelping Kennels are best designed on the fox box principle. The best example of practical design I came across was one built of small straw bales described to me by Colonel Ted Walsh, the lurcher expert. He tells me they are used by greyhound breeders who build an igloo out of small bales making a small compartment inside just large enough for the bitch and her pups. The wall of bales can be secured by driving steel rods down through them into the ground. A roof is made by placing a piece of weld-mesh above the compartment and more bales (with polythene sheet waterpoofing) over this. After use, the whole lot can be burnt. A more permanent whelping box can be made out of 6mm ply sheets with 50mm expanded polystyrene sandwiched between on 50mm x 50mm timber framing as above, but with the entrance at ground level to allow pups to walk in and out. The insulation needs to be continued round all sides, including both the roof and the floor. Such a structure is draught proof and allows the bitches body heat to warm up the interior to the correct temperature, but some additional provision for ventilation (apart from the entrance) might be needed in hot weather . . . something that is seldom a problem in Scotland.

The traditionalist often uses an open wooden bench for whelping with a heat lamp suspended above the pups. In my experience this system has a number of flaws. The wooden bed becomes soaked with fluids during whelping and urine from the pups after they are born. The heat under the pups is conducted away through the damp boards. Damp is a good conductor of heat. This could be prevented by insulation but that is never considered. On the other hand, the heat lamp provides warmth to the tops of the pups' heads and bodies so they are cooked on one side and frozen on the other. The bitch is even closer to the lamp and gets over-heated. The bed is probably positioned in one of those old fashioned living room sized kennels and draughts and a build-up of humidity compound the problems. Presumably, someone will also have to pay for the heavy electricity consumption! I have known of at least three serious kennel fires caused by these lamps in recent years with the loss of valuable buildings, dogs, and pups. The insulated fox box provides heat at the bitch's own temperature, is draught free, and costs nothing to run. I have now reared many litters in these kennels through severe Highland winters without any additional heating except a sack over the entrance in very cold weather to retain the heat.

If fox boxes of the correct internal height (i.e. approximately the height of the dog at the shoulder) are used, there is seldom any trouble from dogs soiling their bed. Occasionally, where they are used to accommodate several dogs, one may dominate the entrance and fight with others wanting to get in but it is not a serious problem.

Urinating on the traditional bench-type bed can be stopped by suspending a false ceiling of weld-mesh or similar material over the bed slightly above the dog's shoulder height. The psychology involved here is that both dogs and bitches need to raise their heads to urinate or defecate. If they are prevented from doing that, they will jump down to the floor to perform these functions and keep the bed dry and clean.

With an insulated bed, bedding is really unnecessary though a few handfuls of sawdust or shavings keep the coats clean. I like to use clean straw for the bulk of the bedding for a whelping bitch and use soft hay for the inner lining. Straw used to make good bedding for dogs years ago but all corn is now cut with a combine harvester when it has to be over-ripe. Barley straw, particularly, breaks down into a fine and highly irritant dust. Years ago corn was cut with a binder and then dried and the straw made excellent bedding. Hay ought to be given a light dusting of louse powder as it is inclined to harbour mites. The oft recommended suggestion of tacking old carpet or any form of sheet material over the whelping bench has inherent dangers. The bitch will inevitably attempt to dig or rearrange her bed (it is her instinct to do so) making holes in the sheet which can trap a pup.

Breeding

Mating: The signs of a bitch coming into season are well known and have been covered by many other books on practical dog breeding. The correct time of mating is shortly after the bloody vaginal discharge turns to straw colour. If a bitch has to be taken to the dog, it is a useful indication to see if she will allow a dog at home to mount her. But generally a couple of days more should be allowed because the bitch will be quicker to accept a dog she knows than a stranger.

By far the best method of mating a dog and bitch, in my opinion, is to kennel them together and leave them strictly alone for nature to take its course. I have never assisted a dog at mating and do not intend to do so. All the interference necessary ought to be limited to an occasional surreptitious peep every ten minutes or so to see if they are tied. Many dogs, particularly setters, will refuse to mate except at the time they judge to be correct. Pointers are more precocious. Two matings with an interval of a day or two between them are preferable in case one service does not 'take'. After the dogs have mated and 'tied', it is a good plan to tie the dogs' two collars together so they cannot prematurely tear themselves apart.

Gestation: Between mating and the birth of the puppies there is an interval of about sixty-three days. The first thirty days the bitch may give little indication that she is in whelp except an almost imperceptible dropping of the belly and her teats becoming more pronounced. At around the twenty-fourth day it is sometimes possible to actually feel the pups in the bitch as a small succession of swellings like a string of beads but this is best left to a suitably qualified person. These days, professionals skilled in the ultrasonic scanning of sheep can usually give an accurate diagnosis later in pregnancy for a few pounds. This is invaluable if sending a bitch away 'certified in whelp'. But such an assurance is no guarantee and it is possible for a bitch to reabsorb some or all of her pups. A veterinary certificate would seem a wise precaution if the expected litter is a valuable one.

Bitches in whelp should be in good condition but not over-weight. It is wise to worm the bitch around the fortieth day. There is no need for special treatment, except a suitably adjusted diet, until a couple of weeks before whelping. My own feeding includes a lot of meat but there are properly formulated commercial feeds available for brooding bitches. Again, there are plenty of specialist books available on this aspect of kennel management but provided a careful watch is kept on the condition of the bitch, working dogs are generally quite easily whelped. One of my Irish setters, Moanruad Kinty, heavy in whelp, refused to be left behind when I went off for the field trials and all I could think of was to remove the passenger seat of my car and make her up a bed in the space created using plenty of old newspapers. On the morning she was due to whelp I had to run a pointer in a stake. Before leaving for the trials Kinty coursed a rabbit and jumped a standard stock-proof woven wire fence about one and a half metres high. A couple of hours later she gave birth to ten healthy pups! All pups survived and she reared the lot.

Whelping: The bitch ought to be moved to her whelping accommodation at least two weeks before she is due to have her pups so she can settle down and make her bed. She may need some help in making a nice bed from the straw and hay you have provided. Young bitches can be perfect fools and manage to roll their bedding into a tight ball to be pushed into one corner of the box. Patience is the answer. Just quietly make up her bed again . . . and again . . . and again . . .

About twenty-four hours before a bitch starts to whelp a few drops of milk may be squeezed from her nipples and her parts begin to produce a quantity of mucous which is nature's lubrication to help the birth of the pups. The bitch may become agitated and all that can be done is to make sure the bed is all right and then leave her in peace. Many of my own bitches come and tell me when their pups are due. It is rather nice being taken into their confidence in this way. The more fussing on your part over the whelping, the less chance of the natural instincts taking over and everything going as it should do. When the pups start to come the bitch will lick them clean and they will make their way to a nipple and start to suck. It really is best to leave the bitch well alone while this is happening. Sometimes a pup is dropped away from the nest as the bitch takes an impromptu walk. Nothing to worry about, just put it in with the others and reassure the bitch.

There is a chance that the bitch may lie on a pup but it is a small chance and on balance I believe more damage is done by interfering than leaving the bitch to get on with things herself. It is fairly straight forward to decide whether the noises coming from the box are normal contented murmurings or distress calls and act accordingly. I might take a quick look at a whelping bitch, make sure no pups are laid on, and move any laggards to a nipple, but generally I prefer to leave well alone. Frequent opening of the kennel allows heat to dissipate and disturbs the bitch. Except for maiden bitches, which can be very stupid, I seldom lose a pup so I guess I must be doing something right.

Once the pups are born, or if they are slow to come, it is not a bad idea to watch the bitch in case she is continuing to strain. I really do mean she will be in obvious distress and clearly trying to give birth to a pup which will not come. In that case, the vet ought to be called without delay. Having said that, I can think of only two or three such cases in over thirty years. Working dogs are generally very tough and if reasonably fit not at all prone to the problems associated with some show strains.

There is nothing unusual in a newly whelped bitch refusing food for a day or two after the birth of her pups. In fact, it is quite natural for her to do so. But I feel better if I make sure some fairly rich laxative type of food (such as well boiled meat or offal) is available in case she wants it, plus, of course, fresh water at all times. Some old hands are very casual about the whole business and get back to normal after just a few hours, other stay laid up for days.

After the birth, the bitch may still discharge a dark matter from her rear end which looks horrific but is in fact quite normal. This is usually faecal material from the pups before they were born. You can safely leave this for the bitch to clear up as nature intended although it does no harm to wipe away the worst with a damp cloth.

There is a condition called 'fading' which affects some litters. Soon after birth, the puppies fail to thrive, feel cold, become more and more dehydrated, are rejected by the bitch and slowly die, emitting pathetic mewing noises as they do so. Over a period of days, the pups die off one by one. In spite of a great deal of theorizing, little appears to be known about this condition though a course of broad spectrum antibiotic treatment for the bitch before the pups are born is said to help. In my experience, the problem is inherited and over the years I have gradually bred the condition out though, occasionally, puppies still fade and there appears to be nothing to be done. Presumably, natural selection will eventually solve the problem.

Culling: No one should contemplate breeding a litter unless they are prepared to cull both puppies and older dogs. This ought to be made quite clear. What we are talking about here is the humane destruction of unwanted dogs. Every breeder will occasionally be faced with too many puppies in a litter, malformed puppies, even unwanted puppies from an accidental mating. It is gross ill-responsibility, in my opinion, to rear puppies which nobody wants and which do not have suitable working homes to go to. The excuse that pet homes will be found for them is simply untenable. These are working dogs.

Most bitches will find six puppies more than enough to cope with. She will make a good job of half a dozen and they will grow all the better for less competition. At around a week old, the litter should be carefully examined for under-sized pups, bad jaws, kinked tails, faulty colouring, etc. These pups should be disposed of. The Highland shepherd has a saying that some are meant to die. A hard maxim but a true one, especially in nature. Yet due to the 'wonders of veterinary science', many nowadays survive which nature would have selected out. If an owner is unable to face up to the fact that this is one of the responsibilities of breeding working dogs, then it is better not to breed at all.

There is a defect called 'dwarfism' in some strains of pointers and it is by no means rare. Lack of size ought to be considered a serious fault in pointers and setters. Paling, a factor which dilutes colouring, produces grey-and-whites in pointers rather than black-and-whites. This may sound rather attractive but the eyes also lack pigment, are pink like an albino ferret's, and so are unable to protect the dog against the intrusion of strong sunlight. Afflicted dogs squint in discomfort in strong light and for humanitarian reasons should be culled.

Kinked tails are a blemish on what might be an otherwise perfect dog. There is another fault which produces a cork-screw tail. Bad jaws may be 'under-shot' (bottom jaw longer than top jaw) or 'over-shot' (top jaw longer than bottom jaw). The lower jaw continues to grow after the top jaw has stopped growing, so slightly over-shot jaw in a young puppy may be tolerated as it can improve. Under-shot jaw, or 'pig jaw', just gets worse. Temperament problems may appear later. I have come across occasional excessive nervousness, hysterical screaming, hyperactivity, insensitivity, and so on, though thankfully not often. Some defects are the more serious as they may not become evident until the pup is mature and a lot of time and money has been wasted in its upbringing and training. But that is where good breeding comes in. The genetic faults in dogs are truly legion; they are not *caused* through close breeding and an elementary knowledge of the inheritance of most will help the breeder avoid or eliminate them completely. Breed societies, if members could be persuaded to be honest about congenital faults, could do much to eradicate such problems, especially as there are now cheap and efficient computer systems available for recording pedigrees.

Rearing puppies: Pups can benefit from additional feeding as soon as they will take solid food which is from about a month old. Mixing finely minced cooked meat and warm milk to make a thick porridge is food the pups can lap up without harm. Very young pups can easily inhale milk with fatal consequences.

As pups get older, I feed them and their mother *ad lib*. What goes into mother will eventually go into the pups. The choice of food is important. Perhaps I am lucky but I have always been able to feed a lot of meat. Proprietary feeds need to be chosen with care. Some are just cereal and roughage which may be fine for a pet but is not a complete diet for a growing pup, let alone a nursing mother or a working dog. There are no meal times for pups in my kennel. Puppies have food available at all times though it may be removed and replaced with fresh food several times a day. There is usually someone quite willing to clear up what the pups leave! I do not like to hear pups calling hungrily for food at any time.

As soon as pups get reasonably sensible, at, say, five weeks, they get *ad lib* milk. This is calf replacer milk and a twenty-five kilo bag takes a litter of pups through to weaning and beyond. Fresh water ought to be available at all times and I greatly favour self-fill water bowls connected up to the main supply. If this is not possible, provide at least two bowls and make sure they are kept filled at all times. If there are two bowls, only one need get empty before there is a clear warning that they need a refill.

I suppose I ought to recommend that pups have a few bones to chew but that is taken for granted in my kennel. Butchers ought to give these free as a public relations exercise but most will make you pay. These days it costs £100 a tonne to get bones removed by the knackery so we are doing them a favour . . .

When the pups begin to get active, they can be moved to a grass run. I have never experienced problems rearing pups on concrete possibly because mine get out for a run almost daily but there is no doubt there are enormous benefits to letting pups have the partial liberty of a large grass run. Small birds usually drop in for a free meal and I have seen quite small pups teaching themselves to point and back. These kennels will just about keep themselves clean if large enough and exposed to the wind and the rain. Large stones can be dropped into the holes pups inevitably dig around the edges in an attempt to get under the wire or better still a strip of concrete about 450mm wide can be laid alongside the wire. This need only be about 25mm thick as it will not have to bear much weight but will effectively stop pups digging out. Muddy areas should have a load of heavy gravel dumped on them. The puppies' feet will soon have this stamped down almost as good as a concrete yard. A number of whisky barrels or old packing cases kept off the ground with concrete blocks or railway sleepers provide ideal kennels. If there is a squabble, there are other barrels and no pup need get left out in the cold. Pups just love piling on top of each other in these barrels which, after all, is the natural thing for pups to do.

Fences are best constructed out of chain link. The heavy grade is preferable. It can often be picked up quite cheaply on the completion of some building project or other and if they ever get the problems sorted out in Northern Ireland there are going to be some great kennels made with all that wire!

Feeding dogs can be expensive. But it need not be. I have fed dogs on table scraps and left-overs from schools, surplus herring in the Outer Hebrides, seals, chicken off-cuts, butchers' offal, and various by-products of the food processing industry. Many working sheepdogs are fed on nothing more than porridge with what meat they can scavenge when out at work on the farm. The agricultural advisory services provide information on farm livestock feeding for a small fee and I argued that the working sheepdog came into that category. Eventually, I got lists of the basic feed components but the advisers admitted they had encountered extreme difficulties in obtaining the information. The reason appears to be the huge profits made by some pet food manufacturers. It is easy to work out the profit margin on a bag of feed by taking the most expensive ingredient (usually dried meat or fish meal) and finding out the wholesale price of this constituent per tonne from an agricultural feed merchant. A simple computation will give an idea of the profits involved. Since the meal will almost certainly be bulked out with cheaper cereal all will soon be clear. The solution should be obvious. When it is considered that the dog's first function on domestication was that of scavenger and the remover of rubbish and excrement around the human camp, we could say the dog has come a long way!

The feeding of dogs doing hard daily exercise, growing pups, and nursing bitches needs to be considered with special care. Dogs worked hard on the wrong diet will first break down fat and then muscle to provide energy. Pregnant bitches will also go thin for the same reason, breaking down muscle to feed puppies. A starved bitch will, in the extreme, kill and eat her own pups so that the remainder can survive. Of course, this ought never happen and it is essential to feed a high protein ration with an adequate quantity of fat, vitamins, and minerals. The protein ought to be of animal origin, as found in meat, not soya as in many canned feeds. Over feeding can be almost as dangerous as under feeding.

Chapter 10
Hunting

Case Study No 1: Grouse Shooting

What could be nicer than to find yourself in good company, with half a dozen young dogs all ready to go, and an expanse of purple heather in front of you with a soft breeze in your face? There are grouse calling in the distance and the haze of a summer's day makes the far off hills look like something out of a fairy story. Everything is set right and we are full of expectation and anticipation. It is early August and we are out to get some of the young pups shot over. None of us wants to kill a large bag, just a bird or two each to reward the young dogs, and the main enjoyment will come from seeing the results of last year's breeding and all that hard work training on broods during July. But we have brought along one of the older dogs, too, just in case.

Going dogging may seem to be something that needs no organization but we are all old hands and a little planning can make everything go a little smoother. My host is a sheep farmer who has some upland grazing with a few grouse. He has brought along the local doctor, a close personal friend of us both for many years. The farmer and his son, both keen sheepdog trialers, have come to help carry the bag and lead spare dogs as none will be worked for long. All out today are real dogmen. Like myself, they want to see a bit of style, pace, and good dog work rather than a lot of shooting. I am here to give my dogs some experience and to enjoy seeing others appreciating good dogs. But I am not adverse to borrowing a gun later on, when everyone else has had a shot, and there will be a lot of leg-pulling about the accuracy of the shooting. Maybe running bird dogs is a personal thing, but none of us is impervious to the odd word of praise or appreciative nod.

Jim, our host, knows how these things should be done. As a farmer he is an avid watcher of the weather and we have got onto the moor with a cheek wind carefully angled so the dogs will get the benefit of the breeze in their faces. As birds are disturbed they will feed back into the ground we have yet to shoot. He has also arranged for one of his daughters to meet us with the farm truck about three miles upwind. Usually, the girl takes her knitting with her and waits until we arrive, but in this high-tech age he has a walkie-talkie and can call up lunch to meet us at the end of the beat. The truck will also move us to a new point on the moor for a fresh beat with a favourable wind, bring up a couple more young dogs, and take home some youngsters that have already been tried. We also hope there will be a reasonable bag of grouse for her to take back!

To start the day, we run a young dog that got some light shooting last year. He's a black-and-white pointer dog, and he's off at a cracking pace, quartering out the ground like a veteran. This dog has already had experience of broods in July and early August and he should know what it is all about. I start forward at a steady walk signalling the dog to drive out further at each cast so he is covering a front perhaps three hundred yards wide. This is wide enough for this moor as there is a good population of birds. Jim and Doc follow on behind, chatting quietly and remarking on the dog's work. There is no need for a 'line', or for us to walk the usual half gunshot apart, because the dog should leave nothing behind. With myself out front, the dog can clearly see me and respond to my signals, perhaps a wave to tell him to search out a heathery bank, perhaps a cautionary signal as a hare jumps up out of the heather, but mostly he is expected to get on with it without hand signals or whistle. At the last, I glance back, but the lads are doing a great job dropping the young dogs and talking to them gently as they watch the hare. It is good to have people who understand dogs leading the puppies; each pup gets a scratch behind the ears as they patiently watch the hare loping away.

The author, shooting grouse over F.T. Ch. Advie Gunsmoke in 1975. (Willie Newlands)

As we walk along enjoying the day, great clouds of pollen rise from the heather in the wake of the dog and from our feet. The sticky yellow dust adheres to our boots and trousers; it's a wonder any dog can scent grouse in such conditions. Perhaps he can't. Nothing much seems to be happening. Almost as I think it, the pointer throws up his head, hesitates in his stride, but continues running across the wind. 'Birds on the next cast', I remark to my companions; and I can almost hear the quickening pulse rates. Privately, I congratulate myself on having a good 'un. Many dogs would have altered their cast to investigate the scent, this one has the brains to make a mental note and check next time across. Sure enough as the youngster comes across the wind he curves abruptly round, runs forward a dozen paces, and comes to a firm and confident point. 'A good covey by the look of him', I remark, glancing back and gesturing to the shepherd and his son to bring the other young dogs up so they can see what is happening and smell the birds. My prospect is trembling with the thrill of the scent and he champs his jaws as he sucks in the sweet stench of grouse.

There is no need to say more. The Guns know the drill. One starts to walk up either side of me as I head for the dog, each walking parallel to my line and about fifteen yards out and slightly ahead. As we draw level with the dog I softly call his name and he glances sideways as if to check that the Guns are in position. Then we all move forward together, the dog walking confidently up to his birds as I encourage him on with a snap of my fingers and a brief word. Just as I think the birds must be running ahead, the grouse rise with a cackle and a cloud of pollen. It seems an age before I hear the shots, but Jim and Doc know their business. Count one – two – three, at the same time select a target, bring up the gun, swing, and pull. There is no great haste and the object is to fire at about thirty-five yards when the shot spread and penetration are at maximum. Four birds with four shots. Both have taken their birds from their side of the covey, firing well away from the dog, and birds which go back are left strictly alone for safety considerations. As the birds rose, the pointer dropped instantly; now he's straining forward, still dropped, eager to see what is going on out there and to see why the birds so mysteriously dropped and to hear the rustle of their wings in the heather as they flap their last. My small black cocker which has remained steadfast at my heels until now looks fit to burst. This is her chance and she knows it; she is a mass of excitement just waiting for the command, 'Fetch it!'. Just think, if we taught our bird dogs to retrieve, there would be no excuse to own such a spaniel; sent up from Hades with red hot coals for eyes to torment mortal man, didn't Keith say?

Now we have a dog-leg of the heather moorland to cover, a high spur jutting into better grazing land that surrounds us lower down. This can only be worked down wind. The pup is put back on the lead after a sniff of the grouse he found for us and the old dog unleashed. He sets off straight down wind for about six hundred yards, then turns and begins to quarter towards us. This spur seems a favourite for grouse and before long the dog spins round on a flash point. It looks most spectacular but we all know it is a find of the 'after-thought' variety. The dog has come on the grouse unawares; he should have scented them further back but we will never know why this was not possible since we can never fully understand scent. We line out and walk towards him, heading him face on. I would never do this with a young dog, but this fellow is an old campaigner. As we walk, a covey gets up and it is safe for Jim to take a single shot which results in another bird in the bag. Such actions would be completely out of order if we were running a youngster. This covey, although lying between us and the dog, was not missed by the dog as he is now working towards us (see quartering diagrams). We would only be killing birds to a young dog's point. As we approach the point, the dog becomes even more intense. He can see us approaching and knows that the grouse must burst at any moment. And there they go, a great covey of perhaps fifteen or sixteen birds. Four shots again but only two birds for the cocker to pick this time.

The day continues as it has started, the young dogs in turn performing as they have been trained to do, all happily steady on the occasional hare and not one running in to shot, all pointing nicely and having birds shot to them. By lunch we have a respectable bag and everyone is mildly tired and contented. The Doc even manages a short snooze after lunch.

Case History No 2: Wild Sport

Grouse shooting is all very nice but it lasts only a few weeks before the real sport begins. If I did not have my friends, there is no way I could afford such shooting. But I've managed to lease some 'white ground', degenerated heather moorland which, through over-grazing by sheep, has become replaced by poor grasses and rushes. There is nothing on it according to previous bag records. It comprises a few thousand acres of grazings, forestry in various ages, and odd corners of rushes and bracken.

When I leased the ground I got permission to site feeders at various strategic points. These are forty-five gallon oil drums filled with wheat; slots cut into the sides near the base allow a thin stream of corn to spill out for the birds to find. I have also constructed silos out of small square straw bales. These points are fenced against the sheep. Feed is collected from a variety of sources and I have unofficial contracts with workers in grain processing mills and feed compounders. A brace of pheasants or half a sheep in exchange for an unlimited quality of spoilt corn, cream buns, and spilt sheep and cattle nuts from burst bags gets me some wild and varied shooting. Duck on the hill lochans, incidentally, go mad for cream buns! Hill pheasants and partridges are too hungry to be particular and being wild birds they are opportunistic in their feeding habits. Occasionally, I grow wheat or barley on the farm which is mown when almost ripe and baled without threshing. This makes good feed to hold birds, keeping them exercised as they hunt for ears of grain amongst the straw but once again, the sheep have to be excluded or they would eat every grain, the straw too.

This time I am alone. It will be a hard slog on foot up the hill but the wind is in my favour and I get the dog working ahead of me. Frankly I do not expect a point and this is just a training session but in November there could be a snipe, occasionally a woodcock in a clump of bracken, perhaps even a grouse, maybe two. After an hour we have encountered nothing more exciting than a mountain hare and I am pleased to see my dog watches it going away with casual indifference.

After half a mile we are into the ground I have been heading for. The flat basin, perhaps one hundred acres in extent, is really an over-grown loch. The soggy peaty soil carries a heavy crop of rushes which floods in wet weather. Pheasants migrate from the far side of the hill from a low ground shoot to the sanctuary of this isolated marsh. Occasionally there are snipe. A few strategically placed feeders encourage the odd pheasant to linger. But for the hope of a marsh long-tail it would be a thankless slog up the hill with the prospect of little reward.

I am accompanied by a three year old Irish setter which is now settling to be a consistently reliable worker. She is one of those dogs which will run all day and keep going on no more than a hint of scent from a snipe. If I can get a pheasant today it will make her the happiest dog in the world. But for the dog, I would buy my pheasants at the game dealers; I have shot enough during my ten year stint as a sporting agent to last several lifetimes.

The dog seems to perk up considerably when we reach the marsh. She knows the form. First I examine the feeder, make sure that the corn is flowing freely and that there is still enough left; then look round about for tell-tale signs. Sure enough, there appears to be a pheasant about as it has left a few droppings and a couple of feathers. As I let the setter off the lead she bounds into the rushes as if her tail was on fire. I just hope she does not run up the pheasant in her enthusiasm! But, no, she soon begins to settle down to quarter out the rushes with fair precision. After ten minutes she is 'on'. A flash point out to one side after 'poking' over occasional ground scent. Bare open hill above her and rushes on three sides. I run like a stag as cocks are liable to break, run, or just lie doggo. And it is a cock, I feel sure. It is, of course, dangerous to run with a loaded gun, but I am alone. No one should run carrying a gun in company; the dangers are too horrendous to contemplate. A shotgun blast can cut a fence post in two and human flesh is a lot less resistant.

As I approach the dog she begins to move and I know the pheasant is going to try to out-smart us by running through the cover. But I also know what the pheasant, almost surely a cock, does not know; that running birds are my setters specialty! We set off in procession, the cock, my dog, and myself in the rear. Fortunately, the setter is anything but sticky. She trots off through the rushes with that shuffling, sinuous motion of an Irish setter working birds I know so well, and weaves her way after the retreating pheasant. Occasionally, the dog pauses to drop her nose and check ground scent. Sometimes, she pauses to push her nose up high to search for air scent. A thin veil of mist lingers over the marsh, the scent no doubt caught between the heavy vapour and layer of clear air just above the rushes. I urge the dog on as fast as I can. Pheasants will run like the proverbial hare in cover and the dog will have to get up close to force the bird to fly before I can get a shot. Then the dog seems at a loss. She casts slightly to one side, then the other, checking the air. Nothing. Suddenly, the dog starts to run out to the side, turns down wind, runs directly downwind about fifty yards and starts to quarter the ground we have already covered. She wavers, hesitates, moves on. This time the dog slinks along at what for her is a snail's pace. Her casts barely cover a thirty yards beat. While I am admiring her style and cunning, she draws to a quiet but firm point. Surely we have him now! But no. She is on the move again. Then suddenly the red bitch casts out to the side and runs in a wide circle, perhaps fifty yards in diameter, until she is facing me, directly up wind of me. Then she stalks forward. This dog, clever as she is, has headed the bird like a cunning old sheepdog turns a ewe. It is a rare talent in a dog these days and I mentally hug myself for having such a paragon.

As I race towards her, closing the ground between us where I know the bird must lie, a magnificent cock pheasant breaks from the rushes just ahead of her and between us with that chortling cackle that sets the nerves tingling. Shooting birds up the backside? Easy? Ha! This bird explodes from cover catching me off balance and out of breath. My gun is up and swinging, everything seemingly skewed around at the wrong angle, my gun on a slant and the barrels tilted sideways, then my feet slide in the mud. As I sweep the barrels through the catapulting figure, it twirls and curls changing direction frantically as it seeks to avoid the first danger from the dog and now me. Bang! A miss. Steady the Buffs! Bang! And down he comes! A mass of glorious, shining red and gold feathering. The dog is dropped but watching. A brief pause, and 'Fetch 'im!', the setter bounds forward, gently gathers up the bird and retrieves it to hand. A moment of joyous congratulations and we set off again adding a brace of snipe to the bag, both retrieved, before the marsh is worked out. Both the dog and myself would have been almost as happy with just the snipe. That's dogging. The pheasant is a bonus. Now twenty minutes for a sandwich, shared between us, and we head home through the barren grassland again.

Case Study No 3: The Invitation

'Wonder if you'd care to come down for a day's grouse shooting?', says the voice on the other end of the telephone. The name does not ring a bell and the accent is not local. I'm too old and wily a bird to accept invitations from strangers out of the blue. Thank you, but I am engaged that day; perhaps I'll call by if I get finished early. No feelings hurt and I say how grateful I am. Not to worry, another name is mentioned and my caller rings off.

In Scotland it is possible to find out what any man has had for breakfast that day by making two telephone calls. At least, that is my boast. So a couple of calls later I am the possessor of the information that my kind enquirer is the new owner of a nearby estate. It is apparently the company of my dogs he seeks as his reputation for generosity, or rather lack of it, is already established in the district. That afternoon I have to pass by the moor on which shooting is scheduled so I can see how they are getting on. From a lay-by on the county road I can see a line of perhaps a dozen Guns with two white dogs, obviously bird dogs, moving to-and-fro before them and I begin to thank my guardian angel that I had the foresight to avoid that scenario.

As I reach for the binoculars a regular staccato of whistle blowing echoes across the glen from the direction of the shooting party. I can see both dogs now, moving like two flies across a window pane as they course some unseen hare over the moorland landscape.

Half the line stops as if in acknowledgement of the handlers' panic measures to call the dogs off, the other half wanders forward unaware of the drama that is unfolding further down the hill. Another fifteen minutes and all is total confusion. One dog has returned, the other has given up hare chasing and has started working again; the trouble is it works alone, out of sight of the shooters and its handler. Meantime, the first dog has got a point and four hurrying figures converge on the dog. The handler must be the one at the top of the line now running hard down the line in front of advancing Guns to get to his dog before the shooters pre-empt the

Lady Auckland shooting over F.T. Ch. Lark of Cromlix (Champion Stake winner 1961), Gordon setter F.T. Ch. Joker of Cromlix backing, with Angie Handling.

situation. Before he arrives, there is more a machine-gun staccato of shots and I dumbly thank the heavens that that dog is not mine. The upper dog remains firm on point, waiting in vain for its handler, someone, anyone, to come and honour its find. More shots below and the line gradually starts off again, now looking very ragged. Two figures remain behind, clearly looking for a lost bird. Then, I can see the dog further up the hill moving in on its point, birds rise, and, clearly out of sheer frustration, the dog is soon chasing a good covey of grouse. The birds swing down the hill, the dog chasing but losing ground. The grouse are caught by the wind, and hurtle towards and over 'the line'. There is more firing, sporadic now, and I hear voices shouting. Figures converge to where one of the Guns had stayed back to find a lost bird. Later I learn that the man has been fortunate. The shot lodged in his chest and face but he will live. They operated to remove an eye that same afternoon. I heard later that one of the Guns, paying an exorbitant fee for his sport through some agency, had refused to go out and was suing the organizers for misrepresenting 'walked up' shooting as 'grouse shooting over dogs'. If I am asked, I'll be delighted to appear as an expert witness. Adding a couple of pointers to a walking party does not create the traditional sport of shooting over pointers and setters, just the ideal scene for a nasty accident and some ruined dogs.

These days I politely decline any invitation to work my dogs where there are likely to be more than two Guns. If I know the people involved I might accept three, more rarely four, one to take each side and another birds going behind, Guns taking it in turn to go up at each point. Even then, great discipline is needed as the side Guns can only shoot forward and the back Gun can only shoot behind. Each Gun must at all times be aware of the position of the dog boy and gamekeeper who have to stay somewhere in the middle ground. Two Guns is really the optimum number, especially if they have an unknown record for safety, and non-shooting participants, perhaps wives and girl friends, should be strictly limited and stay near the dog boy or keeper.

Case Study No 4: Sport is where you find it

Another day, later in the season, I share sport with a friend who is as keen on dogs as I am. Every year we meet to try something different to test ourselves and our bird dogs. Last year we headed off for the west of Scotland when the first decent fall of snow came. Someone had told us the woodcock are concentrated in the milder areas in such conditions and it sounded worth a try. Before the first snow, we did a tour of what seemed a suitable area, mostly knocking on doors and asking around in the local hotels. We ended up on the doorstep of another sporting farmer who, in typical Highland generosity, told us to help ourselves. But where, we enquired, were the boundaries of his ground? No point in upsetting his neighbours. He vaguely waved his arm in the direction of a couple of mountain ranges, so long as we kept between the two we would be all right, he told us.

The next few days we ran our dogs on the open heather moorland, in open mature forestry, amongst newly planted trees, and amongst the birch woodland and rough grassland of abandoned crofts. We shot twenty-nine woodcock in the two days and so many snipe I don't think we bothered to count. It was all a question of reading the conditions and being in the right place at the right time. Most sportsmen *want* to help another get some sport. And it is generally sport which is unlettable because the next day the woodcock had all moved on and there are not many who have dogs that will work any sort of country, have an established reputation of being safe with stock and deer, and adjust range and pace according to the varied conditions.

The following year we heard of pheasants straying from a low ground shoot into some forestry. The shooting tenant of the forestry was traced and bribed with a couple of bottles of whisky. He just dismissed us a couple of eccentrics who had clearly lost our minds. He told us he had tried to get to grips with the pheasants, working an aged labrador amongst the lop and top, but gave it up as a bad job. How could anyone find pheasants in thousands of acres of trees? But we did, by tying bells on the collars of our dogs and calling them back if they tended to range too wide. That winter we shot pheasants and woodcock amongst Sitka and Norway Spruce. It was tremendous fun and almost impossible sport trying to work out where the birds would fly before ordering the dog in to flush and then trying for a snap shot in some clear space amongst the tree tops just yards wide. American and Japanese hunters have the latest electronic gadgetry to guide them to a dog on point in thick cover but we think there is little to beat a couple of old hawk bells tied to the dog's collar.

Woodcock shooting on the open moorland is a different proposition. The birds are easier but not that much easier. And they tend to fly a couple of hundred yards and drop in again. We try amongst the old rank heather around abandoned peat cuttings; along the shores of lochs where dead bracken provides cover. Where the dogs could not go, the cocker spaniels went, even out to the islands on the lochs with the flushed woodcock being marked down as they dropped into long heather on our side of the water. On these forays we also found snipe. These birds could be anywhere on the open hill when migration flights are in full swing and it was very pretty to see a dog finding and pointing such a small bird miles out on the open moor where there is virtually no cover.

In Scotland, game is scarce and it is a big country but that is what dogging is all about. I have enjoyed as much sport working the dogs in turnip fields for pheasants in my native Devonshire. It is different sport but just as much fun. The pheasants were just as likely to be found in thick field hedges and the dog had to go in like a spaniel and flush them out. An intelligent dog can soon be taught to come off a point and go round the other side of the hedge to put the bird out for a lone Gun. Almost anywhere will provide sport for those with an adventurous spirit and a bit of imagination. The dogs get very clever, too, adjusting their style of work to whatever the conditions demand.

From just these few examples it is easy to see that shooting over dogs can be as traditional as grouse shooting in August or as unconventional as rough shooting in thick forestry. The more work and experience the dogs get, the cleverer they become. Shooting over pointers and setters can take place anywhere, and at any time of the open season, provided there are two essential elements. These are sufficient ground cover to encourage birds to lie to a dog's point, and game of a type (red grouse, black grouse, capercailzie, partridges, pheasants, woodcock, and snipe) that will lie to a point. And on every occasion there is some added dimension totally unexpected. This could be the point your dog gets on a stoat struggling with the last death throes of a rabbit, or a pair of roe kids lying concealed where their mother left them on a bank of heather bathed by the afternoon sun. Cautious bird dogs will point anything strange so mine have found merlins' and harriers' nests, baby hares in their forms, the remains of some predator's still warm kill, even, once, a wrist watch I had lost a year before! The delight of dogging is the extra dimension of the unexpected.

Commercial Shooting

A handler with a good team of bird dogs can usually find work on the grouse moors early in the season. Shooting over dogs is still a minority sport in Britain because of our history but many visiting sportsmen prefer to shoot game over dogs. This is what they are used to. Being experienced, these people are not fooled by bad dogs and are usually prepared to pay for the privilege of shooting over the best in the traditional manner.

But a word of caution. In the eagerness to show off one's dogs it is all too easy to find oneself in the middle of an impossible situation. Before taking on the responsibility of working dogs for such a shoot, a few details ought to be considered. No one will think any less of a dog owner for being business-like. It follows that the shoot organizer will expect the dog handler to produce good dogs, sufficient for the day's sport, and to conduct himself in something approaching a professional manner. A few ground rules would not go amiss.

Ground rules
(1) When and where are the dogs required? A few shoot owners are notorious for changing the dates and venues of their shooting at the last minute. This is fine if

someone else is paying, but if the handler has to frequently change his own arrangements, taking time off work and adjusting his holidays to suit, it could cost him money. Get agreed dates confirmed in writing and agree a cancellation fee. You can be sure the shooting organizer will be wise enough to arrange for a substantial deposit in advance from paying Guns, who in turn will take out cancellation insurance.

(2) What is the dog owner expected to provide? The usual requirement is for 'sufficient experienced, well-trained pointers and/or setters for each day's shooting', together with their handler and transport to the moor or a mutually acceptable meeting place. Dog handlers are not usually expected to provide off-the-road transport or the various helpers needed to run these things smoothly. Nor do clients expect the handler to use the opportunity to train dogs. However, the handler who can provide the complete package clearly ought to be worthy of his hire.

(3) Who provides the retrievers? Most gamekeepers and shoots have their own, but some do not. Estates which are run predominately for stalking come into this last category. If the dog handler is expected to provide a retriever, too, he ought to be so advised and paid an additional sum for that service.

(4) Who provides accommodation? The dog handler and his helpers, if any, will have to live and eat somewhere. Someone, either the handler or the shoot organizer, will have to pay. Better arrange this in advance to avoid problems and conflicts later. 'Accommodation provided' may mean the handler lives as one of the guests in the lodge, or it may mean an unfurnished bothy or caravan scarcely fit to house a dog! Lodgings with a gamekeeper or farm worker, accommodation in a local hotel or bed-and-breakfast, estate holiday cottage, beaters' bothy, caravan, etc. can all be valued differently and that is something that should be taken into account when the fee is fixed.

(5) Who provides lunch on the hill? Even lunch every day for the handler alone will amount to a substantial sum over a week or two. Lunch for friends or members of the handler's family who lead dogs as well will add up to a significant amount over the season. Who pays?

(6) Who is to lead spare dogs, carry the game bag, etc? It is a very frustrating experience for the handler to try to lead spare dogs and work another. At every point, dogs trying to act correctly and 'back' have to be dragged up to the point so the pointing dog can be taken forward to raise the birds. The answer is a 'dog boy' to lead spare dogs, an invaluable aid who can also groom up young dogs and get them backing, dropping to wing and shot, etc. before they are ever off the lead. Sometimes the dog handler provides members of his own family to help. If a gamekeeper is released for duties elsewhere the dog handler ought to be compensated. Otherwise, at least one strong and fit person (other than the handler) will be needed to lead spare dogs and carry the bag. That could mean an additional man's wages each day.

(7) Who is the hirer? Some sporting owners and agents have neatly side-stepped the responsibility of hiring, saying this is a matter between the Guns themselves and the dog handler. But it could equally be the landowner, sporting agent, or one or all of the shooting clients. Clearly, the client needs to be identified. And what happens if those charming overseas sportsmen 'forget' to pay the handler before they leave the country? Worse still, suppose they are not insured and a dog or handler gets shot and injured or even killed? Far better to contract with a British property owning resident who is properly insured and who can be sued than a possible 'fly-by-night'.

(8) Who insures and for what? When everyone is on holiday and out to enjoy themselves, it seems inconceivable that things could go wrong. But Murphy's Law states that if things can go wrong, they will go wrong. An estate owner will normally carry an 'all risks third party' policy which will cover the handler and his helpers and dogs. A sporting agent or shoot organizer may not be so covered. What if the handler is asked to drive his car up a private hill road and it gets damaged? If a dog gets off and kills a sheep? The handler ought at least to check with his insurer and explain the risks. Dogs ought to be valued by some knowledgeable person before an accident happens, not just as shooting dogs (which can be replaced) but as future breeding prospects (which may be virtually irreplaceable).

(9) Just what has the handler contracted to do? What if there are no grouse? Perhaps it would be worth inserting a 'get out clause' in the event of there being too few grouse or there being some irretrievable breakdown in arrangements not the handler's fault. Perhaps bird dogs are bred to find game where it is scarce but running dogs where there is no game at all will quickly ruin the best. A clause automatically cancelling shooting where there are fewer than a specified number of points per day or shorter period will at least ensure the organizers allocate reasonably productive ground. Otherwise the handler seriously risks a suit for breach of contract if he declines to work his dogs on barren ground.

(10) Who is in charge of the shooting party and the shooting arrangements? Generally, shooting on the moor is under the overall control of the gamekeeper who acts as the owner's agent but only the dog handler can control the dogs or specify matters relating to shooting which might affect the dogs. That ought to be specified in the agreement. For example, the handler will usually not want hares and rabbits to be shot as this merely awakens the dogs' interest in these animals as legitimate game. He may not want any game shot when young dogs are being worked except that pointed by the dogs. The positioning of the Guns at the point is usually left to the handler because he should know, from the attitude of the dogs, where birds lie and where they can be expected to fly. At least one sporting agent of my acquaintance disputes the handler's right to control these factors and too bad if dogs are ruined as a result! Understandably, his handlers change every season! The handler's control over shooting might reasonably include some measure of control over the keeper's retriever which should normally be kept on the lead until required, as specified by the handler, to retrieve game. Some retrievers very quickly learn to rush in to every point to prematurely put up the birds with a predictable effect on the pointers.

(11) How many Guns and 'spectators' will there be? I neglected this item when I arranged to work my dogs for a Highland estate. I expected them to know how dogging should be conducted. I got the shock of my life when twenty-one people turned out, twelve carrying guns! A *maximum* number might be three Guns and two non-shooting spectators, but remember there will also be the handler, gamekeeper, and dog boy, making a total of eight persons at least which, to my mind, is already three too many for safety.

Having a note of these points in an exchange of letters is to the benefit of all parties and it is naive to dismiss such details on the grounds that it is 'just sport and a holiday'. The agreement need not be drawn up by a solicitor but should certainly be included in a letter of agreement. These days most owners and handlers of pointers and setters are amateurs, not business people, and as a sporting agent I experienced many last minute let downs. Such capriciousness is generally taken into consideration when fixing the fee and the true professional is rightly in great demand. Unprofessional people do not deserve to be paid professional rates. Had these inconsiderate people been sued for breach of contract I have no doubt the damages would have been considerable. The fact that some wretched visitor has possibly saved for years and travelled thousands of miles to enjoy his sport does not enter into the considerations of such self-centred people.

Dog handlers and shoot organizers make contact through the classified advertising columns of the sporting press, and also through the considerable communications network of the shooting/sporting agent community. It always pays to get several opinions of the abilities of a dog owner and his dogs; also the organizational expertise (or lack of it) and character of shoot organisers. Some handlers are prepared to lower their standards, accepting a nominal fee to get their dogs shot over. Others work their dogs for long lines of Guns, not worrying about their dogs which are often past further ruination. Generally, the labourer is worthy of his hire and you get what you pay for. Handlers who lunch with the Guns and neglect to play the role of the humble peasant can forget the tip! My own view is that the quality of sportsmanship can be far greater reward than any fee and it is a great thing to receive a justly deserved accolade for some brilliant piece of dogwork. On the other hand, keeping a kennel of specialist gundogs is an expensive business and I have never found the true sportsman hesitant when it comes to contributing a fair price for his sport.

Dogs for Falconry

Game hawking with falcons over dogs must be the most exciting sport ever created by man. I was fortunate to be asked to work my team of pointers and setters for Geoffrey Pollard in Caithness in the 1970s. There is no doubt that Geoffrey is the most proficient expert in this exacting field of falconry and I doubt if anyone will ever be able to emulate the sport we enjoyed during those years. Much of the ground the hawks were flown over has now been planted up with forestry and the best of this sport is quite impossible where there are trees.

At that time, Geoffrey, an Uxbridge solicitor, insisted in flying only wild-caught passage falcons, something that would not be possible today. These are peregrine falcons trapped on migration in the autumn of their first year. Today, it would probably be illegal to import such birds but at that time it did less harm than might be imagined as the natural mortality amongst wild falcons in their first season is around seventy per cent, then over fifty per cent the following year. The Arab falconers would purchase a bird, train it and fly it during the season, then release it or sell it for falconry in Britain before the eastern hot weather set in. Grouse hawking is a hazardous sport and birds, well able to fend for themselves in the wild, are regularly lost.

Grouse hawking: the falconer, Geoffrey Pollard, has unhoooded and cast off his falcon, which will now ring up high above the dog's point. (Derry Argue)

The word peregrine means 'the wanderer' and every year trappers in the Middle East would catch these birds on their autumn migration for the big annual auction in Arabia. Geoff had contacts who would purchase a bird on his behalf and fly it back to the U.K. Having already learnt to make full use of their wings in the wild such birds were skilled fliers. Yet they were still young enough to take training quite easily.

On arrival in Caithness, the whole team of wild-caught falcons would be released. For a while, they were too unfit to fly far, just down to the river for a bathe and to the lure in the afternoon for their feed. Gradually, they would be brought into condition and taught to respond to the lure and 'wait on', or fly high above the falconer, in anticipation of the day grouse would be flushed beneath them. Daily repetition brought the birds to a peak of fitness so that in a week or so they would be flying like wild birds, but trained, too, to return when called.

The traditional British pointing breeds are preferred for falconry because they were bred for this sport long before guns were invented. Frankly, they have the temperament for it and even a dog new to falcons seems to know that the birds must not be harmed and must be treated with the utmost respect.

The falcon is trained to expect the lure to be thrown out when it flies above the falconer. (And I am sticking to that explanation!) Each day it is kept waiting a little longer and its natural inclination in that situation is to rise higher in the air the fitter it gets and the longer it is kept on the wing. When the conditions are judged right, the dog is worked until it comes to a firm point, then the falcon's hood is removed and it is cast off to fly high above the falconer as usual. This time, instead of the lure, birds are flushed and everyone prays that the falcon will make a kill. If she does, each successful flight encourages the falcon to fly higher as she realizes, through experience and trial and error, the higher she goes, the greater area she can cover and the greater the force behind her downward stoop onto her quarry below. Naturally, it pays to start the falcons early in the season so they learn to catch young inexperienced grouse. But both birds learn quickly as the days go by, each getting stronger and better flyers, and within a week or two the flights are quite spectacular. It has been estimated that a grouse can fly in excess of 55 mph on level flight and a falcon can achieve 180 mph in that near vertical, downward stoop. I have seen a grouse all but cut in half by the strike of a falcon.

Since the falcon is learning its role by trial and error it is absolutely vital, in those early days especially, that there are grouse in front of the dog's point. Also, it is important to get the grouse up at exactly the right moment which is usually when the falcon is slightly upwind of the point and with her head pointed towards where the birds lie. If the falcon is to be encouraged to fly high, she must be sure that birds will be flushed for her. Gaining height, for a falcon, is like climbing a long flight of stairs to us. Neither will repeat the experience if there is no benefit to be gained from the exercise. The falcon wants, at least, the *chance* to catch a grouse. One of my falcons was so annoyed by a dog that false pointed that she struck the dog on the side of the head so hard it would not work for the rest of the day!

Unfortunately, falconers these days are seldom dogmen. When I was involved in the sport, my fellow falconers seemed convinced that they could pick up some reject from the shooting field for around £30 which would turn out a superb hawking dog. It became one of those boasts falconers like to make and 'I never pay more than £30 for a dog' became a well hackneyed phrase. And everyone wondered why they could not emulate the performances of the Gilbert Blaines and William Humphreys of past generations of falconers who achieved top style and record bags by using the best dogs available!

With the falcon waiting on at a good pitch and the dog firm on point, the falconer must choose the critical moment to put up the game. Generally, the falcon needs to be up-wind of the grouse when they flush because her wings are designed for rapid down-wind flight and the grouse, travelling down wind, are less able to jink as she comes up behind at colossal speed. But to put grouse up when *you* want is another story. Grouse are fully aware of the dangers of a falcon flying over head and they would much prefer to stay quiet and still, when they know they will be invisible to the falcon, than expose themselves to attack from an avian predator designed by thousands of years of evolution to pluck them out of the sky!

Flushing the grouse at exactly the right moment is the problem. The falcon will be at her pitch, as high as she will go, and we cannot wait too long or she will be off on the soar, see some passing pigeon or rook to rake off after, or decide to fly off to the river for a bath, or, even worse, tire and come down to pitch on some fence post or rock. We must put the grouse out when she is headed towards where they lie and we must stage events so she is upwind to insure a downwind stoop. So correct timing is vital. At the exact moment it is judged she will go no higher, at precisely the moment she is up wind and headed towards where the birds lie, that, exactly to the split second, is the moment we want the grouse in the air. The problem is the sport cannot be organised to that degree of precision. Assuredly, the pointing dog knows where the grouse lie. It points because it has located the air scent of the birds. That scent states where they lie and from the dog's own experience it knows how far ahead they will be. Getting these birds into the air with split second timing is the problem; and we can be quite sure the grouse know that this is when they would be better keeping a very low profile indeed!

Grouse hawking: the falconer has unhooded and cast off his falcon. The dog handler, leading a spare setter, looks on. (Derry Argue)

Traditionally, falconers form a human line and rushed downwind towards the pointing dog in the hope that they can raise the grouse at the critical moment. A few may keep a cocker spaniel, leashed and ready, to be slipped like some fighting bull terrier to rush up behind the pointing dog, up the scent cone, and amongst the grouse. It is a horrendously mismanaged, shoddy form of dogmanship but it does get grouse into the air in double-quick time. The only problem is, canine discipline soon collapses and the whole scene degenerates into a rat hunt. Inevitably, the pursuit involves not only the falcon after the grouse but a pack of ill-disciplined dogs after the retreating birds.

I think it was the celebrated Mr St Quintin, a very experienced amateur falconer, who had lemon-and-white setters perfectly trained to work with falcons. When they came onto point, they would wait while the falcon was unhooded and it reached its pitch high above. Then, when the falcon was judged to be in the correct position the dogs would be commanded to bound forward to put the grouse up at exactly the most strategic moment. As soon as the grouse were raised, the dogs would drop down in the heather into the correct 'down' position. There is no reason why setters should not be trained in the same way today. Some falconers manage to get their dogs to flush on command (which is really no great feat) but cannot manage the subsequent control. Obviously, it is better to have the dogs worked by one person concentrating on that job. And that was my role in Caithness. I am afraid my problem was to communicate to the falconer that my dogs could, and would, run in to put the birds up exactly when told and then drop to wing. The falconer insisted in allowing too long for the dogs to raise the birds with the consequence that the falcon was regularly badly placed. Unless there is a good rapport between all the component parts of the team, game hawking fails to deliver the pinnacle of perfection achievable in field sports. But when things do go right, perhaps once in every generation, the very finest spectacle possible in the field sports will be witnessed by a privileged few.

These days falconry is in the midst of a revival. No one could have foreseen that the captive breeding of falcons would be possible or that radio-telemetry (radio tracking) would allow falcons to be flown on almost any moor where previously only the lunar landscape of Caithness was considered suitable. For me, the sport has lost much its magic. The mere thought of some peak-capped official tapping at my door to check my licences to own hawks and practice the sport has me wincing, but I expect I'm getting old. Thankfully, I lived through those wonderful times when it was all possible if you got up and made an effort to do it. That, of course, is falconry with style and few can these days afford to do things on such a scale.

Even so, it is surely no sin to dream. Most of us today will fall short of falconry at this level. Pointers and setters are still the most useful dogs to search wide open country where game is scarce. The ideal programme for a falconer's dog is to concentrate on dogwork for the first season and try to get the dog shot over, as was described earlier, so hunting makes sense to the dog. From this firm foundation of practical experience, the dog ought to begin to understand what it is all about and go from strength to strength.

Many falconers make the mistake of not involving the dog in the kill. This is assuming the dog to be some stupid creature having the sole function of locating game and possessing little or no intelligence to understand what it is doing and why. Nothing could be more short-sighted. Dogs are quite capable of working out what is going on and they ought to be involved in the success just as much as the bird when a kill is made. Every falconer knows that his bird ought to be given the reward of the head or some other part of the kill after a successful flight, but how many reward their dog with a few tit-bits or even a kind word?

Chapter 11
Breeding, Field Trials, Selection, etc

Breeding

Anyone can breed dogs. As humane society statistics repeatedly show, the problem is to prevent dogs breeding. There is little point in breeding pointers and setters to add to the already huge population of unwanted and uncared for pets. The number of suitable homes in Britain, where pointers and setters are going to be worked and cared for as they deserve, is extremely limited and those contemplating the export market should realize that even breeders with an established reputation find it an uphill struggle. Certainly, big prices are occasionally paid for working pointers and setters, but they are paid by people who know what they want and where to find it. They know how they will recover their costs, either through breeding or the pleasure they obtain from hunting over a top class bird dog.

So it is even more important that when we set out to breed we do so with the aim of reproducing the best. Also, that we plan ahead and make sure there are homes for the puppies to go to when they are reared. Anyone who has gone through the experience of rearing a litter of working gundog puppies and has still not got rid of them when they have reached several months of age will readily confirm what I say. I would rather give house-room to a pack of hungry wolverines than have a litter of well-grown bird dog pups about the place without the proper facilities to keep them!

From the previous chapters it will be apparent that there is more to the make-up of the working dog than mere external appearance. So, when choosing dogs to breed together to produce good workers we need to consider a lot more than just looks. Of course conformation is important, but what can broadly be called mental characters are equally so in a working dog. The problem is, as we have seen, that these mental characteristics can often be materially and inadvertently changed by environmental factors. For example, a young dog that has been badly reared will grow up stunted both mentally and physically. A pup off the best of stock may never make a worker if it is badly socialized and denied access to game before its ideas on 'hunting' become fixed. (I have seen setter puppies brought through six months quarantine which were obsessed by hunting flies on the kennel wall to the exclusion of all else.) On the other hand, a moderately well-bred dog may become an excellent performer in the field with careful education and appropriate experience in the hands of a skilled trainer so appearing better than it actually is. These are factors the experienced breeder will carefully consider.

It might be thought that all one has to do to breed perfect working gundogs is to breed field trial champion to field trial champion. It doesn't work like that. It might well be possible to breed show winners by breeding the top show dogs together; I have no experience of that subject, but I can state with some authority that simply mating what field trial judges have decided are the best workers together without any further analysis is the road to ruin in working gundog breeding.

Before starting seriously to consider breeding, it is necessary to evaluate what makes a good working pointer or setter. I can see little point in breeding top performers if they take months of hard work to train. Most professionals want an early maturing dog that trains easily and then retains what is learnt. Amateurs, on the other hand, need a dog that will be a lot more forgiving of their mistakes even though it may take a lot longer to train and need 'maintenance training' right through to old age. Training ought, in my opinion, to be a once-only routine, but that also means training must be completed within a specific period of the dog's life or it will become very difficult to achieve later. And if the wrong things are taught to such a dog, or it gets the wrong experiences, those faulty behaviour patterns will become even more firmly ingrained than the ones the skilled trainer took so much care to implant. So that 'good dog' is no longer such a straightforward proposition. Such a dog may be the perfect prospect in one man's hands, and a 'hard headed, stubborn, nervy brute' in another's.

Five-month-old pointer pups.
(Derry Argue)

We have already discussed the desirable characteristics of a working pointer or setter in Chapter 2 but what we want in the finished dog is not quite the same thing as what we want in a puppy ready for training. Olfactory powers are probably the first requirement, but they are not always easy to assess. No nose, no bird dog. Temperament, to take training and respond to the handler, is as important. But that really needs further analysis. I would say a soft nature was essential, but not so soft that the slightest harsh word makes the dog creep and cower, nor so hard that every effort in inhibiting undesirable behaviour becomes a battle of wills, only to be accomplished by harsh measures. Response to the handler must be associated with a dog's natural affection for his handler which must have something to do with the pack instinct and willingness to take a subordinate role in that pack, i.e. to subject itself to man's directions and control. The development of this is dependant on correct socialization and some dogs socialize better than others which is yet another variable. Precocity (the ability to develop early) has already been mentioned. Keenness for work? Yes, but for 'work' read 'birds'. A keenness to hunt is a prerequisite. Even a shy dog will overcome its fears of strangers and the gun for love of hunting. Freedom from 'killer instinct' is mentioned by most authorities. That is an absence of the will to kill and a willingness to pass on this role to the human partner. Most would consider natural pointing and backing high on the list, but not so that the pup will exhibit stickiness or a tendency to back anything that looks remotely like another dog (some dogs back to such an excess that they will back every white stone or sheep on the hill). Of course, we want pace and stamina. Style and good conformation are important too. Personally, I prefer big dogs to small ones as they can manage the long heather better and cover more ground. There are genetic faults we ought to avoid but these are often so obviously undesirable that they need little special consideration here. The hidden defects, the undesirable recessives, are not going to be seen from an external examination of either parent and few breeders are so honest as to include a note of these defects on the pedigree *as they undoubtedly should*.

Unfortunately, very little is known about the inheritance of the working characteristics we have mentioned so far. A knowledge of genetics is the form book of the breeder. A form book is the reference book used by gamblers to calculate the betting odds on race horses and greyhounds. It lists the previous performance of these racing animals and with intelligence a form book can help choose which dogs or horses are likely to win. But a form book cannot prove an absolute guide, only improve your chances of picking a winner; if it did, we would all be millionaires and the bookies would be bankrupt . . . and, as you may have noticed, that is certainly not the case! Some prefer to pick their winners with a pin. Some breed dogs in much the same way even stating that a knowledge of genetics 'would take the fun out of it'. All I can say is that if anything will help breed better dogs and avoid the production of more genetically unsound animals we have a duty to learn as much about the subject as possible. This ought to be done on a club level, with the Kennel Club taking the lead. But it isn't.

So genetics can provide an insight into what puppies any two dogs may produce when they are mated together. Their previous 'form' *may* be known from information contained in the pedigree. A knowledge of genetics merely helps reduce the element of chance and seldom provides an infallible guide. Most of the work done in the genetics of the dog has been in the inheritance of coat colour which is not a lot of use to the breeder of working dogs but you may wonder if anyone has ever tried to breed these dogs on a scientific basis. The answer is an emphatic 'yes' but the success stories are few and far between. Most successful pedigree breeding is achieved through the possession of a good instinct and judgement for livestock, not breeding 'too close', and a certain amount of trial and error. A knowledge of the animals involved, gleaned through many years of hard work and experience, is the best recipe for success.

There are three problems to the scientific breeding of working dogs. The first is the difficulty of identifying those characteristics which are inherited and which are environmental. The second is to provide an environment in which all pups get identical rearing, training, and opportunity so that we are able to compare like with like and select the best. The third is to measure these mental characteristics so that one dog can fairly be compared with another keeping all other things equal. These factors present real problems.

Very slight differences in the raising of puppies can profoundly affect temperament. When attempting to assess puppies to be retained for future breeding, I have occasionally found perhaps one in the litter to be very nervous at four or five weeks of age. Most breeders would condemn such a pup as not worth keeping yet with a little individual attention such puppies often recover quickly becoming indistinguishable from their siblings. Naturally, I do not breed from excessively nervous dogs so I can only conclude that these pups have suffered some traumatic shock, perhaps being over-enthusiastically 'corrected' by the bitch or some other upsetting influence. Given time and reassurance they recover. Time and again, I have condemned a pup because it is slower than its litter mates only to realize later that it has missed out on some vital lesson, perhaps a lesson taking only a few moments, that the others have absorbed. The effect of that omission can be cumulative. These days I mark each pup with sheep marking crayon as it is taken out of the run for some lesson so mistakes are few. But seemingly insignificant environmental factors applied during the critical periods can have disproportionate effects on the development of young puppies and this is always worth bearing in mind. When assessing breeding stock the best guide is past performance which means an accurate assessment of the working characteristics of the puppies they produce.

How do you assess 'nose'? It appears to be a simple problem but a dog with excellent olfactory powers may lack the necessary interest in game to encourage it to recognize birds and so it appears to be deficient in this sense. Perhaps the hunting instincts were not properly aroused, or the dog, as a youngster, had little opportunity to apply this skill. It could even be that a sensitive youngster was badly shocked when it first encountered game. The sudden clatter as a cock pheasant takes wing must be quite alarming to a small puppy.

How do we assess a dog's natural fondness for its handler and therefore its willingness to work to and for its human partner? The pup may have been badly socialised (which is a problem of the environment) or it may be naturally shy (which would be a genetic fault). Some dogs show excellent intelligence by distancing themselves from an ignorant handler!

And so the problems of assessing the working dog for breeding begin to mount. It may be wondered if anyone has ever tried scientifically to breed working dogs, so great seem the difficulties. In fact, there have been several successful attempts though I know of none, on strictly scientific lines, with bird dogs. There have, of course, been many successful breeders of working gundogs, this success arising from the skill and experience of the breeder, but here we are attempting to be a bit more analytical.

Dr R. B. Kelley of New South Wales, Australia, was responsible for the creation of the Boveagh strain of working sheepdogs. Dr Kelley carried out what he termed a system of controlled heterosis, starting out with a nucleus of top imported dogs, to create three families which bred consistently good dogs. Occasionally, an outcross was introduced but more usually the families were inbred with occasional crosses between these families to introduce genetic variability, or heterosis as Kelley called it. This system is described in Dr Kelley's book *Sheep Dogs; Their Breeding, Maintenance and Training,* published by Angus and Robertson of Sydney and London, in 1947. Kelley also found that young puppies tested on sheep at a few months of age exhibited the same characteristics at maturity. This early testing of young puppies can often be useful. The Guide Dogs for the Blind Inc., of the USA found the willingness to 'fetch' (retrieve) a useful indicator of guiding potential. My own pups are worked on captive bred game birds from a very early age and it is easy to pick the best from the age of a few months.

A sheepdog shows a similar attitude as a bird dog to game.
(Derry Argue)

Another scientific breeding project was undertaken by the Fortune Fields kennel of German Shepherds in Switzerland to produce good looking working dogs for police and blind leading work. This was done by Elliott Humphrey and Lucien Warner and the results of their work was published by John Hopkins of Baltimore in 1934 under the title *Working Dogs.* However, the authors admitted that part of their success was due to improved knowledge in the training of their dogs over the life of the project though better selection and breeding played a major part.

Another attempt to improve German Shepherds by selective breeding for guiding the blind was undertaken by Guide Dogs for the Blind Inc., San Rafael, California, mentioned above. About the same time, scientific studies in the genetics of behaviour in dogs were being carried out by Dr J Paul Scott at Bar Harbor, Maine, USA, in an attempt to learn more about the inheritance of behavioural characteristics and learning in children. The first project was written up in very readable form by a member of the board of Guide Dogs for the Blind Inc., Clarence J Pfaffenberger, in *The New Knowledge of Dog Behavior,* published by the Howell Book House, New York, in 1976. The Bar Harbor experiments are described in *Dog Behaviour; The Genetic Basis*, by John Paul Scott and John L Fuller, published by the Chicago University Press in 1965. This, too, is worth reading if rather more heavy going. And there are others including on-going projects at the Swedish Army Kennels and the Bio-Sensor project of the US Army.

There is no doubt that the Laverack-Llewellin-Humphrey dynasty, although not scientifically based, is another success story of the selective breeding of working dogs. These breeders followed the family system of inbreeding favoured by Dr R. B. Kelley although almost no outcrosses were used. Again, puppies were trained from a very early age. Interestingly, many of these breeding programmes experienced a 'problem' (if that is the correct word) in that their training and rearing techniques improved over the life of the project so introducing an unforeseen variable. It is sometimes difficult to decide whether improvements have come about because of better breeding or because of better training and rearing techniques. One report of Purcel Llewellin's dogs was that they were three-quarter Laverack at the time of his death which seems to indicate that the great man had learnt how to deal with the unique Laverack temperament towards the end of his career, a problem he seems to have attempted to solve earlier by introducing those outcrosses. The late John Nash once confided in me that he had never managed to train a Llewellin. The technique required is certainly very different from that needed to train the Irish setters with which he made his reputation.

The basis of any breeding project is that characteristics are inherited separately. It would not be correct, for example, to state that 'all liver-and-white pointers have good noses' (which is stated as an example and, so far as I am aware, has no basis in fact), simply because the two characteristics are controlled by different and unrelated genes. It may well be that a line of liver-and-white pointers became noted for excellent olfactory powers but out-crossing to pointers with bad noses would almost certainly give rise, ultimately, to some liver-and-white individuals with bad noses to disprove the hypothesis. On the other hand, it is clear that the pace and stamina of a dog are related to its conformation. But it would be wrong to assume that breeding purely for conformation will, *ipso facto,* produce dogs with great pace and stamina. That is the logic of the show bench and if that were true the Crufts' Champion greyhound would also win the Greyhound Derby. And so far that has not happened. For that reason there are no copies of the Kennel Club breed standards for pointers and setters in this book. The pictures will, I hope, convey a better guide than any written description can ever do.

Both parents contribute towards the genetic make up of the puppies in equal measure. That is not to say that sire and dam contribute equally to what the puppies will become; they do not. The contribution of *genetic material* is, for our purposes, more-or-less equal. The bitch, of course, provides the initial environment in the uterus in which the pup grows, from which it is born, and. then, the care and feeding during rearing. So let's exam this in more detail.

All living plant and animal matter is made up, at some stage, of minute individual cells. Each and every living cell in the dog's body contains, at some point, a nucleus.

This nucleus contains the genetic material, a sort of 'blue print' or specification, for that animal. This material consists of a number of threads called chromosomes arranged in pairs. The dog has thirty-nine pairs of these chromosomes in every nucleus except the sex cells which, in the female, are the eggs and, in the male, the sperm. These sex cells contain *half* the normal number of chromosomes.

The reason for this is that the chromosomes contain the genes, or genetic factors, along their length and when, in fertilization, male and female cells unite, they come together to create a cell (the fertilized egg) with the full compliment of thirty-nine pairs of chromosomes. It is this cell which, by a process of repeated division, eventually grows to form the puppy. Truly a miracle of nature!

With the chromosomes arranged side-by-side in pairs, there are also pairs of genes arranged on the chromosomes. Some characteristics are controlled by a single pair of genes, what is called 'single factor inheritance', others are controlled by several pairs, even very many pairs of genes. Each of a pair of genes controlling a 'single factor inherited characteristic' may not be equally powerful. In such a case one will be dominant over the other, and this second is said to be the recessive. A dominant gene in the pair will mask the effect of the recessive gene.

Whether dogs are pied (parti-coloured) or of one colour (whole- or self-coloured) is an example of single factor inheritance. The gene for self-colour, which is dominant, is usually denoted by the letter T in the shorthand of the genetic scientist, and the gene for parti-colour, recessive to whole-colour, is written t. So a dog having the TT combination of genes is self-coloured in appearance and also in genetic make-up. Because both genes are the same it is said to be *homozygous* (homo=Greek for 'like'). One having the combination Tt is self-coloured in appearance (because the dominant self-coloured gene masks out the recessive parti-colour gene) but is genetically a carrier of the parti-coloured factor (so, *heterozygous*, hetero=different). And one having tt is both parti-coloured in appearance and in genetic make-up. In this last case, the recessive gene has been allowed to come into influence because there is no dominant gene to suppress it. This is evidenced by the scarcity of whole-coloured pointers in Britain which almost became extinct, the pied dogs (tt) not possessing the factor for the whole colour. I am afraid it all sounds horifically complicated! And this is genetics at the most basic level.

The breeders of working dogs are not overly interested in colour. But the inheritance of, say, a high-headed style of hunting in pointers (which is desirable) can be considered in a similar way. According to Winge in *Inheritance in Dogs,* the high-headed style of hunting of pointers and setters is thought to be dominant to the low-headed style in Continental hunting dogs. Assuming this characteristic is controlled by a single gene (which may not be so), the low-headed dog bred from two high-headed parents must have been bred from parents both carrying the low-headed gene. A single recessive gene may be carried through several generations without its influence becoming apparent in the offspring.

One of the dangers of modern dog breeding is the tendency of enthusiasts to take their bitches to some famous and fashionable stud dog which, unbeknown to them, carries some undesirable recessive. It is only when successive generations are inter-bred (as will be inevitable if many bitches are bred to the afflicted dog) that undesirable recessives start to come together so that whole generations of some breeds are riddled with genetic faults. Examples of this are Progressive Retinal Atrophy (PRA) which afflicted large numbers of spaniels and collies and Hip Dysplasia in Labradors and German Shepherds.

Not all inheritance is as described. Some types of inheritance are extremely complicated. It should be emphasized that genetic faults are not created by any particular type of breeding programme though some can make the incidence of such problems higher than it needs to be. Changes in the genetic material can also occur so that 'faults' develop within a breed as a normal process of evolution, called mutations. In the natural world, these would normally be weeded out by 'natural selection'. I hope the need for an elementary knowledge of genetics to all breeders is now clear. Genetics is a subject best studied from specialist books, and some are mentioned in the final chapter of this book.

Ojvind Winge lists some 'mental' characteristics which are inherited in his book, *Inheritance in Dogs with Special Reference to Hunting Breeds,* published by Comstock Publishing Company Inc., of Ithaca, New York, in 1950. Excessive nervousness in dogs is certainly dominant. Excessive barking also appears to be strongly inherited. Hanging ears are dominant over upright ears but semi-erect ears (as in the pointer and most setters) are dominant over both types. Tail type is highly complex and it used to be said that a pointer carried its pedigree in its tail and its character in its head. Incidentally, the ears of pointer puppies should be correct at four and five weeks but may hang down to the age of twelve to fourteen months when they again become correct! Very young puppies are easier to judge than half grown dogs which are growing in all directions and look like gangly awkward children at the same stage of growth. The dish-face with distinctive 'stop', often pronounced in Continental pointers, is recessive to the flat face found in some old strains of British pointers and, for example, the German Shorthaired Pointer. One researcher, an American called Whitney, found that the pointing instinct was incompletely dominant over the instinct to hunt game up, but I suspect the matter is more complex than that. The instinct to back another dog is part inherited, part learned, but is inherited separately to the pointing instinct. 'High style' hunting, with head held high, as has been mentioned, is said to be dominant over low-headed, ground scenting. A keenness to enter water is apparently dominant over reluctance. And so on.

Most breeders will strive to breed dogs which fulfil their ideals in every respect which is where inbreeding can play a part. Inbreeding tends to bring recessives together so they can be retained or discarded as required. This is where pedigrees are important and carefully kept notes on the breeding of dogs will greatly assist in tracking down the inheritance of certain characteristics and help to decide what action must be taken when problems are encountered. Inbreeding brings with it problems of small litters, lack of vigour, and a loss of size called 'inbreeding depression' but these are unlikely to be a problem unless very close inbreeding (i.e. brother to sister) over many generations is practiced. Pfaffenberger's book explains just what degree of inbreeding is possible without problems.

There are really two ways to go about breeding and the best system combines both. One is to record carefully details of the dogs at each generation in a pedigree. This should be much more than a list of names; rather a record showing how each

Dr Jan Martinek of Prague with self-coloured orange pointer Talmberk Angie roading pheasants in the lucerne.

individual was scored on a number of traits considered important to the end in view, the total adding up to a maximum score. Only those dogs with a high score would be included in the breeding programme. This is how cattle and sheep are bred commercially; each individual being scored at various periods of its life for readily identified standards of performance, i.e. the number and growth rate of lambs or calves, milk yield, butter fat content, etc., etc.

The other system, followed in nature, is for those individuals with obvious faults to be dropped from the programme so that only the best are bred from. These quality dogs are compared, possibly in some demanding form of competition, and only the successful retained. The racing greyhound is a perfect example. The fastest dogs are retained regardless of looks. Possibly gundogs ought to be selected on a system somewhere between the two ideals, and it would not be so difficult for a small group of dedicated individuals to get together to work towards some common aim.

Small, wiry, field trial-type Irish setters. The author recommends the dogs, but not the collars. (Derry Argue)

It follows that any form of competition purporting to improve working dogs by awarding prizes to those other than the best selected on the 'first past the post' system will inevitably lead to a gradual deterioration in the breed it claims to be improving. A very good example of this type of selection can been seen in the deterioration of working dogs under the influence of dog shows and the reason the author is so vociferous in his condemnation of modern field trials under Kennel Club Field Trial Regulations and 'negative judging' as practised by some who are unable to recognize a good dog. All these people do is to 'eliminate' dogs according to the mistakes they make awarding what is left the prizes.

Whatever breeding system is used, an element of inbreeding is usually accepted. Inbreeding is a subjective term; all Irish setters are 'inbred' from the viewpoint of colour. Other breeds may be more or less inbred according to the numeric size of their population. Broadly speaking, inbreeding with selection increases uniformity within that inbred population; outcrossing increases variability. Inbreeding is generally considered a 'bad thing' by the layman; and he would usually consider an animal inbred if the same individual appears more than twice in the same four generation pedigree. Inbreeding to the geneticist means something very much more intense. Thirty years ago laboratory mice had been bred litter brother to litter sister for two hundred and fifty generations without serious problems. When I recently enquired whether the number of generations had been increased since, my informant told me that no one would bother. After twenty generations, an inbred strain is now considered to be as genetically pure for the selected traits as might ever be required for experimental purposes. Even so, such a strain will only be uniform in the characteristics selection has been aimed to produce. In other characteristics, variability remained unchanged. It is generally accepted that the influence of an outcross can be effectively bred out after five generations. So those lengthy researches to prove that one's dogs are descended from some famous individual twenty years ago (with outcrosses at every generation since) are really a waste of time!

Some breeders will seek variability, the obvious example being the greyhound breeder who is looking for that exceptional performer that will win. It is of no value to him to breed litter after litter of identical dogs which all complete a two hundred yard race in identical times. He is hoping for an increase in speed, the odd-dog out that completes that two hundred yards a split second faster. His chances of getting this exceptional dog are increased by random changes in the genetic blueprint material, called 'mutations'.

The professional gun dog trainer hopes to produce *some* variation in his dogs but he also wants to produce reasonable uniformity so the majority will at least make shooting dogs with the minimum of effort under his particular system of training. The occasional field trial champion is of little value if ninety per cent of the puppies born have to be rejected for whatever reason or can only be made into useful working dogs by the expenditure of an inordinate amount of time and energy. The amateur, of course, may be quite happy with one outstanding dog in a litter. He can sell the remaining 'duds' to his rivals!

Inbreeding is a subject which causes much disquiet amongst amateur breeders. The subject can be put into perspective if one considers that all the rabbits in Australia are descended from a few imported pairs and various wild animal populations in nature have occasionally crashed to relatively few pairs only to recover again to many hundreds of thousands. Some species seem better able to produce variation than others. There are obvious advantages for a species regularly preyed upon to appear identical as a predator finds it more difficult to single out an individual to pursue and capture. Anyone who has shot driven grouse late in the season when the coveys combine into packs of fifty or sixty birds will agree the peculiar psychological effect which makes one hesitate. The eye follows one bird which we intend to shoot. Before the trigger can be pulled another intrudes on the periphery of our vision, we hesitate and the chance is lost. The same phenomenon must surely be experienced by the wolf attempting to single out a caribou from the herd or the hawk to pluck its victim from a whirring flock of massed identical birds! The wheeling, pirouetting,close-knit flight of a flock of starlings would scarcely be possible if there was not some common, inbred system of communication shared by all.

On the other hand, variation in individual wild dogs hunting in a pack would be of positive advantage. Each member of the pack takes on a different role and adaptation to that role would surely be a survival factor. There is certainly greater variation between breeds of dogs than, say, in breeds of cattle though both must have been subject to man's domestication for a similar period. It is my feeling that there is a greater tendency to variation in dogs than in predated animals, so that some degree of inbreeding is not only desirable in a breeding programme but necessary if all is not to be total confusion. Most amateur breeders have not a clue as to what qualities their dogs will pass on or what puppies will be produced. Far from there being serious dangers in inbreeding (which can be corrected by a single outcross), the very real dangers to modern dog breeds are of 'overbreeding', a situation I mentioned briefly above. Michael W. Fox in *The Dog; Its Domestication and Behavior,* published by Garland, USA, writes, 'Although the negative aspect of excessive inbreeding is now well recognized as a major flaw in the propagation of 'pure breeds' of domesticated dogs, the perhaps more serious problem of 'overbreeding' is not fully recognized (often the former being mistaken for the latter). Overbreeding implies undirected selection where man does not replicate natural (directed) selection processes . . .'. In other words, man must select the best dogs for breeding and eliminate those with undesirable traits as would occur naturally in the wild.

Field Trials

Selecting the best is the problem. With greyhounds, it is simply a matter of picking the fastest dogs over a given distance. (With apologies to all greyhound owners for this gross over-simplification!). Selecting the best working pointer or setter is quite another matter. It might be thought that the best test of a working gundog is to examine it under practical working conditions. And that is exactly what field trials purport to do. 'A Field Trial should be run as nearly as possible to an ordinary day's shooting', states the Kennel Club's *Guide to the Conduct of Field Trials.* The problem is that no one, except the trainer, knows how long, and at what cost, it has taken to achieve the finished article and, in practice, it is extremely difficult to fully test a gundog in the limited time available at a British field trial. I have been an outspoken critic of field trials as run under the Kennel Club system in Britain for many years, not because I do not believe they cannot be a valuable aid to the breeder but because so many who should know better fail to acknowledge the shortcomings of such competitions. In my opinion field trials are increasingly becoming more of a social sport than a means of selecting the best breeding stock. There is, of course, nothing wrong with the social side of field trials, but it is a mistake to confuse the noble aim of finding the best dog with the politics of a social occasion. The fact ought to be recognized so that some, more serious in their objectives, may set up alternative ways of testing gundogs for work. And it is absolute nonsense to suggest there can only be one way to test a working gundog. As much nonsense as to suggest that a dog should only work in one officially prescribed way. It is up to the individual owner to decide how his dog should work and groups of similarly minded individuals should have the right to test their dogs with these aims in view.

Competitors and spectators at a field trial. (Derry Argue)

It is now not unusual for upwards of forty dogs to be tested in the first heat at a Kennel Club licenced field trial for pointers and setters in a matter of a couple of hours and the whole stake to be decided in under four hours. I recently attended such a meeting which started at 11.00 am and finished at 2.40 pm, some dogs not having been tested on game and therefore non-contenders. Thus two thirds of the dogs will be dismissed after a test of perhaps only two or three minutes each. This is effected by applying a number of 'eliminating faults' to dispose of dogs 'of undoubted lack of merit' to reduce the field to a manageable proportions. The question is, can 'undoubted lack of merit' be decided in less than two minutes? Judges say it can, but since they do not see these dogs again, how do they know they do not regularly make glaring mistakes? Such a method of judging, to my mind, produces ridiculous decisions. An old cock grouse seen drying out after a heavy shower caused the judges to dismiss both dogs under their scrutiny for a 'flush' when the bird flew off! That bird was quite capable of judging the distance he could safely allow the dogs to approach. Dogs are put out for travelling in the same direction as a hare or rabbit on the grounds that the particular dog must be chasing! Dogs running into birds straight off the lead are dismissed 'for an upwind flush' yet most experienced dog trainers will admit that dogs often need time to settle to their work, especially after being dragged around on a lead for half a day. The list of minor mistakes which can, in the eyes of the judges, disqualify (or severely penalise) a dog from the competition are endless underlining the pressures to reduce over-subscribed stakes to manageable proportions so the favoured remaining dogs can be given a decent run. Dogs *must* be put out for committing an 'eliminating fault'. The ridiculous situations this can lead to caused judges to recently re-run a second round of a stake because, it seems, the best dogs had been eliminated. A wise man would change the rules, not break them.

The nonsense does not end there. At least twenty years ago the author was warned against touching his dog at the point at a trial by none less than the great John Nash. More recently, I have had cause to study the rules closer than I had done before so when I was 'eliminated' for touching my dog at a trial under KC rules I raised the question with the Kennel Club. The Field Trials Supervisor wrote me in clear terms that touching a dog at a trial is not an 'eliminating fault' and Mr Sinnatt, the Secretary of the Kennel Club, wrote me that he thought the Regulations 'entirely clear' and 'further advice to judges is unnecessary'. It is, by the way, an 'eliminating fault' for a competitor to touch his dog at the point under Irish Kennel Club rules. Perhaps I am unduly pedantic but the fact that such a misunderstanding can exist for over twenty years is indicative of the malaise endemic in the selection of gundogs for working ability.

Yet all the efforts of the Kennel Club committees appear, to my view, to be geared towards increasing entries at trials! And why? A perusal of many field trial schedules will reveal that only twenty-five to thirty per cent of the entry money may be re-cycled as prize money (overseas trials regularly redistribute sixty to seventy-five per cent), the balance, it is alleged, being used to finance dog shows and retriever trials which are more hungry for cash.

In such circumstances, there is considerable pressure on a gundog society to run a trial. For example, at one Open Stake it was declared that due to the severe weather no arm bands would be worn, the draw would be abandoned, and owners would be limited to the running of one dog each. In addition to this, the first few brace down were run on ground used for the winter feeding of deer. There was literally no ground cover whatsoever to hold birds. Since the stake was run in alphabetical order (and not according to the usual draw), some owners would seem to have been unfairly penalized. An objection was lodged with The Kennel Club that the trial was run in breach of the field trial regulations. The Field Trial Committee however concluded that 'no breach of the Regulations had been made' and the awards, presumably, stand. Just why bad weather required the modifications cited above is not clear. The 'winner' of this dubious event was, of course, 'one leg up' to field trial champion but whether this was a fair and reasonable assessment of the worth of a gundog I will leave the reader to decide. The person who complained about this irregular conduct was later informed that 'the Committee of the Club (had) decided to refuse this (his) entry (for a subsequent trial) at their last Committee meeting'. No reason for this refusal was stated. Trade unionists would shout victimization. It is a fair estimate that field trial champion status increases the value of a dog by about three hundred per cent but, on this example, it would seem prudent for the would be breeder or purchaser to make his own assessment.

Chance now plays such a large part in British field trials that any moderate shooting dog *could* win, simply because its fellow competitors, many of them better dogs, may have been put out for some 'eliminating fault'. Of course, this is exactly as things should be if field trials are just 'sport', 'a bit of fun', with everyone having an equally lucky chance to win. If field trials are held to be an assessment of a dog's working ability, as would seem reasonable from the Kennel Club's avowed aim to 'improve dogs', the argument begins to look decidedly thin.

The majority of all KC licenced field trials are held on heavily stocked driving moors so competing dogs may be tested on game in the brief period they are before the judges. Entries for most meetings have to be in long before, sometimes months before, the date of the trial when the owner has no idea which of his dogs will be the best on the date of the meeting. . . so he enters the lot, just in case! Pointer and setter owners can enter up to six dogs. Because trials are over-subscribed, a complicated system of qualifying dogs in junior stakes is implemented supposedly to restrict entries . . . and since owners have to attend these to qualify their novice dogs they tend to enter other stakes too, so swelling the entries yet more. Since it takes years for a new club to become registered by the Kennel Club, then a further delay before it may run trials, the number of field trials is severely limited. To whose benefit?

I believe that, as field trials become increasingly a social event, so judges are chosen because they are socially acceptable rather than for their knowledge and expertise. Decisions based on such criteria, to me, produce ridiculous situations. The suggestion that a very experienced trainer and handler should be asked to judge was opposed because the objector stated he 'made unpopular decisions'. I explained to one field trialer that his dog was blinking its points. I then had to explain to this person, a Kennel Club listed judge, what the term 'blinking' meant. Many KC listed judges have never trained a dog, let alone owned and worked a top performer so it is perhaps not surprising that there is an over-reliance on the application of 'eliminating faults'.

Lunch time at a field trial in the 1970s. Betty McCabe, the late Pat McCabe, Michael Early, Betty Town (hidden), Jimmy Blair, Mr Town, and Bertie McElhinney (standing).
(Derry Argue)

'If trials were judged as you want, Derry', I was told by a Kennel Club Panel 'A' field trial judge, 'the same dog would be winning all the time'. Perhaps this is a fitting footnote to what may seem unnecessarily harsh comments but having attended field trials for over thirty years I feel qualified to comment. Personally, I would prefer to compete in trials open to all-comers where the best dogs win, even if the best dog did 'win all the time'.

The Irish system of field trialing is, to my mind, fairer though because of a shortage game, tending to become victim to what I would term 'technical judging'. Winning dogs are awarded 'Green Stars' which accumulate to qualify a dog for higher events, somewhat after the sheepdog trial system. The standard of sportsmanship, too, is generally very high on the other side of the Irish Sea as most entrants to field trials are from the shooting community. Sadly, game is increasingly scarce in Ireland and the traditional 'free shooting' is not so freely available any more.

Field trials for pointers and setters are held in the Spring, on paired grouse, partridges and pheasants, then about mid-July to mid-August on grouse. In September there are trials on partridges and pheasants in England. In Ireland there are also autumn trials on pheasants and special trials on snipe. The main British trials start in England around 15 July and continue up through the country, moving to a new venue further north each couple of days, until the day before the opening of the grouse season, to the North of Scotland on 11 August. The best way to find out about these events is to contact someone who regularly attends. Alternatively, write to the individual clubs and societies involved as listed in the *Kennel Club Year Book* (obtainable from The Publication Department, The Kennel Club, 1 Clarges Street, Piccadilly, London W1Y 8AB). Unfortunately, there will often be delays in your letter being forwarded to the field trial secretary so it pays to enquire well in advance. The public ought to have the opportunity to witness these competitions for it is on the results of these that purchasers and breeders are expected to rely when making decisions to buy or breed. There is scant enough information of individual dogs in Kennel Club pedigrees or in the Stud Books.

Entering dogs for trials is, unfortunately, something of an obstacle course, the objective of many societies appearing to be to limit entries to the privileged few. The reason for having a 'circuit' with trials organized at different locations around the country on successive days was apparently to encourage the proper training and handling of dogs at a local level. But this aim seems to have been abandoned as field trialing becomes a sport for an affluent minority who have the time and money to travel around attending such events. Gamekeepers and the young are conspicuous by their absence and some young trainee gamekeepers who recently attended a trial here in the north were kept so far back from the action they must have left knowing less than when they arrived, utterly convinced that they ought never attend a field trial again. I find this sort of thing very, very sad and a complete contrast to the way I was treated when I attended my first field trial in the Irish Republic thirty years ago. One youngster remarked that he would like to compete but did not understand how the dogs were judged. Some of us have not managed to work that out in half a life time!

About twenty years ago I remember brace stakes at field trials where one competitor ran two dogs in co-operation with each other but these were dropped as so few were able to train their dogs to this standard. I remember seeing Alf Manners, trainer and handler for the late Lord (J. Arthur) Rank, run a brace for this exacting type of work, both dogs being evenly matched and with perfect manners, pointing and backing without jealousy. Another competitor was Arnold White-Robinson, trainer and handler for the Duke of Wellington, and it was wonderful to see these two handlers battle it out for the awards.

Puppy Stakes, too, are no longer the event they were when professionals took pains to produce young dogs with a similar degree of polish and natural flare to dogs many years older. The old time professional is now extinct and more's the pity.

All field trials for pointers and setters in Britain are held by societies registered with the Kennel Club in London. These trials are run under the KC Field Trial Regulations published, with the names and addresses of the Secretaries of Societies holding field trials, in *The Kennel Club Year Book* mentioned above.

Details of dogs winning field trials are published in the *Kennel Club Stud Books*. The information published is, according to the Regulations, limited to 'registered name of the dog, its sex, colour, date of birth, owner, breeder, and an extension of its pedigree limited to three generations . . .'. Such limited information is of very little use to the serious breeder. My own practice has been to purchase any dog I intend to use so that I get to know all its faults and virtues from personal experience but this is an extreme measure born out of hard experience.

For reasons I have mentioned, breeding to pedigree and field trial results can, in my opinion, be a hazardous business. It also ought to be mentioned that both show and working dogs are recorded on the same registry at the Kennel Club. An examination of the pedigree may give some clue. The letters 'F T Ch' denote a Field Trial Champion and this dog has either won the Pointer and Setter Champion Stake or 'two First Prizes under different Judges at two different Field trials in Open Stakes for Pointers and Setters in which there are no fewer than sixteen runners. One of these wins must be in a Stake open to Pointers and all breeds of Setters'. The wording 'Open Stake' is misleading. Dogs now need to qualify to enter Open Stakes and then preference is given to members' dogs. The membership of many societies is restricted in number. Membership applications are considered at an annual committee meeting so it could take, assuming the dog has qualified in a Novice Stake, anything up to two years to get a dog into an Open Stake. Entries may also be decided by ballot. In effect, the winner of an Open Stake has won against a small number of other dogs decided largely by luck. And I personally feel there is already far too much luck in selecting the better dog in field trials as it is. There is no shortage of excellent working dogs which never compete in field trials, some far better suited to the average shooting man's needs than any bred purely for trials.

The letters 'Sh Ch' denote a show bench winner. The letters 'F T W' or 'F T A W' are sometimes used by breeders to denote Field Trial Winners and Field Trial Award Winners respectively and should be treated with caution. Some owners of show dogs mention 'F T A W' when in point of fact the dog has won a show gundog working certificate which is an award of no practical significance to the breeder of working gundogs whatsoever. There will be no information of the ratio of wins to failures at trials on the pedigree and therefore no distinction between the dog which, say, won two Open Stakes out of four entered and the dog which won two out of twenty-four entered, nor whether the stakes were on grouse in Sutherland or pheasants and partridges in Suffolk . . .

Field trialers occasionally take themselves rather too seriously so when I overheard a conversation at a trial where a certain member of the clergy, famous for the quality of his setters, was alleged to have been fraternising with a certain lady member of the aristocracy, equally famous for her pointers, I naturally pricked up my journalistic ears. It was only later I learned that that field trial enthusiast had another hobby, the breeding of ornamental fancy pigeons. It appeared that this person had named individual pigeons after various field trial personalities and the discussions I had overheard concerned the difficulties of breeding these birds and the misalliances which inevitably occur even, or so I am told, in the best regulated pigeon lofts. I absolutely decline to reveal which particular dog owner was the pouter pigeon and which the fantail . . . . However, field trialing was never quite the same for me after that and if I had any problem swallowing some particularly absurd judging decision it was an easy matter to mentally transform the offending judge into his or her feathered counterpart!

By the time this book gets into print it may be possible for working gundogs to compete in independent trials not licenced by the Kennel Club. This is the position of very many non-affiliated gundog clubs in other countries where the official kennel club events are regarded as something of a joke. This, in my view, could be a tremendous advance if followed in Britain. Experiences of totalitarian rule by committee in Eastern Europe have apparently taught the dog world nothing. If independent field trials were allowed (and this change might soon be forced on the Kennel Club) it would then be possible for owners to get together to decide on fairer and exacting forms of competition for their dogs. Not only that but rapid improvement in dogs by better breeding is possible if individuals pool information, organize trials with specific aims in view, perhaps score dogs for particular traits and use the latest computer technology to selectively breed for desirable qualities and eliminate genetic faults. A number of computer programmes for the serious dog breeder were listed in the June 1991 edition of *Dogs in Canada,* the journal published by the Canadian Kennel Club and I currently have two under test. These techniques are used by the modern breeders of farm livestock and it is these techniques which show up selection under the Kennel Club field trialing system as little better than archaic.

Independent field trials would require no more than the adoption of Rule 11 of the Kennel Club Working Trials Regulations into the Kennel Club Field Trial Regulations. This rule allows certain unlicensed events to be recognized by the General Committee. In effect, Rule 11 allows Kennel Club registered sheepdogs to compete in sheepdog trials not licensed by the Kennel Club. Anyone may hold a sheepdog trial, anyone may compete, and anyone may judge. I have not noticed that this causes any harm to the competing sheep dogs or their owners, rather the reverse and the owners of KC registered sheepdogs tell me they believe the KC would be rather pleased if more dogs registered with them would compete in such trials. It would help, they feel, to counter the argument that KC registration leads to the degeneration of working dogs (on which I will refrain to comment!)

I would suggest that trials for pointers and setters could very simply be run in Britain under a successful American system. The 'minimum requirements', as adopted by the Amateur Field Trial Clubs of America, American Field, and Field Dog Stud Book, provide a broad framework under which the results of trials are accepted by the American Field. This system found favour amongst British sportsmen almost a century ago when it was praised by such stalwarts of the pointer and setter scene as Mr William Humphrey and Captain Gilbert Blaine. Briefly, trials under this system must have heats with a minimum duration of thirty minutes. (They may be up to three hours in National events.) There are no eliminating faults and the only other requirements for wins to be recorded is that the dogs must be registered with the American Field Dog Stud Book and the events must be advertised. About three thousand stakes are run under this system in the USA, Hawaii, Japan, and Canada each year. The late Bill Brown, Editor of *The American Field,* wrote to me indicating that there would be no problem in organizing such trials in Britain from their point of view. Under such a system, the element of luck is reduced to a minimum and after thirty minutes it is quite clear to all which is the best dog.

Perhaps thirty minutes is too long for heats under British conditions. Fifteen minutes would be a useful compromise, winning dogs being awarded points which accumulate over the year to a National event run with heats of longer duration. In America the judges and field would be mounted. In Britain, the judges at least might be mounted on ATVs which are so popular with shepherds. Eliminating faults could themselves be eliminated and the dogs judged on their performance the whole time they are down before the judges as they are under the American rules.

A similar system of 'minimum requirements' is operated by the International Sheep Dog Society in Britain and it has been responsible for an enormous increase in the understanding and enthusiasm for better sheepdog training and handling at grass roots level. This system lays down minimum rules under which sheep dog trials must be run for their results to be accepted by the Society. But not all trials are run to these requirements. Anyone may run a sheep dog trial in Britain and anyone may judge. Dogs may or may not be registered with the ISDS. Briefly, for wins to be accepted by the Society, the trials must be advertised and open to all, the course must approximate to the specification laid down by the Society, and the dogs for whom the results are to be recorded must be registered with the ISDS. The openness of the proceedings ensures fair play and there is no need for top heavy bureaucracy and a lot of rules and regulations. Winning dogs score points which accumulate towards qualification to enter 'National' events run by the Society. I believe the International Sheep Dog Society registers around eight thousand dogs a year and is run by just two people backed by an unpaid committee. An organization which did not register dogs (the Kennel Club, though expensive, runs the registration side efficiently enough) could be organized on an even simpler basis.

Although field trials are supposed to be organized as an ordinary shooting day, the techniques needed for training and handling field trial dogs are different to those for ordinary shooting dogs. Dogs are run in braces, not *against* each other as field trial officials are so fond of announcing, but *with* each other to demonstrate what each can do in company. The handlers are required to walk together as if out shooting. The emphasis at trials, as compared to shooting, will be on speed. Pace 'catches the judge's eye'. A fast dog is not necessarily an efficient dog but there is no doubt that a fast dog that does its job reasonably well looks a lot better than a slower dog that finds the same number of birds.

The 'fast' dog is all too often the dog that *appears* fast. Small dogs, because of their rapid movements, often appear faster than bigger dogs, but compare the amount of ground the larger animal covers in the same time and the truth of the matter soon becomes apparent. Can a maximum of ten minutes running really be any test of stamina in a working gundog? Half the technique of producing field trial dogs is to cultivate this speed. Let them out to exercise for a strictly limited period; run them each day for a few minutes only. Very soon you have a 'mean machine' which eats up the ground as soon as the lead is taken off. Carefully rationing game contacts and the careful choice of ground will also increase speed. But for how long? It is now the practice to run shooting dogs for twenty minutes at a time. This is necessary because most modern dogs do not possess the stamina to run for longer periods. Running trial dogs for long periods causes them to 'pack up'. Many a fast trial dog has been spoilt for life by running it on too long. Some of the top trial dogs are never shot over in the conventional manner; that would quickly spoil them! Contrast this to the stories of endurance competitions in the chapter on the Llewellin Setter! Small dogs, too, are easier to get fit and keep fit. They pull less on the lead and are easier for today's unfit handlers to handle. And so working pointers and setters, due to the influence of Kennel Club, are becoming smaller and smaller. The other day I saw an English pointer dwarfed by a cocker spaniel though I admit this was an extreme example.

The best description of how to judge trials I have come across is contained in a little book published by the South African Field Trial Club. South Africa has ideal conditions to show pointers and setters off to their best advantage and they inherited their ideas about field trials from England when things here were at their peak. The booklet is the published speech by a former Vice President of the Club, Mr H. W. Ardler, at their annual prize giving in 1938. The original style of writing is a little stilted and too verbose for modern readers so I have taken the liberty of publishing an edited version here:

Natural Instincts: Gundogs are born with instincts adaptable to the aid of man, in finding and bagging game, and no amount of training will develop these where they don't exist (i.e. nose and pointing instincts). A gundog must have these instincts controlled in order to render them adaptable. The first without the latter is potentially a perfect gundog, the second can never be a gundog at all.

What to look for

Nose: The whole basis of the dog's work is manoeuvring to bring this organ into play to enable him to draw to his prey. A dog's negative work, i.e. when there is no scent and he is trying for it, is as important a part of the hunting instinct as his work on scent; in fact, his mode of performance under 'no scent' conditions is worthier of study by the judge than that on proven scent.

Hunting for Scent (windless conditions): Experienced dogs will cover their ground quickly or slowly according to temperament, quartering and raising or grounding their noses according to the conditions. They will range in search of wind and cover. Bare ground will be searched by sight, and thoroughly and closely searched with nose to ground. Note, a barren point under these conditions is not to be under-valued, it is merely a cautionary investigation of some residual scent.

With the Wind: Here there should be no difference between the experienced and inexperienced dog. It is in them to use the wind and the base of their operations is their handler. Generations of handling by man and recent training limit the beat to controlled dimensions. Therefore, if the wind is blowing in the handler's face, he will range from the handler's right hand to his left on a fairly wide front. This is called quartering and in a marked and persistent wind the proper distance for the dog to be ahead of the handler will not be too far for the dog will scent game ahead of himself and the handler.

Down Wind: Note, this is a test for the dog of quality. He must run down wind as far out as control permits and work back ranging from right to left as wide as control will allow. He must not quarter going out for his chances of flushing down wind are tremendously increased.

Crossing Wind: The dog must go out to the windward of him and quarter back up the wind, i.e. decreasing and increasing his distance from the handler, until he is well to the leeward of his handler, about the same distance as when he went to the windward. (This is easiest explained through the diagrams on page 00.)

   These exact conditions often do not apply and a dog will adjust his quartering and pattern to tackle changing or inconsistent conditions. A judge will be aware of the weather and these factors and judge the dog's behaviour in the light of these considerations.

Quartering: This much abused term is applied to the ranging from side to side by the dog of an area in front of the handler, advancing at a rate suitable to the handler. Provided there is no wind or the wind is head on, this is the best means of picking up scent. Quartering, in fact, applies to the dog's running to and fro while advancing up wind, *irrespective of the position of the handler*. Therefore, while quartering at right angles to the handler's advance is not a virtue but a necessity when there is a head wind or no wind, it becomes a *fault* when the wind is coming from any other direction. This fault lies with the trainer who has subjected the dog's natural instincts to his own incorrect conceptions of the significance of ranging.

Working on Scent: The dog will immediately indicate his discovery of the presence of living game, or the recent presence of living game, by his actions which vary according to the proximity of his find and his temperament or character. This indication is best referred to as an acknowledgement.

   First, the acknowledgement of birds that are not game that his handler has persistently ignored. If an experienced dog, he must be allowed *a brief pause* or period of enquiry by draw or quest to satisfy himself that scent or presence he is conscious of is not game; thereafter he must ignore both its presence and its flush.

Remember, therefore, that the dog who is cautious before proof should not suffer by comparison with the more determined dog who entirely, and possibly willingly, gallops through birds which are not game. Also handlers must remember that a good dog will stand on anything that his master has often shot. The judge will probably interpret such behaviour unfavourably in comparison with the dog who conserves his work for true game. (Passing snipe is not considered a fault at British trials for this reason though a point would usually be credited. There are, of course, trials run exclusively on snipe in Ireland.)

When, however, the pup you judge in the Derby stake has a non-game find, you must allow him more time to prove his discovery and it may even be a virtue for a very young dog to defer to his handler's dictation in the matter.

Acknowledgement of Game

Point: When a dog ranging comes suddenly to his find without previous indications, acknowledgement and point are simultaneous. This should happen when there is occasional or no wind, or when a dog ranging down wind has very slightly over run his find. Let me say at once that this performance, spectacular though it is and most entertaining, is not by any means to be compared to the draw, or quest and find. It is usually first a tribute to the dog's physical prowess and industry, and secondly to his alertness; and the judge must give this only its due value on these scores.

I must add that the conditions may also occur on a very recently pitched bird which has not moved since it has alighted. I can offer no help to a judge in deciding whether this is the case or not, beyond correlating this point with the rest of the dog's performance.

Finding from the Ground: If the dog is ranging correctly in wind, scent found on the ground should be some distance from the game and the dog will then cross the tracks if recently left, going towards it (the game) when it has gone up wind, and away from it when it has gone down wind. In the former case and when game has remained on the ground he will advance directly to his point, lifting his nose until he locates it. Then, if the latter lies, he should remain motionless on point. Should the game move he may keep pace with it cautiously by a series of quick advances and points, or a slow stalk *as long as game is not disturbed*. Note that the dog may finally follow the moving game by sight. This is called 'roading' and must not be confused with following by scent.

When the game has gone down wind or flushed before his arrival the dog will quest, in the former case, usually away from the game and, on losing the line, will *cast* for a pick up of his scent. *Casting* is taking a deep detour down wind to head the game for ground scent or direct (body) scent. In the case of a flush his cast will result in the dog becoming puzzled and he will go back to the original pickup, investigate and perhaps cast again; but the more quickly he makes up his mind and starts ranging again, the more credit you must give him for decision. A poor quality dog will nose about too long without casting.

If the game has kept its course the cast will bring the dog either to a hotter scent, in which case he will again cast ahead, or to leeward of his game, when he will act as already described.

Finding
Here you have the best comparative test for dogs. His nose was given to him to find in this way and his intelligence allows him to achieve this purpose. His ranging is a matter of tactics. He finds live scent in the air and immediately points if near to the game or *draws*, i.e. lifts his head and advances steadily and directly upwind to the game, or keeping on the line if the game moves, and coming to a point when correctly distanced.

The final act is the pointer's 'point' and the setter's 'set' (nowadays, such distinctions are generally ignored). The manner of the point is not of great importance so long as it indicates a find by its attitude or pose, combined with an absolute rigidity of stance as an expression of a determination not to disturb the find.

I have frequently seen the final point of a comparatively mediocre dog, because of its spectacular appeal, wipe out the better all round performance of a worthier dog who has come to point perhaps less showily, but by great industry and cleverness. I do admit that no matter how clever a dog's work may be, if no point results he should not win, but I nevertheless am strongly against giving undue credit to the dog who is brought to his point or who has done no spade work of his own. Good judges will consider *all the acts* in a dog's performance when they have been greatly impressed by one outstanding act.

Added Qualities of Outstanding Dogs
Some of these habits. acquired by patient training, are not always noticed by judges. who are often prone to penalise faults in a manner out of proportion to the credit they give for, say, obedience.

The dog of quality must get well out in the open and work at a good pace. There is no excuse for 'pottering', i.e. slowly covering a circumscribed area about his handler. We, in this country (i.e. South Africa), where in the open game is scarce, are best served by the dog that covers the most ground in the least time, provided his purpose is correct and his methods effective.

Obedience:
The dog should answer to his handler's commands to the following:-

Changing Direction: The dog should occasionally sight his handler to ascertain the latter's movements. Judges should therefore insist on the handler keeping a dictated course until his dog is on real scent. The handler may indicate his change of direction or his wish for the dog to hunt by a well-marked wave of the arm. He must come in immediately when whistled or otherwise called. He should drop or remain stationary when ordered to by his handler from a reasonable distance and not move again until commanded to.

Natural Habits – Dropping on Game: Standing or dropping on find is equally meritorious. A cautious dog will often drop when close to birds so as to prevent disturbing them.

Heading Game: I must refer to this rather rare and great quality of the most gifted of dogs so that judges and critical onlookers may perhaps be saved from confusing it with 'leaving the point' or 'blinking'. Briefly, when a brace is on point or drawing close on persistently running game the header will run out speedily, but with recognition and caution in his every action, to right or left, according to the wind, of the forward line of the advance of birds. He will go far enough out so that his forward run won't frighten or flush. Then he will turn and face oncoming birds, perhaps even working back till scent brings him to a point. The other dog is meanwhile conventionally holding the scent or pointing. I mention a brace because in judging you are always dealing with a brace. Remember, only moving birds are headed. Going round sitting birds must at least be regarded with suspicion as either robbery or lack of decision, but do not fall into the pitiable mistake of calling true heading, which I have attempted to describe, '*leaving point*'; rather give it the top marks it deserves, for only a masterful and courageous dog will do it.

Backing: A dog *must* back another's point; there is no compromise about this be it instinct or training, I think it both. When he views the other dog on true point he must freeze where he views first and not run jealously ahead. When, however, he has backed a false pointer once, he need only pay short attention to the next, sufficient to find out if it is another false point. Remember again, backing is almost as important as pointing, for the lack of it can easily disturb the point and/or flush the game. (In British trials it is generally considered sufficient for a dog to drop on command if it will not back though full credit should be given for a natural back).

Faults
Chasing: If a dog definitely chases he is ruled out and quite properly so, but if he definitely started to chase and is immediately and easily checked by his handler he may still be a good and is certainly an obedient dog and should be given credit for obedience and not ruled out for this alone.

Hunting Trail is questing the scent left by fur, and if the handler knows that it is a recently left scent, he must not be considered to have belittled his dog's chances or character by checking him. If the dog is left and quests steadily and earnestly in enquiry and then gets on with his work without getting out of touch, he must be given credit for perspicacity. If, however, he quests out of range and sight, that means out of control, he must be severely faulted. Should he make a beeline on the trail and not heed his handler he should suffer a severe loss of points and, in good company, be ruled out. (The British view is rather more severe.)
   Last, judge the dog, not the handler.'

   This concludes Mr Ardler's comments which I have edited as appropriate to British conditions.
   The techniques of running dogs in trials have to be learnt by experience. The man to watch has always been the lean-faced man with the ten-year-old car and the home-made dog trailer! That man is at trials to win! Clearly, no one lacking confidence in his dog ought to enter it at a trial but assuming you have done so, it does not assist the dog to let him know how much you doubt his abilities. Remember we ought to have a partnership here between man and dog. Often an air of quiet confidence and

an ability to trust the dog to get on with it produces surprising results. Over-anxiety and excessive whistle blowing upsets both the dog and the judges. It is sometimes difficult to know what to do when your brace mate loses his cool and starts blowing his whistle as if his life depended on it. My own technique is to put my whistle in my pocket and give a hand signal whenever my dogs glances in my direction. I try to reassure the dog that it is not *I* who is upset but the other idiot!

Some dogs get very independent at trials and refuse to follow any commands. This is particularly true of the dog 'doing the circuit' as he gets more and more steamed up seeing the other dogs working and so many birds flying whilst he is on the lead. Incidentally, this is just another technique to get maximum speed out of a dog. The trick to handling the headstrong dog is to give the occasional signal anticipating what the dog is going to do anyway so convincing the judges that you are in complete control. And if things go badly wrong, the best technique is to assume an air of calm confidence which may so befuddle the judges that they have been known to overlook the most outrageous incident. Personally, I have never had the confidence to return from retrieving my dog after a hare chase to relate a masterly piece of dogwork over the rise and out of sight to the judges but I know a man who can. But the judges are there to judge, that is not the job of the competitor, and it is a mistake to assume that one is out of the stake because our dog has committed some apparently blatant fault. After a good lunch, it is surprising what judges fail to see, whether by design or accident.

Field trials: left to right, handler casts her dog to the left as a judge watches, right-hand competitor casts his dog right, second judge watches; official Gun and Steward look on.
(Derry Argue)

Sportsmanship at trials amongst competitors is usually of the highest order and the après-trials social life was always a high light, sadly now very much diminished because of the high cost of 'doing the circuit' and the drink-drive laws. Just before trials started one year a competitor broke his false teeth. Arrangements were made for the offending gnashers to be repaired and duly forwarded to another competitor's home en route. A couple of trialers managed to intercept the package and substitute a set of dentures rescued from someone's tool shed shelf where they had lain collecting dust and verdigris for a couple of decades. Our victim did really well and won the first stake, all managed quite successfully with a spare set of dentures with half the front incisors missing. Some said he had dispensed with his whistle and simply blown through the gap but I cannot attestify to the truth of that. Anyway, although looking fairly respectable, the set dropped out every time our victim opened his mouth. At the last moment, just before going forward to collect the silver, he was handed the substitute verdigrised set. With a muffled oath against all dentists for the lying cheating brutes they are he wiped the worst of the green mold and cobwebs off on his pants and crammed them into his mouth. Before anyone had time to stop him (the truth is our intentions were good and the joke was not meant to go so far – laughter rendered us all helpless) our victim had started forward to collect his awards. I believe what followed was the shortest speech of thanks ever recorded in the history of field trialing.

Chapter 12
Learning More

No one book can tell everything about training dogs. Some authorities advise sticking to one book on the grounds that reading more will give rise to confusion. If the reader is that easily confused he would do well to take up some less demanding hobby and leave the poor misunderstood working bird dog well alone. Far better, in my opinion, to read as many books on the subject as possible and try to get a general understanding of what is involved than attempt to blindly follow a manual on 'How To Do It' without any real comprehension of the workings of the dog's mind. Once the basics are understood it becomes possible to solve many problems with commonsense.

When I first became interested in training pointers and setters I found the advice on the subject conflicting. My first researches led me to *Dog Breaking – The Most Expeditious, Certain and Easy Method whether great excellence or only mediocrity be required with odds and ends for those who love the Dog and Gun* by General W. N. Hutchinson! Yes, that really is the full title of this delightful little book! First published in 1848 the book went to ten editions in the next forty years. Copies used to be available from any second-hand book shop for a pound or so but the book is now collected and both scarce and expensive. So many novices asked me to direct them to a suitable book on training that I re-published Hutchinson in 1977 but this is currently out-of-print. As might be expected from the title, the General was not short of words and to get the best effect one should read the 10th Edition (published in 1898 and 1977) which even has footnotes to the footnotes! Very interesting reading and a guarantee against insomnia. For all that, Hutchinson's was one of the first books on psychological gundog training and his advice is, for the most part, as applicable today as it was then.

My next port of call was William Arkwright's *The Pointer and His Predecessors – An Illustrated History of the Pointing Dog from the Earliest Times,* first published in a 'coffee table edition' in 1902. Arkwright followed this up with a 'cheaper, more portable edition, which shall be suitable for everyday use' published in 1906. This, of course, is the authority on the 'English' pointer though the student of training ought to exercise a little caution for Arkwright (who probably had little first hand experience of dog training) quotes earlier authors without any distinction between pointers and setters. Both editions of Arkwright's book are collector's items and my own reprints (published in 1977 and 1989) should be relatively easy to find.

Edward Laverack's *The Setter* is a book I have come to appreciate more and more in recent years. Published originally in 1872, the sixty-two page book was re-published by C. W. Sorensen in 1976 but is again out of print. There is just a paragraph or two on training, but what wisdom!

Waldermar Marr's *Pointers and Setters,* published in the 1960s and re-published by myself in 1979, is an invaluable book for the serious student of the breeding of working pointers and setters. Written when it was, it gives the background to the breeding of most modern pointers and setters world-wide but it may be necessary to research back a few generations of today's dogs to find the ones he mentions.

Starting as I did with a badly reared and partially ruined Irish setter, I found Konrad Most's *Training Dogs,* very useful. The book is actually about training war, police, and guard dogs for work but it is good (if dated) on canine psychology and excellent on obedience. These days it is considered out-of-date and I am sure there are excellent modern equivalents. Published by Hutchinson in their Popular Dogs series I understand the 1983 edition was remaindered so a new edition seems unlikely.

Writers on British working bird dogs in their country of origin are few in number. One gets the impression that they were all far too busy shooting over their dogs to write about it! I have not yet found time to read *Observations on Dog Breaking* by William Floyd published in 1821. Floyd was dog trainer to Sir John Sebright, a celebrated sportsman, falconer, and writer of the period so I imagine Floyd knew what he was doing. *The Scientific Education of Dogs for the Gun* by 'H.H.' (The Reverend Hely Hutchinson), published in 1890 by the Gresham Press contains much wisdom on the training of pointers and setters. *The Whole Art of Setter Training* by R. L. Russell, published by *The Field* about the same era is excellent, especially on training Irish setters on snipe. Richard Sharpe's *Gundog Training for Amateurs* reprinted by Tideline is a minor classic on training gundogs with good sense on pointers and setters. Richard continued his father's commercial gundog kennel. The authoritative work on the Gordon setter is undoubtedly, *The Gordon Setter – History and Character* by G. St G. M. Gompertz, published privately in 1976. Gompertz did for the Gordon setter what Arkwright did for the pointer.

Training Setters and Pointers for Field Trials by Beasley, Manners, and White-Robinson, published in 1973 by Faber, is still an up-to-date and useful book for the modern field trialer. Another on the same theme, *Training Pointers and Setters,* was written by Dr J. B. Maurice and published in 1974 by David & Charles. *Field Trials – History, Management, and Judging Standards,* an American book by William F. Brown, published in London by Yoseloff Ltd in 1977, tells everything anyone might want to know about organising trials under the American 'minimum requirements' system. It also contains a lot of good sense on working bird dogs. Hopefully, we will all be reading this soon.

It is better to avoid reading books on training hunter-retriever breeds (except for specific information on these breeds) for information applicable to pointers and setters; the two types are not the same. The HPRs generally require a different approach to training.

As might be imagined, there are many excellent American books on training pointers and setters but some allowance must be made for the different methods of working the dogs and different temperament required for their type of training and hunting. *Troubles with Bird Dogs* by G. B. Evans, published by the Winchester Press, New York, in 1975 is a useful book. Paul Long's *Training Pointing Dogs,* published by Nick Lyons, is excellent. K. Roebuck's *Gundog Training; Pointing*

Dogs, published by Stackpole is also good. *Wing and Shot* by Robert Wehle, published by The Country Press, 1964, is very readable and practical. Bill Tarrant's *Best Way to Train Your Gundog – The Delmar Smith Method,* published by David McKay Company Inc. of New York, explains professional methods including force training to retrieve and the use of planted game. *Training Your Own Bird Dog* by Henry Davis, published by Putnam Sons, New York, in 1948 is worth reading. *The Complete Guide to Bird Dog Training* by John Falk, published by the Winchester Press in 1976 is all embracing and excellent. *Practical Education of the Bird Dog* by J. A. Sanchez Antunano; *20th Century Bird Dog Training* by Ed Shelley; and *Practical Pointer Training* by Sherman Webb are all good. *Hunt Close* by J. B. Robinson, published by Winchester; Dave Duffey's *Expert Advice of Gundog Training* and *Hunting Dog Know How* are further suggestions.

Knowing what books to read is one thing; obtaining copies is another. Your local library will usually be helpful and, if necessary, can often obtain books through Inter Library Loan. *The Shooting Times and Country Magazine*, 10 Sheet Street, Windsor, Berkshire SL4 1BG, UK, occasionally publishes articles and advertisements of interest to bird dog enthusiasts. Also, *Shooting News*, 2 Whitehall Mews, Westminster Road, Dublin 18, Eire. American suppliers advertise in magazines such as *Gun Dog Magazine*, P O Box 343, Mt. Morris, Illinois 61054–8088, USA and *The American Field*, 542 S. Dear Born, Chicago, Illinois 60605–1528, USA.

The instructional video is the modern way to learn about gundogs and, as might be expected, there are plenty available from the USA. One word of warning. The American videos run on the NTSC system and most European countries, including Britain, run on the PAL system; conversions can be expensive. *The Complete Pointing Dog, Gun Dog TV Series* (tips by experts on a variety of gundog breeds) – three tapes, and *Gundog Training – Pointing Dogs – Bob West* are a few currently advertised in *Gun Dog Magazine*. No British videos on pointers and setters are currently available in the UK though I have one in production. *The Halti Way of Dog Training* by Dr Roger Mugford is a new video just out.

The serious student of dog training will want to learn something about animal psychology. There are specialist publications almost incomprehensible to the layman but Conrad Lorenz's books (*King Soloman's Ring, Man Meets Dog,* etc.), written about fifty years ago, are a 'must'. I have just read *Dr Mugford's Casebook – Understanding Dogs and Their Companions* by Dr Roger Mugford which is an eye-opener and essential reading. *The Dog – Its Domestication and Behavior* by Michael Fox, published by Garland in 1978, explains in rather technical terms the hunting sequence and other behaviour in dogs.

On breeding dogs there is *Practical Dog Breeding and Genetics* by Eleanor Franklin, published by Hutchinson's Popular Dogs in 1961. *Genetics of the Dog* by Burns and Fraser, published by Oliver and Boyd, Edinburgh, in 1966 is a classic. *Inheritance in Dogs with special reference to Hunting Breeds* by Winge, published by Comstock, New York, in 1950 is relevant. I purchased a copy of *The German Shepherd Dog – History, Development, and Genetics* by Dr M. B. Willis, published by K. & R. Classics, for the content on genetics but H. S. & G. Witherby has since published *The Genetics of the Dog* by Dr Willis in 1990 which must be *the* reference work on the subject. The serious student ought to read Humphrey and Warner's

Working Dogs, published by John Hopkins, Baltimore, in 1934. *Dog Behavior; The Genetic Basis* by Scott and Fuller, published by the University of Chicago Press in 1965, may be rather heavy going but *The New Knowledge of Dog Behavior* by Pfaffenberger, published by Howell, New York, 1976, presents the more important information in very readable form. This last ought to be compulsory reading.

The government has expressed concern over the disappearance of heather uplands in Britain and grouse shooting is one use suggested as an alternative to sheep farming and forestry. As the reader will now be aware, low grouse populations are most efficiently harvested using good bird dogs. Yet education in pointer and setter training and handling is almost totally omitted from gamekeeper education. Lamenting this absence of informed authoritative education for young gamekeepers to the Ministry of Agriculture and Fisheries the author was assured that there were several courses available. No further information has been forthcoming and it appears that this was wishful thinking.

The Scottish Vocational Educational Council, which provides modules for gamekeeper training in Scotland, does not specifically mention pointer and setter handling and training (beyond the identification of three breeds of gundog!) on its modules. The author was advised to write to the Industry Lead Bodies which compile SCOTVEC modules. These bodies, I understand, only respond to demands from the industry. This goes some way to explain the lamentable standards of gundog handling in gamekeeping circles and why there are so many cruelty cases involving the mismanagement of gundogs by gamekeepers. The bottom line appears to be that landowners are not sufficiently concerned about their dogs to make their feelings known to the Industry Lead Bodies. Concerned members of the public, if my own experiences are anything to go by, will be studiously ignored by these people who respond with stereotypical behaviour. Until that situation is remedied the dogs will continue to be mistreated, mishandled, and generally misunderstood. Owners and breeders approached by this sector of the market ought to respond with extreme caution!

Field trials should be a first stop for anyone wanting to learn more about these dogs but bear in mind Thomas Hardy's advice that 'Experience is proportional to intensity, not duration'! Some spend a lifetime doing things the wrong way. But it costs nothing to ask for and listen to advice; you don't have to take it. Wisdom is sometimes found in unexpected quarters. It is sometimes revealing to ask how a particular trainer deals with a certain problem; the advice from the bad trainer will tell you how *not* to do it, the advice you get from the successful trainer may well be worth its weight in gold in saved time and energy. Whatever the price, practical experience with good dogs in the shooting field is always cheap.

Index